PRAXIS-ORIENTED PEDAGOGY FOR NOVICE L2 TEACHERS

In this cutting-edge book on L2 teacher education, experts Johnson, Verity, and Childs demonstrate how praxis-oriented pedagogy grounded in the principles of Vygotskian Sociocultural Theory (VSCT) can have a meaningful impact on L2 teachers' development. Starting with a clear definition of praxis-oriented pedagogy, the authors lay out a theoretical foundation and document how appropriately designed praxis-oriented L2 teacher education pedagogy supports the development of novice teacher reasoning. Drawing from a longitudinal study of L2 novice teachers, chapters address the teachers' understanding, learning, and cognitive development and how their capabilities grow in creating and implementing engaging language learning environments for their ESL students. At the core of the book lies a unique set of pedagogical concepts: linguistically compact, conceptually rich chunks of language that function as psychological tools for learning and teaching. By covering teachers' changes in understanding, reasoning, and pedagogical activities, the book reveals the role that pedagogical concepts play in praxis-oriented pedagogy.

Essential reading for language teacher educators, language teachers, and researchers, this book makes the VSCT principles that inform praxis-oriented pedagogy both clear and accessible.

Karen E. Johnson is Kirby Professor of Language Learning and Applied Linguistics at The Pennsylvania State University, USA.

Deryn P. Verity is a Teaching Professor in Applied Linguistics and Director of ESL/EAP Programs at The Pennsylvania State University, USA.

Sharon S. Childs is an Associate Teaching Professor and Chair of the MA TESL Program at The Pennsylvania State University, USA.

ESL & Applied Linguistics Professional Series
Eli Hinkel, Series Editor

Teaching and Learning Second Language Listening, 2nd Edition
Metacognition in Action
Christine C. M. Goh and Larry Vandergrift

Foundational Principles of Task-Based Language Teaching
Martin East

What English Language Teachers Need to Know Volume III
Designing Curriculum, 2nd Edition
MaryAnn Christison and Denise E. Murray

Doing Reflective Practice in English Language Teaching
120 Activities for Effective Classroom Management, Lesson Planning, and Professional Development
Thomas S. C. Farrell

Creating Classrooms of Peace in English Language Teaching
Edited by Barbara M. Birch

Shaping Learners' Pronunciation
Teaching the Connected Speech of North American English
James Dean Brown and Dustin Crowther

Handbook of Practical Second Language Teaching and Learning
Edited by Eli Hinkel

English L2 Vocabulary Learning and Teaching
Concepts, Principles, and Pedagogy
Lawrence J. Zwier and Frank Boers

Praxis-oriented Pedagogy for Novice L2 Teachers
Developing Teacher Reasoning
Karen E. Johnson, Deryn P. Verity, and Sharon S. Childs

For more information about this series, please visit: www.routledge.com/ESL-Applied-Linguistics-Professional-Series/book-series/LEAESLALP

PRAXIS-ORIENTED PEDAGOGY FOR NOVICE L2 TEACHERS

Developing Teacher Reasoning

Karen E. Johnson, Deryn P. Verity, and Sharon S. Childs

NEW YORK AND LONDON

Cover image: © Getty Images

First published 2023
by Routledge
605 Third Avenue, New York, NY 10158

and by Routledge
4 Park Square, Milton Park, Abingdon, Oxon, OX14 4RN

Routledge is an imprint of the Taylor & Francis Group, an informa business

© 2023 Karen E. Johnson, Deryn P. Verity, and Sharon S. Childs

The right of Karen E. Johnson, Deryn P. Verity, and Sharon S. Childs to be identified as authors of this work has been asserted in accordance with sections 77 and 78 of the Copyright, Designs and Patents Act 1988.

All rights reserved. No part of this book may be reprinted or reproduced or utilised in any form or by any electronic, mechanical, or other means, now known or hereafter invented, including photocopying and recording, or in any information storage or retrieval system, without permission in writing from the publishers.

Trademark notice: Product or corporate names may be trademarks or registered trademarks, and are used only for identification and explanation without intent to infringe.

ISBN: 978-1-032-21568-6 (hbk)
ISBN: 978-1-032-21408-5 (pbk)
ISBN: 978-1-003-26898-7 (ebk)

DOI: 10.4324/9781003268987

Typeset in Bembo
by KnowledgeWorks Global Ltd.

To Glenn, Elizabeth, and Lillian

To the life and memory of Steve Cornwell, extraordinary teacher educator and dear friend

To Karen and Deryn for mediating my professional growth throughout this journey

CONTENTS

List of Figures	ix
Foreword	x
Acknowledgments	xii
Notes on Transcription	xiii

PART I
Defining Praxis-oriented Pedagogy for L2 Teacher Education

1	Vygotskian Sociocultural Theory: Concepts and Principles	3
2	Praxis-oriented Pedagogy for L2 Teacher Education	15

PART II
The Design Features of Praxis-oriented Courses

3	The MA TESL Program	33
4	The MA TESL Capstone Projects	51

PART III
Tracing the Developmental Trajectory of L2 Novice Teacher Reasoning

5 Why Pedagogical Concepts Matter	63
6 Responsive Mediation and Teacher Instructional Stance	91
7 Orienting to Emotion: The Centrality of *Perezhivanie* in Teacher Development	119
8 Internalizing Pedagogical Concepts	144

PART IV
Outcomes, Impact, Opportunities

9 Reconceptualization in Novice L2 Teacher Reasoning	173
10 Post-graduation Trajectories: Our Novice Teachers in the World	201
11 Praxis and Program Design	221
Appendix 1: Pedagogical Concepts in L2 Teaching	*230*
Appendix 2: Teacher Demographics	*233*
Index	*235*

FIGURES

1.1	Pedagogical Concepts in L2 Teaching	6
1.2	Novice L2 Teacher Demographics and Years of Teaching Experience	12
4.1	Elevator Speech for MA Paper Workshop	57
4.2	Preparing Your MA TESL e-Portfolio: Planning Tool	58
5.1	Reaction Paper #1 Visual Depictions	85

FOREWORD

It was Tuesday, July 10, 2018. Outside, the lush green, rolling hills of central Pennsylvania were punctuated by orange day lilies, drenched in the warmth of a July sun. But we—Karen, Deryn, Sharon, and Paula—opted to be inside the windowless four walls of the fluorescent-lit conference room in the Department of Applied Linguistics at Penn State. We were just beginning a two-day discussion about each of the initial subsets of data representing the journeys of novice L2 teachers who had graduated from the MA TESL Program at Penn State.

I now reflect on those initial days of impassioned dialogue and the final book that Karen, Deryn, and Sharon (KDS) have written through the dialectic of being/becoming, a conceptualization through which we, as language teacher educators, typically understand our novice L2 teachers. At that point in time, this book was in the process of organically being/becoming as KDS engaged in thinking together and writing themselves into meaning. How does one craft a theorized, compelling, readable book condensing an abundance of data covering a two-year process of teacher development while foregrounding the teachers' voices? KDS decidedly do this in *Praxis-oriented Pedagogy for Novice L2 Teachers: Developing Teacher Reasoning* through the revolutionary pedagogy of their language teacher education program. I use the words 'revolutionary pedagogy' in the Vygotskian sense, where learning and development are conceptualized as being in a dialectic, through which people make meaning using conceptual tools in socioculturally situated, goal-oriented activities. The book is also revolutionary in the Vygotskian way it actualizes the program as a research laboratory, and, thus, highlights teacher development through their voices within these intentional learning-to-teach activities.

The explanation and exploration of *pedagogical concepts* through the teachers' voices is the most theoretically profound yet practical contribution of this book. The book shows how KDS introduce pedagogical concepts, or "theoretical insights packaged for use by novices" (p. 26), in three pillar courses. They show how novice teachers increasingly make sense of their teaching through conceptual tools; that is, by thinking together with their classmates and teacher educators, they increasingly talk about their instructional activity through the pedagogical concepts, and their practical activity of teaching facilitates a deeper understanding of the concepts. Crucial to this is that as teachers talk through their understandings of their instructional practice through specific pedagogical concepts, the teacher educators gauge teachers' reasoning, identify emerging growth points, co-construct ZPD activity, and engage in responsive mediation. This book enables readers to witness this through what is rare in many published materials—longitudinal, in-depth highlighting of teachers' voices as they externalize their intimate, emotional, individual experiences with learning-to-teach in increasingly reasoned and self-regulated ways. It similarly traces these teacher educators' own understandings and use of these pedagogical concepts, their own being/becoming.

What this book refutes is that teachers do not develop their expertise simply by teaching. The intentionality and quality of the teacher educator mediation in all three courses demonstrates how and why language teacher educators/education matters and the centrality of the novice L2 teacher/teacher educator relationship. The excerpts demonstrate how responsive mediation can be enacted as the teacher educators listen, offer emotional support, offer an instructional alternative, or probe teachers to consider the effects of their instructional choices in the process of teaching the practice teach or after tutoring and teaching in the practicum. What is revolutionary is that the mediation is intentional, orienting, emergent, holistic, and focused on development while enabling teachers to interact with students more thoughtfully in the next class/tutoring session.

KDS note that people ask them "How could I possibly implement these ideas when I'm in a traditional MATESL program and do not have such like-minded colleagues?" I can attest that these pedagogical concepts **do** 'travel': I use them in my undergraduate TESL certificate program with first-time teachers, where I do not have such like-minded colleagues. What this book provides is a vision of possibilities for language teacher education inspired by Vygotskian Sociocultural Theory. This book challenges us as teacher educators to externalize our own being/becoming to create the kinds of intentional and structured mediational spaces that support the teachers with whom we work in their own being/becoming expert language teachers.

Paula Golombek
University of Florida

ACKNOWLEDGMENTS

We want to express our enormous debt of gratitude to the many novice L2 teachers who welcomed us into their learning-to-teach experiences for the two years they spent in our MA TESL program. It is their insights, struggles, joy, and passion for becoming language teachers that make up the lifeblood of our work as teacher educators and it is their voices that bring life to this book. We are lucky to teach in a setting where exploration of praxis-oriented pedagogy is not only welcomed, but nurtured. Professor James P. Lantolf, a mentor, colleague, and inspirational researcher into Vygotsky's theory of mind and human development, has for years been a sounding board for our ideas and questions. His influence is evident in the openness and support we have for our collaborative quest to create innovative educational contexts for our teachers. We also wish to thank the multitude of graduate students in the Department of Applied Linguistics at The Pennsylvania State University who labored over intricate transcriptions of hours of digitally recorded classroom data. They allowed us to see into our teachers' 'inner worlds' in ways that would not have been possible otherwise. We also thank the many instructors who allowed us to come into their classrooms to record lessons and carry out observations, and who thoughtfully mentored our MA TESL students in their practicum teaching experiences. A special thanks goes to our long-time colleague and friend, Paula R. Golombek (University of Florida), who offered us insightful feedback on an initial draft of this book and who pushed us to fully articulate the true potential of praxis-oriented pedagogy for the development of L2 teacher reasoning. We are very grateful to Jacob Rieker for his meticulous copyediting and attention to clarity in the written word. Finally, we would like to thank the reviewers commissioned by Routledge for their constructive feedback and the acquisitions editor, Karen Adler, and series editor, Eli Hinkel, for their professionalism and recognition of the book's potential contribution to the ESL and Applied Linguistics Professional Series.

NOTES ON TRANSCRIPTION

T	teacher
TE	teacher educator
S	student (not identified)
S1, S2, etc.:	identified student
Ss	several students at once or the whole class
CM	classmate, CM1, classmate 1
[	[do you understand? overlap between teacher/student, student/student
=	turn continues, or one turn follows another without any pause
(.)	a dot indicates a just noticeable pause
(2.0)	a number indicates a timed pause, e.g., 2 seconds
?	rising intonation—question or other
___	emphatic speech, usually on a word
CAPITALS	speech that is hearably louder than surrounding speech
wo (h) rd	(h) to indicate the word is expressed with laughter
wor-	a dash indicates a word that has been cut off
wo:rd	colons indicate elongation of a sound
(word)	a guess at unclear or unintelligible talk
()	talk occurs but unintelligible
((laughter))	indicates paralinguistic sounds like laughter, crying, etc.
((italics))	notes on gestures, actions, eye gaze, etc.

Source: Adapted from van Lier (1988) and Johnson (1995).

References

Johnson, K. E. (1995). *Communication in second language classrooms.* New York: Cambridge University Press.

van Lier, L. (1988). *The classroom and the language learner.* London: Longman.

PART I
DEFINING PRAXIS-ORIENTED PEDAGOGY FOR L2 TEACHER EDUCATION

1
VYGOTSKIAN SOCIOCULTURAL THEORY

Concepts and principles

While past L2 teacher cognition research has critically examined what language teachers know, believe, and think (i.e., their mental lives), limited progress has been made in addressing fundamental questions about the developmental trajectory of L2 teachers (people) and teaching (activity) expertise. Kubanyiova and Feryok (2015) maintain that the field of L2 teacher cognition has barely begun to answer fundamental questions about developing L2 teacher/teaching expertise: "How do language teachers create meaningful learning environments for their students?" and "How can teacher education, continuing professional development, and the wider educational and sociocultural context facilitate such learning in language teachers?" (p. 435). That is, the question of "what constitutes a meaningful and worthwhile impact of L2 teacher education is far from resolved" (p. 436).

The dominant discourses that typically get invoked when people talk about teacher education reflect notions such as 'too much theory, not enough practice' and 'teachers learn to teach by teaching.' Surprisingly, even teachers who have gone through teacher education or certificate programs sometimes claim that they did not really learn how to teach until they got into their own classrooms. When we enter the realm of L2 teacher education, an even more misguided notion is typically invoked: 'If you can speak the language, you can teach it.' Often, both language teachers and language learners find themselves buying into this notion: for teachers, 'I speak English, but I don't know how to teach it,' or 'my English is not good enough to teach'; for students, 'I would prefer to study English with a native speaking teacher.'

DOI: 10.4324/9781003268987-2

This book offers a counter narrative to these dominant discourses. We crucially reject the notion that a person can learn to teach 'only by teaching' or can be entrusted with the task of teaching on the basis of being a 'native speaker' of a language. To support this perspective, we make our praxis-oriented pedagogy explicit by longitudinally documenting our interactions with the novice teachers in our MA TESL program, whose L1s may or may not be English, and their responses to our interactions as they unfold within our classrooms and institutional context. At the same time, we explore the influences and consequences of this praxis-oriented pedagogy on the development of novice L2 teacher reasoning. We argue, as Vygotsky (1935/1994) did, that school learning is not the same as learning in the everyday world. Instead, he characterized school learning as 'artificial' in the sense that it relies upon the artifacts of formal and intentional mediation: the classroom (in this case, the classroom for novice teachers) is an ideal venue for systematic, intentional, goal-directed instruction where new psychological tools (artifacts, concepts, and symbols) can be introduced with the goal of restructuring both thinking (teacher cognition) and activity (language teaching). We also argue that language teacher educators can intentionally shape the *social situation of development* (i.e., the social environment) by creating structured mediational spaces where novices can grow into becoming L2 teachers. Therefore, language teacher educators are essential participants in the process of seeing, supporting, and enhancing the development of novice L2 teacher reasoning.

This book lays out a theoretical foundation for praxis-oriented pedagogy as systematically and intentionally informed by the principles and concepts of Vygotskian Sociocultural Theory (VSCT). The book has four primary aims:

- To define praxis-oriented pedagogy as educational innovations that embody the dialectical principle that changes in social activities/relations affect cognitive development
- To document how appropriately designed L2 teacher education pedagogy supports novice teacher understanding, learning, and cognitive development
- To highlight the role that pedagogical concepts, as expressed in brief and accessible phrases, play in praxis-oriented pedagogy and in the development of novice teacher reasoning and instructional expertise
- To trace the developmental trajectory of L2 novice teacher reasoning as well as their emerging capabilities to create and enact engaging language learning environments for the English learners they teach

Specifically, we present and discuss data from our two-year graduate-level L2 teacher education program (MA TESL). The data document how, as language teacher educators, we create cohesively structured, intentionally designed, mediational spaces that expose novice teachers to relevant academic and pedagogical concepts as they engage in a variety of mediated teaching/tutoring activities. To provide more context for the course-driven data, we discuss the intentional design features of three required praxis-oriented courses, Teaching ESL, Tutoring Internship, and Teaching Practicum, what we refer to as our 'pillar' courses. We designate these courses as pillars because they hold up the theoretical framework of the approach we call praxis-oriented pedagogy. In essence, we offer a VSCT theorized rationale for the decision-making processes that lie behind our intentional design features. We hope by making the VSCT principles that inform the courses both clear and accessible, readers may find avenues for making their own L2 teacher education programs more principle-driven, cohesive, and praxis-oriented. We then present empirical data that traces the developmental trajectories of novice L2 teachers from two cohorts of teachers in our MA TESL program as they move through the three pillar courses. These courses, which lie at the center of this book, engage novice teachers in learning how to understand teaching as a reasoned and agentive activity, more so on *how* to teach, rather than on *what* to teach. Through our voices and the voices and experiences of the novice L2 teachers in our program, we illustrate how praxis-oriented pedagogy contributes to crucial intersections of theory and practice, where professional, intentional, and reasoned activity is modeled, enacted, and explored. Our longitudinal findings document the emerging capabilities of novice L2 teachers to articulate, create, and enact engaging language learning environments for the learners they teach. We highlight a unique set of interrelated pedagogical concepts (see Figure 1.1, also Appendix 1), designed to function as psychological tools, that we ask the novice L2 teachers to engage with in order to orient them toward taking on a more reasoned, dialogic, interactive, responsive instructional stance as they plan for and engage with their learners. Our findings are supplemented with post-program interviews with recent MA TESL graduates. These practicing L2 teachers reflect on the significant concepts, experiences, and/or realizations that have traveled with them from our praxis-oriented pedagogy into their early professional years and how these concepts have become important facets of their own pedagogy. We conclude with implications, propositions, and design options for L2 teacher educators interested in implementing VSCT-informed, principle-driven, cohesive, praxis-oriented pedagogy.

Below is a collection of pedagogical concepts that we have extrapolated from our work with Vygotskian Sociocultural Theory (VSCT) L2 novice teacher education. As pedagogical concepts, they are not specific to any particular topic or language skill but are relevant to all L2 instruction and L2 teacher education. We use each of the concepts listed here differently to support the development of novice teacher reasoning, that is, for different purposes and in different ways in our individual courses, but all of them encapsulate fundamental principles of praxis-oriented pedagogy. Taken together, this collection becomes a set of powerful psychological tools that enable novice teachers to instantiate *teaching as dialogic mediation* (Johnson, 2009), or, to phrase its value in the form of a pedagogical concept itself, TEACH OFF YOUR STUDENTS, NOT AT THEM.

ACTIVITY BUILDING
- a. design activities in such a way that they build on one another
- b. sequence activities so that they lead to a final outcome or 'product' that is a demonstration of what learners have learned and are now able to do

BE DIRECT, NOT DIRECTIVE
- a. be explicit about what language point you are focusing on
- b. do not tell the learner what to write or say in place of their own contribution
- c. use targeted mediation to support the learner's use of language

CREATE PREDICTABILITY
- a. explicitly state what learners are expected to say and do
- b. explicitly and overtly link activities through language: provide connections/transitions
- c. if working in pairs or small groups, provide students opportunities to 'practice' before they 'perform' or 'present'

EMBODIMENT IN TEACHING
As a performative act, teaching is filled with gestures and positionings that hold meanings, for both teachers and learners. Consider the following when you teach:
- a. Where do I stand? How do I stand? Where do I look?
- b. How do I use gestures and positioning to support student learning?
- c. What do I do when learners are working in small groups?

ENGINEER PARTICIPATION
- a. don't assume learners know how to participate
- b. be explicit about HOW you want them to participate
- c. arrange the classroom in ways that invite participation
- d. continue to monitor participation throughout the lesson

INSTRUCTIONAL PARAPHRASING
Whatever learners say, rephrase or paraphrase it out loud so that you
- a. acknowledge the learner's contribution
- b. make it comprehensible to everyone
- c. provide appropriate language input/model
- d. relate it to what you are teaching (i.e., take learners from where they are to where you want them to be)
- e. establish a pattern that any and all learner contributions are welcome (i.e., lessen face-saving threats)
- f. give yourself an opportunity to 'comprehend' it

FIGURE 1.1 Pedagogical Concepts in L2 Teaching *(Continued)*

ORIENT STUDENTS
- a. situate/connect the concept, skill, or content within the 'bigger picture'
- b. highlight salient and relevant features that learners should pay attention to and state why
- c. help learners relate to it in some concrete or personally meaningful way

PROVIDE RELEVANCE
- a. tell learners exactly *why* you are doing what you are doing,
- b. tell learners *why* you are asking them to do what they are doing
- c. tell learners what you expect them to know and be able to do by the end of the lesson

REASONING TEACHING
Justify your instructional choices. Are they *P.S. ME?*
- a. P = Purposeful – goal-directed
- b. S = Substantive – content-rich
- c. M = Meaningful – matters for your goals and your learners and their goals
- d. E = Engaging – involves all learners all of the time

TEACHING AS CONNECTING
- a. connect content with learners, learners with content
- b. establish instructional relationship and rapport with and among learners
- c. design activities so learners connect with content/one another in different ways (individually, round-robin, pairs, small groups, whole class)

Note: The pedagogical concepts are listed in alphabetical order, to avoid suggesting that any one of them is 'more important' than any other, or that any particular concept should be taught ahead of any other.

FIGURE 1.1 *(Continued)*

Instruction and Cognition: Vygotsky's Zone of Proximal Development

Vygotsky's theoretical stance on the relationship between instruction and cognitive development is that attention to what learners can do independently at any given point in time says little about the trajectory of learners' development or what their potential may be. A more productive measure, Vygotsky argued, is the difference between independent performance and aided performance, framed conceptually as the *zone of proximal development* (ZPD). In Vygotsky's own words:

> The zone of proximal development of the child is the distance between his actual development, determined with the help of independently solved tasks, and the level of the potential development of the child, determined with the help of tasks solved by the child under the guidance of adults and in cooperation with his more intelligent partners.
>
> (1978, p. 86)

The ZPD can be thought of as a metaphoric space where individual cognition originates in the social collective mind and emerges in and through engagement in social activity. It is not a physical place or a mental level; learners do not have a ZPD per se, but during the activity of aided performance, a ZPD can emerge, and it is in this activity, or arena of potentiality, where we can see what an individual might be able to do with assistance; one's potential versus what one has already internalized and thus can do on one's own. In other words, knowing what a novice teacher can do on her own tells us little about her potential to learn something new. When we see/hear how this same teacher interacts with someone who is more capable while accomplishing a task that is beyond her abilities, this creates a window through which we can see her potential for development and her capabilities as they are emerging. Because the bulk of what we do as teacher educators is to help novice L2 teachers do what they are not yet able to do on their own within the limited time frame of a teacher education program, mediation directed at this metaphoric space of potentiality is essential in developing those maturing capabilities. Attention to the quality and character of that mediation and learners' responsiveness to it are signals of potential cognitive development (Johnson & Golombek, 2016; Poehner & Lantolf, 2021). This is why we approach our L2 teacher education program using praxis-oriented pedagogy.

Critical to the ZPD is the notion of change, and of deliberately creating new circumstances, or *the social situation of development*, where change can occur (Newman & Holzman, 1993). In Vygotsky's (1935/1994) later work, the study of child development (pedology) entailed the study of the environmental structure (*the social situation of development*) as it relates to the psychological organization (*higher-level consciousness*) of the developing child. It is not the environment itself, which may be constant, but the child's personally meaningful experiences and relationship with that environment that guides the process of higher cognitive development. By design, our praxis-oriented pedagogy should forge ZPD activity, putting teachers ahead of themselves, changing the social situation/circumstances so that change in teaching practices, new dispositions, or habits of the mind, and new views of teaching/learning can take hold or be internalized. And in that new *social situation of development*, an *ideal* needs to exist as the end product of development. In VSCT-informed praxis-oriented pedagogy, the *ideal* is represented by the way we conceptualize *teaching as dialogic mediation* (Johnson, 2009) and the development of *reasoning teaching* (Johnson, 1999). Yet, the processes and outcomes of ZPD activity cannot be predetermined or pre-specified—they instead emerge from the relations that form during ZPD activity—so while novice teachers and teacher educators are engaged in joint activity, "learning and development emerges from the fluid social relations and forms of discourse that teachers and teacher educators bring to that activity" (Moll, 2014,

p. 78). This being the case, teacher educators cannot predict the nature of their interactions with novice teachers—these must be negotiated and constituted *in situ* through and by the relational features while co-constructing ZPD activity. ZPD activity is, thus, from this understanding, the crucible of praxis, the space where theory and practice become inseparable from one another.

The Dialectical Unity of Theory-practice: Praxis

To the best of our knowledge, Vygotsky did not specifically write about the concept of praxis [практика], yet his entire enterprise to formulate a new psychology in the early 1900s was based on the notion that there is, or should be, an unbreakable interdependence between theory and practice. The notion of praxis, from the viewpoint of Vygotsky's theory, is the dialectic unity of theory and practice. This means that theory cannot stand alone from practice, or vice versa, but rather the two ways of understanding must be conceptualized as equal partners. From this perspective, theory guides practice but practice, in turn, influences theory. A theory without practice is empty verbalism; practice enacted without theoretical knowledge is mindless activity. Vygotsky understood human consciousness, and in particular the development of higher-level human consciousness, as premised on this synthesis, the reciprocal relationship between theory and practice. In Vygotsky's own words:

> Previously theory was not dependent on practice; instead, practice was the conclusion, the application, an excursion beyond the boundaries of science, an operation which lay outside science and came after science, which began after the scientific operation was considered completed. Success or failure had practically no effect on the fate of the theory ... Now the situation is the opposite. Practice pervades the deepest foundations of the scientific operation and reforms it from beginning to end. Practice sets the tasks and serves as the supreme judge of theory, as its truth criterion. It dictates how to construct the concepts and how to formulate the laws.
>
> (1926/2004, p. 304)

The 'pervading' unity of theory and practice discussed in this quote is what scholars of VSCT mean by the notion of praxis: "material activity adapted to specific goals and informed by theory, while simultaneously testing those same theoretical principles" (Sanchez Vasquez, 1977, p. 95). Vygotsky's ultimate goal was to create a new methodology to uncover the development of human consciousness, which he believed could not be accomplished by looking at a fully formed adult, but instead had to be traced in its formation either from child to adult or from novice to expert. One of Vygotsky's greatest contributions to the theoretical study of human development was his insistence that the process (the trajectory of development) and not just the product (a static, testable outcome) must be considered to fully understand how humans learn and how human cognition develops. Vygotsky's life challenge was to reimagine the psychology of his day by proposing a new psychology based on the principles of dialectical materialism—a psychology to explain the human ability to use symbols to mediate their psyche. He argued that everything in human life (beyond basic biological drives) is derived from and dependent on cultural activity; that is, it is through socially organized practical activity that humans create and change the material conditions in which they live, and in doing so change themselves. He argued that the goal of psychological research was to show how external knowledge and abilities in children become internalized tools of thinking. And because he viewed the development of human consciousness as a profoundly social process, he emphasized the role of dialogue, social relations, and engagement in goal-directed activity all via language as powerful mediators of the development of higher-level cognitive processes.

Overview of the Book

In Part I, Chapter 1, we lay out the principles and concepts of VSCT that inform the goals, design, and enactment of the three required pillar courses that we offer in our MA TESL program. Part I is more theoretically focused than the remainder of the book. This choice is intentional in that to understand praxis-oriented pedagogy, readers need accessible, situated understandings of some of the core concepts and principles of VSCT. However, this section is not a Vygotskian primer but a weaving of VSCT concepts and principles into a coherent rationale for the goals, design, and enactment of praxis-oriented pedagogy with the ultimate aim of developing novice L2 teacher reasoning during experiential coursework in L2 teacher education programs. In Chapter 2, we define the essential elements and design features of praxis-oriented pedagogy for L2 teacher education. This includes the essential principles of praxis-oriented pedagogy, including structured mediational spaces/means, concept development, *responsive mediation, teaching as dialogic mediation*, and *reasoning teaching*. We then provide an overview of the deliberate design features of praxis-oriented pedagogy, including the intentional ways that praxis-oriented pedagogy creates mediational spaces/means that foster ZPD activity, restructures the social situation of teacher conceptual development, and fosters reasoned instructional choices and practices.

In Part II, which includes Chapters 3 and 4, we document how praxis-oriented pedagogy supports novice teacher development and offer an overview of the key components of our MA TESL program. While several aspects of our pillar courses will be familiar to those in the field of L2 teacher education, the purpose of Part II is to illustrate for the reader the stance of the courses, that is, praxis-oriented pedagogy. It includes detailed descriptions and intentional design features of the three pillar courses and the capstone projects MA TESL students must complete to earn the degree. It is important for the reader to know where the empirical data for this book come from. Over four years, ten MA TESL students in cohort one and 17 in cohort two gave us Institutional Review Board permission to collect all of the digitally recorded instruction and written reflections they completed during each of the three pillar courses. Importantly, we, as principal investigators, did not know who had given us permission to access their data until after they had graduated from the MA TESL program. Moreover, these data represent requirements of each course and include not only the novice teachers' talk, actions, and reflections, but also our mediation, both oral and written, on all course requirements.

This massive database includes the following items:

Teaching ESL—Extended Team-Teaching Project (teams of 2, 3, or 4 novice teachers):

- Nine digitally recorded *practice teach* sessions (55–75 minutes each)
- Nine digitally recorded *actual teach* sessions (55–75 minutes each)
- Nine audio recorded stimulated recall sessions (1 hour each)
- 27 written reflection papers (five to seven pages each)

Tutoring Internship

- c. 980 weekly written reflection posts with Internship Supervisor responses
- 27 final written reflection papers (eight pages each)

Teaching Practicum

- c. 351 weekly reflective journal entries with Practicum Supervisor responses
- 27 final reflective journal entries with Practicum Supervisor responses
- 81 digitally recorded teaching sessions (55–75 minutes each)
- 27 teaching philosophies

MA TESL Graduates

- Seven interviews with graduates who had participated in the original research project (c. 1 hour each)

Our novice L2 teachers represent a number of countries and L1s and have taught in a variety of educational contexts. Figure 1.2 (see also Appendix 2) provides a snapshot of their backgrounds and the number of years of teaching experience they bring to the MA TESL program.

Defining Praxis-oriented Pedagogy for L2 Teacher Education

Name	Gender	Home Country	L1	Years of Teaching experience		
				<1 year	1—2 years	3+ years
Ai	F	China	Mandarin	X		
Aisha	F	Saudi Arabia	English	X		
Ana	F	Argentina	Spanish			X
Azadeh	F	Iran	Farsi	X		
Bao	F	China	Mandarin	X		
Bei	M	China/United States	Mandarin			X
Chen	F	China	Mandarin	X		
Chul	M	Korea	Korea		X	
Emine	F	Turkey	Turkish			X
Ethan	M	United States	English		X	
Fang	F	China	Mandarin	X		
Fen	F	China	Mandarin	X		
Gan	M	China	Mandarin	X		
Hannah	F	United States	English		X	
Lai	F	China	Mandarin		X	
Layla	F	Saudi Arabia	Arabic		X	
Leo	M	Brazil	Portuguese			X
Lin	F	China	Mandarin	X		
Mei	F	China	Mandarin	X		
Natalie	F	United States	English		X	
Pavel	M	Kazakhstan	Kazakh, Russian			X
Ping	F	China	Mandarin	X		X
Qiao	F	China	Mandarin	X		
Qing	F	China	Mandarin		X	
Shu	F	Taiwan	Taiwanese, Mandarin		X	
Yan	F	China	Mandarin	X		
Zeina	F	Saudi Arabia	Arabic		X	

*all names are pseudonyms

FIGURE 1.2 Novice L2 Teacher Demographics and Years of Teaching Experience

In Part III, we trace the developmental trajectory of novice teacher reasoning. In Chapters 5–8, we document how the internalization of the pedagogical concepts introduced in the three pillar courses foster novice teachers' self-regulation of their teacher reasoning and teaching activity. We provide empirical evidence from our database of how our novice L2 teachers gradually move from the social plane, in which their thinking and activities are mediated through academic and pedagogical concepts and interactions with us, to the internal plane, where they begin to appropriate the necessary conceptual resources to regulate their own thinking and activities. VSCT defines this process as internalization (Leont'ev, 1981), not simply the transmission of knowledge and/or skills but a transformation of the self and one's activities. We begin Part III, Chapter 5, by discussing the overall role that pedagogical concepts, as expressed in brief and accessible phrases, play in praxis-oriented pedagogy and in the development of novice teacher reasoning and instructional expertise. In other words, what are pedagogical concepts and why do they matter in L2 teacher education? This chapter summarizes our understanding of how these accessible, compact statements share and reflect our VSCT theoretical perspective. In Chapter 6, we focus on the role of *responsive mediation* and its effect upon teacher instructional stance. This chapter is designed to give readers a deeper understanding of how being the recipients of targeted, responsive, contingent mediation helps novice teachers learn how and why to provide *responsive mediation* to the learners they work with in various instructional roles. Chapter 7 traces the development of emotional orientation and engagement of novice L2 teachers and illuminates the role of *growth points* ('collisions') between emotions and cognition (see Veresov, 2017), in the context of their teaching/tutoring activity. The chapter is designed to introduce the reader to the core VSCT concept of *perezhivanie*, the way that lived experience is interpreted in terms of emotional understanding, which is central to the way we view L2 teacher education. We conclude this part, Chapter 8, by offering evidence of the ways in which novice teachers come to internalize the interconnectedness of pedagogical concepts, specifically, as they learn to control pedagogical concepts through strategic, responsive, and contingent selection, design, and sequencing of class activities. The chapter presents evidence from our database that shows the internalization of pedagogical concepts as novice L2 teachers gain fluency and versatility in reasoning their pedagogical choices.

In Part IV, we provide readers with information relating to the outcomes, impact, and opportunities of our praxis-oriented pedagogy. Chapter 9 documents how our novice L2 teachers reorient and reconceptualize language teaching, highlighted through the various ways in which they have come to enact a *teaching as dialogic mediation instructional stance*. Chapter 10 turns to the post-MA TESL program professional activity of seven graduates of our program who participated in the original research project. This chapter is included to offer more detail about how pedagogical concepts and a VSCT orientation toward language teaching can carry over into future work once these teachers leave the context of graduate school. Chapter 11 concludes by providing readers with additional information about the way our praxis-oriented pedagogy offers other forms of mediational spaces and input for our novice teachers. It is provided in the hope that readers who want to explore applying some of the ideas laid out in this book will have a deeper understanding of the many kinds of opportunities that can be used for responsive, contingent, and socioculturally focused mediation of novice teacher reasoning.

References

Johnson, K. E. (1999). *Understanding language teaching: Reasoning in action*. Boston, MA: Heinle & Heinle.
Johnson, K. E. (2009). *Second language teacher education: A sociocultural perspective*. New York: Routledge.
Johnson, K. E., & Golombek, P. R. (2016). *Mindful L2 teacher education: A sociocultural perspective on cultivating teachers' professional development*. New York: Routledge.

Kubanyiova, M., & Feryok, A. (2015). Language teacher cognition in applied linguistics research: Revisiting the territory, redrawing the boundaries, reclaiming the relevance. *The Modern Language Journal, 99*(3), 435–449. https://doi.org/10.1111/modl.12239.

Leont'ev, A. N. (1981). The problem of activity in psychology. In J. Wertsch (Ed.), *The concept of activity in Soviet psychology* (pp. 37–71). Armonk, NY: M.E. Sharpe, Inc.

Moll, L. C. (2014). *L.S. Vygotsky and education*. London: Routledge.

Newman, F., & Holzman, L. (1993). *Lev Vygotsky: Revolutionary scientist*. London: Routledge.

Poehner, M. E., & Lantolf, J. P. (2021). The ZPD, second language learning and the transposition—Transformation dialectic. *Cultural Historical Psychology, 17*(3), 31–41. https://doi.org/10.17759/chp.2021170306.

Sanchez Vasquez, A. (1977). *The philosophy of praxis*. London: Humanities Press.

Veresov, N. (2017). The concept of perezhivanie in cultural-historical theory: Content and contexts. In M. Fleer, F. González Rey, & N. Veresov (Eds.), *Perezhivanie, emotions and subjectivity. Advancing Vygotsky's legacy* (pp. 47–70). Singapore: Springer.

Vygotsky, L. S. (1926/2004). The historical meaning of the crisis in psychology: A methodological investigation. In R. W. Rieber, & D. K. Robinson (Eds.), *The essential Vygotsky* (pp. 227–344). New York: Kluwer/Plenum.

Vygotsky, L. S. (1935/1994). The development of academic concepts in school aged children. In R. van der Veer, & J. Valsiner (Eds.), *The Vygotsky reader* (pp. 355–370). Oxford: Blackwell.

Vygotsky, L. S. (1978). *Mind in society*. Cambridge, MA: Harvard University Press.

2
PRAXIS-ORIENTED PEDAGOGY FOR L2 TEACHER EDUCATION

So, what does Vygotsky's commitment to praxis have to do with the education of novice L2 teachers? Central to Vygotsky's genetic method is the notion that educational practice is a form of scientific research; a theory is not designed to simply explain psychological development but can be used to deploy specific principles and concepts to affect development intentionally and fundamentally through appropriately organized activities. Our claim is that the education of novice teachers, if it is designed to promote the development of both theoretical and practical reasoning, should reflect the dialectical unity of theory and practice as laid out in Vygotskian Sociocultural Theory (VSCT). Specifically, the principles and concepts of VSCT that inform the goals, design, and enactment of the three praxis-oriented courses we offer in our L2 teacher education program should provoke and promote the development of novice L2 teacher reasoning; we act upon the belief that theory influences practice. At the same time, we are committed, by our embrace of the principles of VSCT, to explore and empirically document the influences and consequences of our pedagogy on the development of novice L2 teacher reasoning. Thus, we recognize praxis as a social human activity—since social conditions shape human consciousness, only when the social conditions change can higher-level human consciousness change. Additionally, our praxis-oriented pedagogy is longitudinal in that over the course of two years, through engagement in the three pillar courses, we seek to change the social conditions of our novice teachers as they are becoming L2 teachers.

In line with the *pedagogical imperative* (Lantolf & Poehner, 2014), a fundamental principle of VSCT is to deploy specific VSCT principles and concepts to intentionally promote cognitive development through appropriately organized instructional practice, and to explore what that practice illuminates

DOI: 10.4324/9781003268987-3

about our understanding of the principles by which we teach. That is, true to the dialectical unity of theory-practice, as three teacher educators steeped in VSCT, our work with novice L2 teachers over the past 30 years has changed how we understand Vygotsky's central principles and concepts. In other words, our work with L2 teachers may not have changed VSCT on a universal level, but we as Vygotskians are deepening what the theory brings, and can potentially bring, to our work with novice L2 teachers. We do not see Vygotsky's writings as static texts waiting to be revealed but instead his work engages with us, and we are engaged with it. What we say about it, based on our careful examination of our own activity—reflection—and the data—analysis and interpretation, can and probably should change over time.

A foundational principle of VSCT is the idea that cognition is mediated and develops through engagement with cultural artifacts and activities, concepts, and social relations. The development of novice L2 teacher reasoning in our program is intentionally mediated through engagement with all of these resources:

- Readings in the expert/professional literature
- Observations and engagement with actual instructional contexts
- Engagement with academic and pedagogical concepts
- Social/dialogical interactions (oral and written) with expert others (i.e., faculty, teacher educators, mentors)

On the surface, these resources appear to be what one would expect in most L2 teacher education programs. Indeed, one of our arguments in this volume is that nothing we do is out of reach of any interested teacher educator who wants to understand and instantiate praxis-oriented, structured mediational spaces and activities in their own instructional context. The difference in our program lies, perhaps, in the intentionality of these activities and the fortunate circumstance that we share a rich collaborative space with like-minded colleagues. But each of us (the three authors) ended up in this exceptional and privileged environment through individual experiences and choices; it is a fortuitous but not entirely intentional outcome, which is somewhat ironic given that we emphasize the importance of intentionality in our work.

Thus, to recap, what is crucial to understanding how we conceptualize, mediate, and respond to the development of novice L2 teacher reasoning are the following elements: the mediational role of academic and pedagogical concepts and the quality and character of the social interactions around those concepts. To clarify this stance, in the next paragraph we articulate how we approach praxis-oriented pedagogy on two levels: course design and theoretical orientation and the empirical documentation of the processes of learning.

The first level is the design of our courses, the academic and pedagogical concepts we expect our novice teachers to engage with, the teaching/tutoring activities we ask them to participate in, the reflective stance we encourage them to maintain, and the range of interactions (oral and written) we have with them throughout the three pillar courses, all of which are grounded in a VSCT epistemological stance on the professional development of L2 teachers (Johnson, 2009). With VSCT and praxis-oriented pedagogy as our guiding principle, we design practices that create conditions under which developmental processes may be set in motion, observed, and upon which intervention can take place. As such, the principles of VSCT shape the ways in which we structure our pedagogy, that is, the practices in and through which we engage with novice L2 teachers. The practices and the mediational spaces the courses create constitute a concretization of praxis-oriented pedagogy. In this way, it is not so much about the practices themselves, but rather what we, as "teacher educators are attempting to accomplish through these practices" (Johnson & Golombek, 2016, p. 3) and the goals and intentions upon which they are built.

Additionally, our praxis-oriented pedagogy is informed by the VSCT principle of tool-and-result (Newman & Holzman, 1993; Vygotsky, 1978). We are not using our practices as tools to yield results (i.e., this is how to teach) as is the case in much traditional educational practice. Rather, our praxis-oriented pedagogy is meant to be practiced. As novice L2 teachers engage in and with these practices, this creates the potential for qualitative transformation (i.e., development), and this qualitative transformation is a collective accomplishment. As Holzman (1997) describes Vygotsky's method:

> As "simultaneously tool-and-result", method is practiced, not applied. Knowledge is not separate from the activity of *practicing method*; it is not "out there" waiting to be discovered through the use of an already made tool. ... Practicing method creates the object of knowledge simultaneously with creating the tool by which that knowledge might be known. Tool-and-result come into existence together; their relationship is one of *dialectical unity*, rather than instrumental duality.
>
> (p. 52, original emphasis)

Thus, the second level is to empirically document the processes of novice L2 teacher learning and trace longitudinally the emerging development of novice L2 teacher reasoning. Key to this level are the direct (actual teaching/tutoring) and mediated experiences (reflection on learning to teach/tutor) our novice teachers have throughout our pillar courses. The data presented in this book represent those experiences not purely from our perspectives but also from the perspectives of our novice L2 teachers. As is laid out in the course descriptions, each activity they engage in, whether it is practice teaching, tutoring an ESL student, or teaching an entire ESL class, is empirically documented via digital recordings and/or specifically designed reflective writings.

Embedded in our pillar courses is a collection of VSCT-informed pedagogical concepts that we have developed expressly for the purpose of helping novice L2 teachers develop both more theoretically and pedagogically sound reasoning and instructional practices (see Appendix 1). We refer to these concepts as pedagogical, rather than academic, because they indicate *how* to teach, rather than *what* to teach. According to Vygotsky (1978, 1981), human cultures create categories for organizing events and objects, which over time become concepts, represented in linguistic signs, that are passed from one generation to the next. He distinguishes *everyday concepts* based on concrete experiences in the world from *academic concepts*,[1] which reflects understandings based on systematic observation and theoretical investigations in various academic disciplines. As a simple example, young children see the sun rise in the East and set in the West and assume incorrectly, through their everyday experiences, that the Sun goes around the Earth. When children enter formal schooling and are exposed to academic concepts such as planetary rotation and gravity, they come to understand gravitational pull and the relationship of the Earth to the Sun is transformed. And they, as developing humans thinking in and acting on the world, are transformed as well. Thus, the function of any educational activity, according to Vygotsky, is to modify learners' conceptual systems so they are aligned with the most up-to-date academic knowledge available. Since language has a powerful influence on conceptual development, the ways in which the language and the objects are understood, used, and transformed in purposeful activities set the stage for productive instruction (teaching/learning) and ultimately conceptual development. For L2 teacher education programs, this means altering novice teachers' existing conceptual systems about language teachers/teaching, conceptual systems that have been appropriated through the social and historical processes of schooling (i.e., the infamous 'apprenticeship of observation' (Lortie, 1975)) by giving them new words, as well as new ways, for understanding and enacting the activity of language teaching.

The VSCT-informed pedagogical concepts that undergird our praxis-oriented pedagogy are the same concepts that inform our vision of theoretically and pedagogically sound L2 instruction, or, to use a Vygotskian term, the *ideal*. In other words, praxis-oriented pedagogy is appropriate for learners of teaching (novice teachers) as well as learners of any object of study. Praxis-oriented pedagogy is neither a traditional teacher-centered transmission view of teaching nor unstructured student-centered discovery learning, but rather "a student-centered approach with deliberate teaching" (Johnson, 2009, p. 62). Likewise, praxis-oriented pedagogy is a transformative model of higher-level cognitive development in the sense that individuals transform what is appropriated for their own purposes and come to understand new knowledge and experiences in terms of particular contexts of use. Individuals are both participants in social situations and agents of change upon those social situations in which they are embedded. That is, higher-level psychological processes are at the same time both socially derived, meaning that they are embedded within the historical practices of a culture, and individually unique. To bring it back to L2 teacher education, this means that novice teachers are shaped by their experiences as learners, by the cultural practices of teacher education, and by the particulars of their teaching context, all of which are embedded within larger sociocultural histories and at the same time appropriated in individual ways (see Johnson & Golombek, 2016).

Teaching as Dialogic Mediation

Praxis-oriented pedagogy fundamentally conceptualizes the activity of *teaching as dialogic mediation* (Johnson, 2009): it focuses attention on the quality and character of activity and interaction, while highlighting the mediating role in learners' conceptual and language development that activity and interaction play. To learn to teach from this instructional stance, our novice teachers are asked to focus on the quality and character of the activities they engage in with their learners, the conceptual and linguistic resources they use to engage in those activities, and the educational and developmental goals they are attempting to accomplish through those activities. Novice teachers also, through both illustration and discussion, learn how to offer assistance and guidance that is highly responsive to learners' immediate needs and educational goals. Taking a *teaching as dialogic mediation instructional stance* allows novice L2 teachers to create spaces for learners to make their thinking explicit, thereby opening it up to social influence. Our novice teachers are taught to strive to engage learners with the subject matter content they are teaching in ways that promote deeper understandings and promote conceptual thinking by employing praxis-oriented pedagogy, which links academic knowledge (subject matter content) to practical everyday activity (meaningful language use).

Reasoning Teaching

Our VSCT stance defines the learning of teaching as grounded in concepts, social interactions/relations, artifacts, and experiences and, especially, the shared meanings they carry between teacher educators and novice teachers. As Vygotsky's (1931/1997) often quoted phrase suggests, "through others, we become ourselves" (p. 105). Thus, our praxis-oriented pedagogy supports novice L2 teachers as they learn, through their interactions and engagement (oral and written) with us, their mentor teachers, each other, and their English language learners, to reason through their instructional choices. Johnson (1999) defines *reasoning teaching* as:

> the complex ways in which teachers conceptualize, construct explanations for, and respond to the social interactions and shared meanings that exist within and among teachers, students, parents, and administrators

both inside and outside the classroom. Simply put, reasoning teaching reflects the complex ways in which teachers figure out how to teach a particular topic, with a particular group of students, at a particular time, in a particular classroom, within a particular school.

(p. 1)

Reasoning teaching is an educational stance that involves much more than the delivery of curriculum or the acquisition of skills. It implies and comprises the building of teacher agency by strengthening teachers' knowledge of and ability to manipulate a repertoire of linguistic, cultural, pedagogical, and interactional resources that enable them to support productive language learning. To this end, we believe that the development of novice teacher reasoning is best accomplished through high-quality meditational activities with expert teacher educators engaged in the praxis-oriented pedagogy.

Responsive Mediation

Throughout our three pillar courses, we design experiences that provide the proleptic, or 'future-in-the-present' experience of letting novices be, if only temporarily, what they have not yet fully become. Each course is designed to create structured mediational spaces where novice teachers are supported as they attempt to 'jump ahead of themselves,' to try out and try on being and becoming a language teacher/tutor. As we assist and guide them through these experiences, we engage in responsive mediation (Johnson & Golombek, 2016) (oral and written), that is dialogic, intentional, and contingent upon the nature of the interactions and activities. *Responsive mediation* is not just mediation by a more-knowledgeable expert, but rather collaborative, or co-regulated, dialogue between teacher educators and novice teachers. In other words, it is not only teacher educators responding to novice teachers' needs but also novice teachers responding to teacher educators' mediation. Thus, *responsive mediation* is multidirectional, dynamic, and contingent upon the interactions and activities in which teacher educators and novice teachers participate.

Pedagogical Concepts as a Means of Mediation

Praxis-oriented pedagogy is neither scripted nor formulaic; rather, it is highly intentional. As L2 teacher educators, we need to help novice L2 teachers understand the goals of *reasoning teaching*. To that end, we have forged a set of pedagogical concepts that are presented to novice L2 teachers as a set of practical and conceptual tools, grounded in the seminal research on classroom discourse which argues that how teachers and students talk and act in classrooms greatly influences what they learn (Barnes, 1976; Cazden, 1981;

Johnson, 1995, also see Appendix 1). Therefore, one characteristic of our courses is the cohesive way in which these pedagogical concepts—tools for conceptual understanding and for *reasoning teaching* choices—are woven through the three pillar courses. We provide our novice teachers with these pedagogical concepts to enable them to foster greater levels of student participation and engagement in their instructional activities (see Johnson & Dellagnelo, 2013). Throughout our three pillar courses, these pedagogical concepts are operationally defined, modeled, and analyzed in the activity of actual teaching/tutoring. One basic outcome of learning to control these pedagogical concepts is that novice teachers can be seen to shift their instructional stance from teacher-fronted instruction to *teaching as dialogic mediation instructional stance*, which is an outcome, from a VSCT perspective, that is the *ideal*. Likewise, we encourage and support novice teachers in their attempts to use these pedagogical concepts when they prepare and teach lessons or engage in tutoring sessions. For example, a set of pedagogical concepts that we have reported on in a previous publication (Johnson, Verity, & Childs, 2020) includes these three:

a. TEACH OFF YOUR STUDENTS, NOT AT THEM.
b. BE DIRECT, NOT DIRECTIVE.
c. TEACHING AS CONNECTING.[2]

A pedagogical concept is not just an 'idea,' and it is not just a guideline. It is a kind of 'package' comprised of accessible language, theoretical insight, and practical utility. Likewise, pedagogical concepts are not 'plug and play'—they will not solve an instructional impasse if the teacher or tutor has no idea of what to do—but they can help a teacher/tutor evaluate, quickly, a choice or direction. In the case of this list of three, these pedagogical concepts were not written in mantra-like phrases nor were they fully understood as pedagogical concepts until we had used them for several years. It was in the activity of beginning the research project that makes up the core of this book and exploring our own practice that we realized how central pedagogical concepts—theoretical insights packaged for use by novices—are to praxis-oriented pedagogy.

a. TEACH OFF YOUR STUDENTS, NOT AT THEM is a simple play on prepositions, but as a pedagogical concept it has powerful consequences for how teachers orient to their learners and how learners' histories and current understandings are both valued and made part of any instructional conversation. It does not negate the important role of the teacher in the processes of teaching/learning, but it encourages more dialogic, collaborative, co-constructed interactions between teachers and learners. This shift is notoriously difficult for novice teachers as their preconceived notions about language teaching tend to be based in their experiences as students: teacher-fronted delivery of some predefined content and more often than not, explicit instruction *about* the language rather than engagement in actual language use. Additionally, as novices they often overprepare, sometimes scripting out what they intend to say and do without consideration for how their learners may experience and/or respond to their instruction. TEACH OFF YOUR STUDENTS, NOT AT THEM requires that teachers open spaces for learners to make their understandings explicit, listen carefully to their understandings and make links to new concepts or new ways of thinking about the content they teach. It also shifts teachers' attention to the norms that govern participation in an activity and the extent to which learners are able (or not) to participate in that activity. It requires teachers to pay attention to the resources, semiotic, linguistic, and interactional, that learners are using, attempting to use, or need to be aware of in order to fully and successfully, or even partially, participate in an instructional activity. In essence, TEACH OFF YOUR STUDENTS, NOT AT THEM enables novice teachers to shift their instructional stance from teacher-fronted to *teaching as dialogic mediation*.

b. BE DIRECT, NOT DIRECTIVE is a simple way of making this rather complicated point: then working with an L2 writer or speaker of English, novice teachers cannot assume that the learner's orientation to the text or to the linguistic work at hand matches his/her own, which is more expert, by definition, and possibly much more automatic, if English is one's first language. Therefore, novice teachers should BE DIRECT when making a point: say explicitly what level of the text, or of the language, they are giving feedback on. They need to be absolutely clear when they are providing input on, for example, a basic grammatical 'mistake' (such as a missing plural -s on a noun) and a more complex consideration of which grammatical structure (e.g., a relative clause or a separate free-standing sentence) works best in a given context. On the other hand, they should not just 'tell the learner what to say or what to write' (that is, NOT DIRECTIVE). Instead, they need to use targeted mediation to find out what the learner already knows about the point at hand and whether that knowledge is useful for a particular example.

Novice tutors/teachers, not surprisingly, often misconstrue this pedagogical concept as saying 'don't ever tell the tutee/learner what the problem is'—the problem and (a) solution are often conflated in the mind of the novice tutor/teacher, for whom the 'right answer' is always, or always has been, the ultimate goal. When the goal becomes developing expertise in the L2 learner, then identifying the problem clearly (BE DIRECT) can be seen quite easily as separate from just telling the tutee/learner how to 'fix' it. Indeed, one of the solutions to the problem might very well be that there is no way to 'fix' the problem, only to rework the sentence or paragraph.

c. TEACHING AS CONNECTING is another seemingly simple phrase, yet it can help novice teachers begin to understand and make sense of the complex nature of language teaching. Teachers are responsive to multiple stakeholders at multiple levels at the same time. At the classroom level, TEACHING AS CONNECTING reminds novice teachers to connect with their most immediate stakeholders, their learners, and get to know them both as learners and individuals. While this may sound obvious to seasoned teachers, novice teachers tend to focus on learning the content they are to teach and designing activities to teach the content without considering how the learners will respond to their instructional choices. When novice teachers reason their teaching through the concept of TEACHING AS CONNECTING, they learn the importance of keeping their focus on their learners as they design instructional activities. They begin to understand the meaning of intentionality in their teaching as they help their learners connect with the content in meaningful ways. TEACHING AS CONNECTING is a useful pedagogical concept for novice teachers to begin to design cohesive, coherent lesson plans. At the same time, TEACHING AS CONNECTING reminds novice L2 teachers that there is another level of stakeholders in the learning process, administrators and ministries of education who establish institutional, state, and/or national mandates and standards to which teachers must connect their instructional choices. Language teacher educators can help novice teachers make sense of the complexity of teaching by explicitly making visible for novice teachers the many connections inherent in teaching and asking them to do the same.

Pedagogical Concepts and the Dialectic Tension of Teaching/Learning

If there is one way in which teacher education programs are alike, it is that the 'students' are also 'teachers.' The inherent tension in the development and maintenance of these two identities can pose challenges, but from a VSCT perspective, this dialectical tension provides rich opportunities for mediation and development. Indeed, it is one of the motivating factors for our offering, and requiring, three pillar courses that require interaction with actual L2 learners, as well as voluntary extra-curricular instructional opportunities to the novice teachers (see Chapter 11). Toggling between student-identity and teacher-identity, sometimes literally in the same hour, helps novice teachers confront the reality that teaching and learning cannot be construed as separate activities. In theory, this dialectical unity underlies much of our program design; in practice, it means that nearly everything the novice teacher learns in her student identity can be transferred to her teacher identity.

As teacher educators, we build upon existing novice teachers' understandings using pedagogical concepts to materialize what teaching activity means while construing it from a learner-oriented perspective. VSCT encapsulates the dialectic tension that novice teachers experience as 'student teachers' with its use of the term from Russian, *obuchenie*. This word can be translated as either *teaching* or *learning* (similar to the non-standard use of the English word 'learn' to mean 'teach') or, as is often written in translated texts, as the combined term teaching/learning.' As Daniels explains, the term signifies "the process of teaching and learning in which to learn one has to teach (communicate one's understanding with the teacher) and to teach one has to learn (about the understandings of the pupil/learner)" (Daniels, 2018, p. 39).

In a dialectic unity, without the one half of the pair, the other half cannot exist. Teaching depends upon learning and vice versa. In our program, we heighten novice L2 teachers' awareness of this tension/unity in simple ways: at times, by invoking pedagogical concepts 'in the moment' during our own teaching of the three pillar courses. We frequently encourage novice L2 teachers to adopt, literally, words and actions that they see us use in our own teaching. We sometimes 'give them words' as part of our mediation. Even though we are expert teachers, and we understand that a novice L2 teacher might use a pedagogical concept, or an action slightly differently than we do, we need to put tools, literally, into their hands sometimes. As Johnson and Golombek (2018) point out,

> Because *obuchenie* leads rather than follows cognitive development, teacher educators need to relate and respond to teachers as if they can do more than they are capable of—as being in advance of themselves.
>
> (p. 444)

One way we know that the novice teacher is beginning to make sense of this productive duality is when we see them identifying moments of recognition—'oh, I can use what I learned as a MA TESL student in my activity as a teacher! —in their reflective writings. This externalization of their attempts to create links can be seen in all three pillar courses, though it may occur most frequently in the Tutoring Internship, when they are teaching autonomously for the first time, and have a relatively generous window of time to ponder each tutoring session. The carefully designed minimalist instructional space of the tutoring session acts as a kind of fulcrum, balancing high levels of instructional authority with low levels of classroom management, paperwork, and distraction. With its focus on one-to-one encounters, the Tutoring Internship gives novice teachers a unique space for *obuchenie*, in which they can interrogate and consolidate both their student identity and their teacher identity.

Pedagogical Concepts Link Novice Thought and Expert Thought

A great benefit of formulating dense expert knowledge into the format of a light, novice-friendly phrase is that it makes such knowledge both palatable and portable. Pedagogical concepts are not intimidating, and they are, by intention, mnemonically powerful. It is difficult to remember the outlines and complexities of VSCT while coping with a class or a lesson, but it is relatively easy to keep at the front of one's mind the phrase, TEACH OFF YOUR STUDENTS, NOT AT THEM. Being immersed in the complexity of teaching real learners demands a lot of cognitive work; being able to recall a short phrase to help shape a good response to those learners does not.

The 'bite-size' nature of pedagogical concepts makes them particularly palatable when they are first encountered, that is, in the first pillar course, Teaching ESL. And their portability means that they travel well through the program. Just telling a group of novice L2 teachers something simple in a phrase does not make that phrase a pedagogical concept, and the fact that the phrase is pithy does not mean that the novice teachers will retain it. But hearing the same basic ideas—be flexible and responsive when it comes to your talking in the lesson; don't assume you can predict everything about what your learners are thinking, planning, or getting; work hard at supporting student learning by actively and explicitly engineering the way they engage with the materials—repeated in various contexts but always tied to the same brief, memorable encoding means that the novice teachers are more likely to retain the words of the pedagogical concepts even while full understanding of it is emerging.

Pedagogical Concepts Are Tools for Conceptual Development of Academic Concepts

The formulation of a pedagogical concept as compact, memorable but at the same time ordinary phrases is intentional and grows out of our understanding of the VSCT perspective on conceptual development. Novices, especially adult novice teachers, do not arrive at an educational program as 'blank slates' or, to recall John Locke's famous phrase, 'empty cabinets.' They bring a good deal of conceptual knowledge with them, though in many cases their grasp of what we consider to be key concepts is incomplete, informal, or unexamined. In our praxis-oriented pedagogy, we do not typically begin with verbal explanations but engage the novice L2 teachers with material and symbolic representations of what we want them to learn, such as concept maps, analogies, reflective tasks, and so forth. Pedagogical concepts serve as useful bridges between novice teachers' everyday understanding of what it means to PREDICT or ORIENT and our specifically pedagogical and classroom-focused usages of those words. Even the lowly preposition, TEACH OFF

YOUR STUDENTS, NOT AT THEM, opens itself up to interrogation. These new meanings are, in the VSCT use of the term, "scientific [academic]" concepts: they "shape how we perceive, understand, and act in and on the world" (Lantolf & Poehner, 2014, p. 61). Throughout this book, we introduce data that we believe provides evidence of the transformation of novice thinking and acting into more-expert-like reasoned activity. The novice teachers become very aware, especially when they engage in reflective actions such as writing posts or journals, that they can articulate the goal of praxis-oriented pedagogy.

Pedagogical Concepts Work Well with Other Mediational Modalities

It might be seen as a little bit ironic that this entire volume argues for the necessity of responsiveness and contingency in successful instruction, yet we actually provide a list of fixed, static phrases and imbue them with immense power! Recognizing this paradox as part of the dialectical unity between symbolic and material activity, we embrace it. More specifically, pedagogical concepts are expressed in very ordinary (or at least, ordinary-looking) language. Some of their power certainly derives from the fact they are not constructed out of jargon. They represent expert knowledge, but they do not make expertise more opaque. Instead, by talking about BE DIRECT, NOT DIRECTIVE or TEACHING AS CONNECTING in an L2 teacher education course, the teacher educator highlights the polysemy not only of English vocabulary words, but of activity itself.

For most of the two-year program, the pedagogical concepts are threaded through the three pillar courses in various ways, both implicitly and explicitly. Sometimes a teacher educator engages in a 'see what I just did there?' moment, and sometimes they are introduced during a formal discussion of readings or mentioned in a written response to a paper or online post. Indeed, the pedagogical concepts are invoked, both specifically and broadly, every time a teacher educator helps a novice L2 teacher develop a task, an activity, or a lesson, interprets a pedagogical episode, or reflects on a personal choice.

To begin mediating novice teachers toward being able to understand and engage in praxis-oriented pedagogy, we must seek footholds for their learning, just as we help them create such footholds for their own learners. As academics and former language teachers, of course we love to speak! But as teacher educators, we recognize that language is only one of the semiotic systems at our disposal, and we often consciously resort to other forms of mediation to explore meanings and support understanding.

Many approaches to pedagogy value multimodal input and instruction for the supposed benefit it provides to different styles of learning and learner preference. For VSCT, though, the role of multi-modality is not seen as peripheral (let's be nice to the visual learners today) and it is not seen as supplementary (here's a chart that summarizes the main points of the video we watched). Instead, the VSCT theoretical justification for recoding information is that semiotic recasting can provide a starting point for a successful episode of mediation. Using a non-linguistic form of mediation can animate ZPD activity more quickly and can help novice teachers more quickly call up their personally relevant meanings that we then begin transforming into expert understanding.

It is a cliché, yes, but sometimes a picture is really worth 1,000 words; personal meanings can come out more quickly and more immediately in the form of a drawing than a verbal explanation. For example, if a novice L2 teacher draws a picture of a teacher TEACHING OFF STUDENTS, NOT AT THEM by showing the teacher lecturing to the group, that picture clearly demonstrates that the novice L2 teacher sees teaching as 'information giving' (as they probably experienced as students) and it clearly demonstrates that the novice L2 teacher does not yet grasp the pedagogically focused, VSCT meaning of this phrase as we use it in our pillar courses.

Gestures, visual aids (charts, diagrams, sketches), audio cues…anything that a teacher does to help remind learners or point their attention in the desired direction, to orient them toward the importance of not only retention but experimentation and explanation can be used by teacher educators to mediate novice teachers, and, through meaningful imitation, by novice teachers to teach their learners. A quick review of the lesson planning documents prepared by novice L2 teachers in the first pillar course, Teaching ESL, for example, shows that the lesson plans all include some kind of visual or multimodal element, from a student-drawn concept map to a video, to a photograph, to a piece of realia, to a colorfully highlighted PowerPoint slide. While there is no pedagogical concept that strictly relates to the use of other sign systems besides language, visual components of a lesson such as color, video, photographs, fonts, graphic organizers, charts, etc., and other multimodal elements such as music, gesture, audio recordings, and tactile tasks can all play a vital role in TEACHING OFF learners rather than AT THEM.

Conclusion

While the pedagogical concepts themselves, as represented by these pithy sayings, may appear simple, they actually represent a theoretical orientation to the activity of teaching that is built up through engagement in both theoretical understanding and practical activity, in short, through praxis. Our praxis-oriented pedagogy, as L2 teacher educators, is to give our novice L2 teachers many chances to experience the tensions and complementarity of theory and practice in many different forms and formats. One format is to present them with these memorable conceptual expressions. But we do not expect them, or let them, just guess at what the expressions represent: that work is the work of our praxis-oriented coursework, which is the focus of PART II: The Design Features of Praxis-oriented Courses.

Notes

1 We recognize scientific and academic concepts as interchangeable but have given preference to academic concepts as this is how Vygotsky (1935/1994) referenced them in his later writings about formal (schooling) education.
2 We made the intentional choice to use capitalization when referring to all pedagogical concepts. This allows them to stand out for readers as well as to be inserted into our analyses and data sets when they are not explicitly used but referenced in our and/or our novice teachers' own words.

References

Barnes, D. (1976). *From communication to curriculum*. Middlesex: Penguin.
Cazden, C. (1981). Performance before competence: Assistance to child discourse in the zone of proximal development. *Quarterly Newsletter of the Laboratory of Comparative Human Cognition, 3*, 5–8.
Daniels, H. (2018). Vygotsky: Between socio-cultural relativism and historical materialism. From a psychological to a pedagogical perspective. *Cultural-Historical Psychology, 14*(3), 36–42. https://doi.org/10.17759/chp.2018140303.
Holzman, L. (1997). *Schools for growth: Radical alternatives to current educational models*. Mahwah, NJ: Lawrence Erlbaum.
Johnson, K. E. (1995). *Understanding communication in second language classrooms*. New York: Cambridge University Press.
Johnson, K. E. (1999). *Understanding language teaching: Reasoning in action*. Boston, MA: Heinle, Cengage Learning.
Johnson, K. E. (2009). *Second language teacher education: A sociocultural perspective*. New York: Routledge.
Johnson, K. E., & Dellagnelo, A. (2013). How 'sign meaning develops': Strategic mediation in learning to teach. *Language Teaching Research, 17*(4), 409–432. https://doi.org/10.1177/1362168813494126.
Johnson, K. E., & Golombek, P. R. (2016). *Mindful L2 teacher education: A sociocultural perspective on cultivating teachers' professional development*. New York: Routledge.
Johnson, K. E., & Golombek, P. R. (2018). Making L2 teacher education matter through Vygotskian-inspired pedagogy and research. In J. Lantolf, M. Poehner, & M. Swain (Eds.), *Handbook of sociocultural theory and second language development* (pp. 443–456). New York: Routledge.
Johnson, K. E., Verity, D. P., & Childs, S. S. (2020). Praxis-oriented pedagogy and the development of L2 novice teacher expertise. *The European Journal of Applied Linguistics and TEFL, 9*(2), 3–23.
Lantolf, J. P., & Poehner, M. (2014). *Sociocultural theory and the pedagogical imperative in L2 education*. New York: Routledge.
Lortie, D. (1975). *Schoolteacher: A sociological study*. Chicago, IL: University of Chicago.
Newman, F., & Holzman, L. (1993). *Lev Vygotsky: Revolutionary scientist*. London: Routledge.

Vygotsky, L. S. (1931/1997). Development of thinking and formation of concepts in the adolescent. In R. W. Rieber (Ed.), *Collected works of L. S. Vygotsky. Vol. 5: Child psychology* (pp. 29–81). New York: Plenum Press.

Vygotsky, L. S. (1935/1994). The development of academic concepts in school aged children. In R. van der Veer, & J. Valsiner (Eds.), *The Vygotsky reader* (pp. 355–370). Oxford: Blackwell.

Vygotsky, L. S. (1978). *Mind in society.* Cambridge, MA: Harvard University Press.

Vygotsky, L. S. (1981). The genesis of higher mental functions. In J. V. Wertsch (Ed.), *The concept of activity in Soviet psychology* (pp. 144–188). Armonk, NY: Sharpe.

PART II
THE DESIGN FEATURES OF PRAXIS-ORIENTED COURSES

3
THE MA TESL PROGRAM

In many ways, our MA TESL program is similar to other graduate-level TESL programs in North America. It is designed for individuals seeking advanced professional preparation in the teaching of English as a Second Language (ESL) or English as a Foreign Language (EFL) with adult learners in the US and abroad. Our program does not provide certification to teach ESL in US public schools, so the majority of the teachers who graduate from our program seek teaching positions at post-secondary institutions, such as Intensive English Language programs and private language schools, or, if they are international, they may plan to return to their home countries where an MA TESL degree from an English-medium-instruction institution is often highly valued. Still others seek work in non-governmental agencies, such as resettlement or adult literacy programs, and some end up teaching in industries that employ large numbers of persons for whom English is an additional language. Finally, many of our teachers apply to and are accepted into PhD programs at other universities, clearly energized by taking advanced graduate seminars alongside PhD students in our department and the experience of designing, carrying out, and writing the required capstone MA paper.

The degree itself consists of 36 credit hours of coursework that provide authentic, integrated opportunities that prepare teachers to plan, teach, reflect, research, and lead ESL and EFL programs for post-secondary and adult learners. There are three *Foundation* courses (nine credits) designed to develop an understanding of the social, historical, and theoretical foundations of the field of TESL. These include:

- Discourse Functional Grammar
- Second Language Acquisition
- Teaching English as a Second Language

The *Professional Core* (six credits) offers students opportunities to integrate their foundational understandings of specific content-area knowledge with practical experiences in ESL instructional settings. Teachers select at least two courses from the following:

- Teaching American English Pronunciation
- Teaching Second Language Writing
- Second Language Reading
- Methods of Language Assessment

Teachers also take two required field experience courses that provide opportunities to apply and enact their understandings in ESL instructional settings. These consist of:

- The Tutoring Internship
- The Teaching Practicum

As a graduate degree, the department offers a range of Research Methods courses, of which one (three credits) is required. These courses specialize in corpus methods, qualitative methods, quantitative methods, discourse analysis, conversation analysis, and analysis of classroom discourse. Teachers then fill out their remaining courses (12 credits) with electives, such as Language Ideology, Usage-based Second Language Acquisition, and/or Technology in FL/SL Education, to name a few popular choices.

It is perhaps because our program is not essentially different from many other MA TESL programs that we are writing this volume. We have structured a unique and—we believe—powerful framework for supporting, mediating, and framing L2 teacher development, one that focuses especially on the development of teacher reasoning through situated, mediated, and purposeful engagement with actual learners. But we engage in this work within a relatively traditional program context, and we want to underscore the point that anyone can infuse a course, or a sequence of courses, with Vygotskian Sociocultural Theory (VSCT) and praxis-oriented perspectives. It is one of the main goals of this volume to illuminate the accessibility of such perspectives, and the concrete, sometimes even mundane, ways in which we instantiate them. Although the authors feel lucky to work with like-minded colleagues, and there is no question that collaboration is a powerful element in program and curriculum development, a single course designer, teacher supervisor, or class instructor can make choices that align their work with novice teachers with the principles outlined in this chapter and in the other chapters of this book. Our own collaborative work developed out of years of shared interests, but we all came to the authorship of the volume you have in your hand through individual journeys.

At conferences we are frequently asked about the possibility of adapting our findings to other contexts, and our answer is always the same: It helps to have partners, but you can do a lot working by yourself, if you have to. The concept of praxis, and the related task of understanding how to structure a mediational space within a teacher education program, can take many material forms, but by engaging with the pedagogical concepts we offer here, building frequent and mediated reflective tasks into the educational program, and providing support for the reimagined and reasoned choices that novice teachers are learning how to make can be done within a single class or semester.

In the following section, we describe the ways in which we enlist our novice L2 teachers from their very first days with us into this new and mostly unfamiliar way of thinking about, looking at, and understanding, language teaching in the classroom.

Program Goals: Material and Conceptual Tools

As VSCT predicts, most newly arrived novice teachers do not align themselves particularly closely with the stated goals of the MA TESL program. Although they probably have reviewed the program website as part of their application and preparation process, the goals that are listed there are entirely external to their identities. Just as they tend to view classroom teaching as the one-way transmission of knowledge, they see the program as a whole as a relatively random set of experiences and requirements that they are subject to, but which do not particularly have meaning for their day-to-day decisions or for the trajectory of their professional development. Therefore, in our roles as academic advisors and orientation leaders, we structure our first encounters with each new cohort of novice teachers intentionally and engage them in ways that we hope will make these program goals more 'real' to the novice teachers from the first day. The aim is to reorient them to the goals as concepts that can, and should, be appropriated by them, as program participants, in personal ways. To this end, we go over the program website with them in the orientation meeting, and they are introduced to several program documents, such as the MA TESL Handbook (an online program description that includes policies, goals, requirements, capstone projects, and relevant university policies and resources); the MA Checklist, a kind of concept map of the internal requirements that govern course selection (24 credits from a set of required categories, and 12 credits that can be chosen from elective courses); and an overview, typically in the form of a brief slide show, of resources available to them on the campus and within the department. In subsequent advisor meetings, the MA Checklist is referenced, and completed, by the novice teacher working in collaboration with the academic advisor. Final graduation paperwork includes, among other items, a completed Checklist with signatures from the program coordinator, the academic advisor, and other program authorities.

This materialization of the program means that we have a shared vocabulary from the very first encounter and it places the program goals, along with other requirements and expectations, literally into the hands of the novice teachers themselves.

Of all these resources, it is the program objectives, a list of broad and even abstract expectations, that can feel the most distant to the new novice L2 teachers. Yet at the same time, these objectives are fully meaningful and relevant to the novice L2 teachers because they are, at one level, brief descriptions of the future. So, we make a point of referring to the program objectives—both in their list form as it appears on the website and in the continuous materialization of them through their educational and extra-curricular experiences—to inform not only our sessions with them as new and continuing graduate students, but also their own work as developing professionals.

Specifically, the goals of the program (they appear on the website as MA TESL Program Objectives) are listed as follows. Graduates of this program are expected to have, at the time they earn their degree:

- The ability to design and evaluate instructional materials, technology, media, and other resources that meet the specific instructional and language related needs and abilities of students
- The ability to reflect on, critically analyze, and evaluate your own teaching practices
- The ability to articulate a philosophy of language teaching grounded in current language and learning theories
- An understanding of the complex social, cultural, political, and institutional factors that affect language teaching and students' language learning
- Knowledge of research and research methods for studying language teaching and learning
- Knowledge of the teaching field (English as a Second Language)
- Evidence of successful participation in collaborative projects with others

The list becomes particularly relevant at the time when they are making final preparations of the professional e-Portfolio, one of the required capstone projects for the program (see Chapter 4).

The Three Pillar Courses

Since the goal of this book is to define and illustrate praxis-oriented pedagogy as well as trace the developmental trajectory of novice teacher reasoning, our focus is on novice L2 teachers' experiences with us in what we refer to as our three pillar courses: Teaching ESL, the Tutoring Internship, and the Teaching Practicum. This is another intentional choice on our part as each course has an extensive, supervised, field experience where teachers prepare for, engage in, and reflect on the actual activities of planning/teaching/tutoring. The three teacher educators (co-authors of this book) who teach these courses are thoroughly grounded in VSCT on teacher professional development (Johnson, 2009) and have worked collaboratively for a decade or more to offer praxis-oriented pedagogy for our MA TESL students. As teacher educators, we place enormous value on all the courses available to our novice teachers as well as the many departmental and community opportunities for teaching and professional development which enrich their overall experience in our program. Therefore, we emphasize that it is not only the three pillar courses that enable our novice teachers to achieve a high level of professional expertise; however, we focus on the three pillar courses because they have an intense focus on the process of becoming a reasoned, agentive, professional language teacher. The 'becoming' part is critical in that the pillar courses are designed to be future-oriented, to push novice teachers to be what they are not, at least not yet. From a VSCT perspective, this constitutes *prolepsis*. And the mediational spaces/activities and *responsive mediation* that permeate these courses are aimed at novice teachers' ZPD activity, which no doubt shifts and changes throughout their four semesters in the program. In what follows, special attention is given to the intentional design features of each pillar course as well as the nature of the mediational spaces/activities that constitute praxis-oriented pedagogy.

Teaching ESL

The Course

Most MA TESL programs offer what is typically referred to as a 'methods course' with a focus on pedagogical approaches and techniques. In our program, Teaching ESL is designed to be a *non-methods methods course*. This is an intentional design feature, reflecting the fact that for decades TESOL International, the largest professional organization in the field and representing a body of scholarship in L2 teacher education, has recognized that there is no 'best method.' Despite this, novice teachers often enter this course with the *everyday concept* that there is a best method and if they could only learn this method, they would be good language teachers. Most novice teachers also conceptualize language as a stable, neutral, and naturally ordered hierarchical system of syntactic and phonological rules, and teaching language to be the delivery of this organized content to students who have been grouped by measurable levels of proficiency. To challenge these *everyday concepts*, the course begins with collectively reading about, deconstructing, and engaging with alternative conceptions of methods (*post-method pedagogies*, see Kumaravadivelu, 2006), socially oriented views of language (*language as social practice*, see Gee, 2004), and the notion of teaching as principled and agentive reasoning (*reasoning teaching*, see Johnson, 1999).

By design, Teaching ESL has three major sections based on Freeman and Johnson's (1998) reconceptualization of the knowledge base of language teacher education (see also Freeman, Johnson & Peercy, 2020). These include the teacher as a learner of teaching, where novice teachers retrace their own learning and learn about other teachers' knowledge, beliefs, and learning-to-teach experiences and are introduced to the concept of *reasoning teaching*. In the context of schools and schooling section, they delve into how institutions construct language learners, how culture shapes learners and the activity of language learning, how to utilize and adapt curricula, media, and materials to meet learners' specific needs, and an array of alternative assessments. The third section of the course focuses on the activities and content of language teaching, covering (a) critical literacy, genre-based pedagogies, and L2 writing instruction, (b) situated listening and communicative speaking, (c) functional discourse grammar, and (d) task-based, content-based, and English for Specific Purposes (ESP) based approaches to L2 teaching. Teachers complete weekly reaction papers (one to two page prompted reactions) that are responded to by the teacher educator in terms of how they are making sense of the key concepts embedded in the required reading(s).

Mid-way through the course, working in teams of two to four members, the novice teachers complete an Extended Team-Teaching Project. The project is designed to create multiple opportunities for novice teachers to participate in a range of simulated and authentic activities associated with language teaching. It also creates multiple opportunities for expert mediation and supports novice teachers through multiple attempts at materializing and enacting their teaching practices, all with the ultimate goal of moving them toward greater self-regulation over their reasoning and instructional practices. The design features of the project are outlined below.

During the latter half of the semester, novice teachers complete a course development project in which they consider the givens, resources, and challenges of a particular teaching context they choose to work with, and then create a course (in the form of a detailed syllabus) that meets the specific instructional goals and objectives identified in that teaching context. The syllabus includes a list of goals and objectives, a needs assessment, a representation of how they have conceptualized, selected, and adapted the content and activities, and various means of evaluation (see Graves, 1999). In addition, they create a detailed three-week instructional unit (lesson plans) that materializes one aspect/concept of their course. The instructional unit may cover a single objective, a more general course goal, or an assigned project, but it must include directions, activities, materials, assessment measures, projects and/or assignments, handouts, and/or homework.

The Extended Team-Teaching Project

Team members are assigned to teach one session (50–75 minutes) of an actual university-level ESL course. Host classes include a first-year academic writing course for L2 learners, an international teaching assistant (ITA) oral communication course of L2 teaching assistants who are on funding offered by other academic units, or a range of academic language courses offered through our Intensive English Communication Program for non-matriculated L2 learners. Team members complete the project through the following chronology of mediational spaces and activities:

a. *Classroom observation:* In order to establish a better sense of the situated context in which the team will eventually teach, each team member observes at least one session (most observe two) of the assigned ESL course they will eventually teach. The observations enable the team to gain a greater sense of the ESL students' goals, motivation, and L2 proficiency, the particulars of this instructional setting, including the curricular materials and required assessments, and the local settings that the ESL students will be expected to function in once they complete the ESL course. The observations also create opportunities for team members to speak informally with the ESL students and course instructor before and after the class and to gather course syllabi and other relevant instructional materials.

b. *Collaborative lesson planning*: Based on content provided by the ESL course instructor, team members collaboratively construct a lesson plan for the class session they are assigned to teach. They are encouraged to supplement the required curriculum to meet the instructional objectives articulated for that session in the course syllabi. Through both face-to-face and virtual meetings, the teams create a lesson plan that includes instructional objectives, how they have conceptualized the content, the organization of the lesson, strategies for supporting student learning, and an assessment plan.

c. *The practice teach:* Each team completes a one-hour *practice teach* in the Teaching ESL course. During the *practice teach*, instruction is halted at numerous points to allow peers and the teacher educator, henceforth referred to as the Team-Teach Supervisor, to ask questions, provide feedback, and/or make suggestions. Such intermittent probing, commentary, and suggestions prove to be a critical form of mediation as the team members attempt to reconcile what they had planned for the lesson with how it is being experienced by their peers, and how the lesson might be reconceptualized to better meet the instructional needs of the ESL students. The *practice teach* also creates an opportunity for the team to materialize their lesson, both in concrete artifacts, such as handouts and PowerPoint presentations, and also in the ways in which they organized student participation in the activities they were attempting to enact in the lesson. The entire *practice teach* session is digitally recorded and team members receive digital copies of the session within 24 hours.

d. *Collaborative lesson planning:* Based on mediation during the practice teach, each team typically revises their original lesson plan. Some teams meet face-to-face with the ESL instructor and/or the Team-Teach Supervisor while others meet virtually and then submit their final lesson plan for feedback prior to teaching the lesson. This activity creates an opportunity for the teams to rematerialize the lesson plan by focusing on how it might be experienced by the ESL students, to reorient the sequencing of activities, and for some teams, to restructure or supplement the content to be covered in order to better achieve the goals of the lesson.

e. *The actual teach:* Each team teaches the redesigned lesson in their assigned ESL course. During the *actual teach*, the teams make many in-flight decisions as it becomes clear that in the activity of actual teaching, they need to alter or adjust their plans depending on how the English learners respond to teacher-initiated questions and/or engage in certain instructional activities. In addition, team members support each other; for example, if one team member struggles to explain an activity or fails to understand a student's question/comment. Like the *practice teach* session, the *actual teach* session is digitally recorded, and team members receive digital copies of the session within 24 hours.

f. *Stimulated recall session:* Within 48 hours of delivering their lesson, the teams watch their digitally recorded *actual teach* with the Team-Teach Supervisor. They are allowed to stop the recording at any point to comment on what they are doing, what they are thinking, or how they are feeling. They are encouraged to externalize their thinking and consider alternative instructional strategies that might have been appropriate in the lesson. This activity creates an opportunity for the novice teachers to externalize their thoughts while at the same time receiving mediation from their fellow team members and the Team-Teach Supervisor. The stimulated recall session lasts 60 minutes, is audio recorded, and team members receive digital copies of the session within 24 hours.

g. *Reflection paper:* Each team member is then asked to write a reflection paper of five to seven pages in which they focus on these three points: what they learned about themselves as teachers, about the activity of L2 teaching, and about their learning-to-teach experiences throughout the entire project. This activity creates a final opportunity for team members to externalize their understandings of themselves as teachers and the activity of L2 teaching based on their experiences throughout the project.

The Mediation

The design features of the Extended Team-Teaching Project are intended to walk novice teachers through the 'steps' of teaching in an elongated, intentional way so that they can pull teaching apart in ways that they may not have thought about before. Observing helps them know who the students are since they are not familiar with the kind of student who enrolls in the course and their level of English proficiency and intellect can be intimidating.

Teaching content from the actual ESL curriculum forces them to develop a deep conceptual understanding of what they are going to teach. Planning a lesson makes them reenvision that content in ways that make it accessible and comprehensible to English learners. The activity of teaching is dynamic and emerges through social interaction, which is all wrapped up in how they use talk-in-interaction to foster greater levels of student participation and engagement. Reflecting creates a space for a richer understanding of why teachers do what they do, or how they might think differently about what they did. In the real world of teaching, this all happens at lightning speed, but the Extended Team-Teaching Project is intentionally designed to slow the whole process down and allow teachers to experience these essential elements more fully and in more detail.

In a typical semester, between 15 and 20 first-semester novice L2 teachers enroll in Teaching ESL. Teams complete their *practice teach* each week for five to six weeks so the experiences of the first team and the last team are substantively different. Particularly relevant pedagogical concepts (i.e., TEACH OFF YOUR STUDENTS, NOT AT THEM, ORIENTING, INSTRUCTIONAL PARAPHRASING) get repeatedly inserted into the *practice teach* so the later teams are already highly conscious of the interactional and pedagogical expectations of a *teaching as dialogic mediation instructional stance* and the importance of REASONING TEACHING. Since each novice teacher participates in one *practice teach* but experiences four or five others, they become socialized into taking on *a teaching as dialogic mediation instructional stance* while simultaneously attempting to enact it.

Another design feature of the Extended Team-Teaching Project is when the novice L2 teachers are not responsible for the *practice teach*, they are expected to play multiple roles: English learners, peer teachers, and classmates who have or will experience the *practice teach* and *actual teach*. Playing these multiple roles gives them insights into how English learners may experience their instruction, how they might enact their lesson to better achieve their instructional goals, how teachers think about why they are doing what they are doing and share in the emotional and cognitive struggles of being and becoming a language teacher.

In summary, a central design feature of the Extended Team-Teaching Project is the socially mediated, collaborative, and co-constructed nature of the entire project. During the lesson planning, both before and after the *practice teach*, the team must externalize their understanding of the lesson content and how to teach it. This often entails multiple meetings and sometimes intense negotiation between team members with a great deal of REASONING TEACHING; in other words, how should we teach this content, to these students, in this particular course? During the *practice teach*, the Team-Teach Supervisor, the team and their classmates co-construct the lesson as it is unfolding and the reasoning behind any and all instructional decisions is made abundantly clear. During the *actual teach*, the team collaborates to enact the lesson, often making many in-flight decisions as they see and feel how the ESL students are responding to their instruction. During the *stimulated recall session*, the Team-Teach Supervisor is able to stop the digitally recorded actual teach at critical junctures, ask questions, allow the team to elaborate and/or explain their reasoning, express their feelings, and reimagine how they might teach in the future. The *reflection paper* allows novice teachers to step back and closely examine this extended team learning-to-teach experience, externalize their feelings and thinking, and reimagine themselves as future language teachers.

The Tutoring Internship

The Course

The Tutoring Internship is typically the second class in the sequence of the three required praxis-oriented courses. It is the first of two field experiences, or practice teaching classes, required for all students in the program. This class is normally, and preferably, taken in the second or third semester (of four), though occasionally students will take it concurrently with Teaching ESL in their first semester of the program or concurrently with the Teaching Practicum in the fourth semester, usually due to scheduling or other constraints. The Tutoring Internship course provides a hands-on experience of tutoring first-year writing students, with frequent, intensive reflective writing built into it. There is a one-hour weekly class meeting with the teacher educator, plus the core activity of the internship: holding weekly individual tutoring sessions with a small number of tutees (normally three). In conjunction with the tutoring activity, each tutor also writes and posts a reflective commentary after each tutoring session. Tutors meet with the same tutees for 12 weeks and work for 40–50 minutes a week with each tutee separately. The tutees are matriculated international students enrolled in the first-year composition program for L2 writers of English, a credit-bearing 'freshman comp'-style course. Individual tutoring sessions begin in the third week of classes and continue for an average of 12 sessions. A minimum of 420 minutes of tutoring time is required per tutee. Tutors are also required to observe their tutees' ESL composition classes at least twice and are encouraged to be in active communication with the ESL course instructors.

The Instructional Work

The focus of the instructional work in the Tutoring Internship is to participate in a long-term (12-week) individual instructional relationship with three individual tutees. The tutoring focuses on the preparation of several specific class assignments while building a stronger understanding of general academic writing conventions and practices. This support takes many forms, ranging from the tutor asking a tutee 'What did you go over in class this week?' to sitting with a text and talking through the logical flow of information and coming up with suggestions to make the rhetorical structure of the text clearer or more robust, to practicing an oral presentation about the tutee's ongoing research work for the last three assignments of the semester, a sequence of three research-based texts. There is, as the tutors quickly learn, no formula that can be used to predict or plan a tutoring session; it is an immediate, if limited, immersion into the activity of *responsive mediation* and targeted instruction.

Because the goals of any specific tutoring session must be formed in dialogue between the tutor and tutee, expert knowledge (of English grammar or even of academic writing conventions) plays only a limited role in the tutoring activity. We expect the tutors to learn how to listen, how to use instructional time productively, and how to respond to tutee questions and concerns by using knowledge gained in previous sessions as a primary resource. In other words, experiential knowledge of the tutee's progress is privileged over external 'book knowledge.' Tutors learn that having the 'right answer' to a tutee's question is rarely expected or important; rather, they learn that successful tutoring, especially in a long-term instructional relationship, comprises the ability to develop and use questions strategically, present brief but illuminating examples, and draw out reluctant or unclear thinkers to articulate their understandings and (mis)conceptions.

This means that an important goal of the weekly class meetings for the Tutoring Internship is to help the tutors come to a new understanding of what tutoring can be. Many of our tutoring interns received their own English-language education in exam-oriented systems of higher education, where tutoring is often used as a shorthand for both editing and getting better grades and test scores. In contrast, our tutoring internship is designed to help the tutoring interns understand that tutoring does not necessarily involve 'grammar checking' (i.e., correction of errors and proofreading) and are not expected to help their tutees 'get better grades' on class assignments. Rather, their overarching goal is to help their tutees develop into more self-aware, versatile academic writers. Thus, the tutors are expected to focus on building a dialogic instructional relationship with each tutee, and to discuss and engage with the recursive focus on the drafting, revision, and rewriting process that is presented and practiced in the writing classes those tutees are enrolled in. Given that many MA TESL students who received their higher education in countries where the writing process is not as explicitly taught or practiced, this shift of focus can be very challenging for them not only to understand, but even to accept as having face validity (Verity, 2018). Nevertheless, tutors are not prohibited from talking about grammar and word choice, and indeed are encouraged to pay some attention to grammar and sentence-level concerns that the tutees may raise; the continuing challenge is to help the tutoring interns to contextualize such concerns in terms of when and how relevant it is, in the overall academic writing process of preparing a text for submission, to focus on them.

Other elements that the tutors may end up working with include library research in online databases, citation usage and formatting, genre identification, understanding the basics of the assignment guidelines, and interpreting instructor feedback on drafts.

The Writing Work

After each 40-minute tutoring session (occasionally a session is significantly shorter but more often, somewhat longer, than 40 minutes, but this is the guideline we use to calculate contact hours), tutors are required to write and post on the online class platform a reflective commentary on the session. The timeframe for posting is within 48 hours of the session, sooner if possible. These reflective posts can be minimal at c. 250 words, but normally they tend to run long, sometimes more than 500 words; some posts include attachments of visuals from the session or a screenshot of a text with hand-written or computer-made markings. The online platform is designed in such a way that the most convenient option is to assign each tutor an individual discussion board, on which the tutor submits their reflective posts and the Tutoring Supervisor replies. All the discussion boards are accessible to everyone registered into the class that semester, and while they are not required to do so, tutors are encouraged to read and respond to their fellow tutors' posts periodically.

These reflective posts form the bulk of the writing work that is done for the course: over the 12 weeks of active tutoring, most students write approximately 8000–10,000 words, a total which includes the three weekly reflective posts and an eight-page final reflective paper. The Tutoring Supervisor writes a response to every post that every tutor makes, normally within 24 hours of the original post going up. These responses provide feedback that ranges from practical suggestions to conceptual clarification. Occasionally, the tutoring intern responds on the board, and a dialogue ensues, though typically the exchange involves just one post and one response.

In addition to original writing, tutors are asked to submit rough transcripts of two tutoring sessions, one from the first few weeks and one from the last couple of weeks. These transcripts, all the reflective posts, and notes from class readings and discussions, furnish the data for the final paper. This paper, which has a reflective focus, asks the tutors to write retrospectively on their own development. To avoid a simplistic review of the semester's reflective posts, the tutors are encouraged to choose a guiding analogy to shape their final paper and to view their writings and insights through this metaphorical lens. A very common choice is 'a challenging journey' but tutoring is also regularly compared to gardening, cooking, competing in a marathon, kayaking, doing a chemistry experiment, and picking fruit in an orchard, to name a few examples.

Tutoring as Real Teaching

For many tutors, the Tutoring Internship is the first time that they find themselves in an autonomous instructional role face to face with an actual learner. The instructional context is, by design, extremely 'stripped down'—there are no lesson plans, the tutors do not assign grades, and classroom management issues are vanishingly rare, with lateness being the only one that occurs with any frequency. Nevertheless, there is a pressure in the tutoring sessions that does not exist in the Extended Team-Teaching Project as experienced in the Teaching ESL course. In the tutoring work, every meeting is the real thing; the novice teacher is the tutor, not a guest. This means that the tutee can be expected to bring to the encounter, as learners do everywhere, agency, unspoken needs and wishes, and unpredictable responses; it also means that the tutor enters the relationship as a representative of institutional authority, which is typically a new professional identity for an MA TESL student. Of course, this authority is shaped by strict limits, but there is a different sense of responsibility for the tutor than in the Extended Team-Teaching Project. In addition, the importance of incorporating theoretical insights into the practical activity of actual instruction becomes much clearer, as feedback from the teacher educator, readings from the professional literature, and reflective insights combine to give such insights real-world meaning.

Mediation in the Tutoring Internship

A major difference between the instructional experience of the Extended Team-Teaching Project and that of the Tutoring Internship is that mediation by the Tutoring Supervisor is no longer immediate. It is available only at a distance, that is, through post-tutoring consultation and through writing reflectively and receiving written feedback in return. Instead of getting real-time feedback, the tutor has to learn how to draw upon mediational resources through recall and reflection. This displacement is explicitly designed to encourage a sense of professional autonomy and agency. The tutors come to realize that they are the key players in bringing theory and practice together. Their own activity becomes more expert as they become more aware and more conceptually insightful about what they are doing. At the same time, they realize that knowing facts is not the same as skillful instruction. While they learn to incorporate the mediation, they are receiving into their own activity, at the same time, they are helping their tutees incorporate the mediation of the artifacts of the writing class (assignment sheets, model texts, instructor feedback, library research tools, and so forth) into the activity of producing academic texts. The tutors come to learn that it is not just inadvisable, it is actually impossible, to expect to be able to 'direct' a novice writer. Their instructional work in the tutoring sessions becomes more about clarifying and working toward goals, just as the Tutoring Supervisor's work is about helping the tutors work toward goals rather than making them into experts on academic writing.

The Tutoring Supervisor does not do direct observations of tutoring sessions, given the fragility of the one-on-one instructional relationship established by novice tutor and novice student writer. So, from the beginning of the semester, the Tutoring Supervisor tries to help the tutors practice taking in and storing up mediational input for later use. Through role play, discussion, trouble-shooting sessions, and readings, the Tutoring Supervisor's goal is to engage the tutors in a continuing and relatively intensive experience of learning to reason their teaching activity by building connections between what they are learning about in the weekly course meeting and what they are doing in their weekly tutoring sessions. Like the teacher educators in the other two courses, the Tutoring Supervisor tries to both model and present the notion of praxis—understanding what you have read by actually teaching while at the same time shaping your teaching in response to the theoretical insights you have been exposed to—when interacting with the tutors in the weekly meeting and on the reflective discussion boards.

The Teaching Practicum

The Course

MA TESL programs generally require their students to complete some type of teaching practicum, and our program is no exception. Very similar to the typical US student teaching experience for K-12 teachers, our MA TESL students complete a three-credit, semester-long (15-week) practicum either fall or spring semester of the final year in their program. The practicum course is designed from a VSCT perspective as a dialogic and reflective experience in which practicum teachers engage in two intentionally structured learning spaces, a required twice-weekly practicum class with the Practicum Supervisor and other practicum teachers, and the placement class with a mentor teacher.

Practicum Class

In the twice-weekly practicum class, novice teachers engage in activities that ask them to share and reflect on their classroom teaching experiences and begin to make sense of the dialectical unity of theory and practice. To help them with this learning process, the first class of each week is designated a planning day and teachers bring completed activities or ideas for activities to share with others and give and receive feedback from one another. This encourages them to verbalize their thinking, negotiate their way through an instructional activity, and consolidate their ideas into a more reasoned lesson plan for their upcoming placement class. The second of the two weekly practicum classes centers around a particular reading on an aspect of L2 pedagogy and/or instructional question or dilemma the practicum teachers may be trying to navigate.

One of the essential mediational tools for the practicum teachers is the reflective teaching journal. The goal of the reflective teaching journal is to encourage novice teachers to carefully consider their teaching activity each week and reimagine their lessons by considering what they have learned and how their new understandings would shape future instructional choices. They are asked to follow this structure in their journals:

Recall: Briefly describe the lessons for the week and focus on moments that were particularly memorable
Reflect: Discuss why the moments were memorable and what they learned about language teaching, learning, and their teacher selves
Re-Imagine: Reflect on their own learning and consider how what they learned that week can inform their future teaching and development as a language teacher

Based on what they have discussed in their reflective teaching journals, they write one professional goal for the upcoming week with two action steps. The reflective teaching journal is shared with the Practicum Supervisor each week who provides feedback that might include encouraging comments, questions aimed at getting the practicum teachers to dig deeper and think critically about their teaching and their students' learning, and recommendations for other approaches and activities they might use in their classrooms. Oftentimes, the Practicum Supervisor asks the practicum teacher to share a particular question, teaching situation, or dilemma she has written about with the other practicum teachers in the dialogic space provided by the weekly practicum class.

Another important mediational activity is the professional development plan, which is designed to engage novice teachers in choosing professional development activities beyond those that are part of the practicum course. The professional development plan is a mediational tool that encourages novice teachers to recognize that they have agency in their own learning and development. Based on their weekly goals, novice teachers choose professional development activities such as webinars, workshops, readings, conferences, guest speakers, to participate in that can help them move toward achieving their professional goals. They share their professional development experiences with one another in the practicum class and reflect on them in their teaching journals.

In addition to the reflective teaching journal and professional development plans, the practicum teachers write a teaching philosophy as part of the practicum course. The initial draft is completed at the beginning of the semester drawing on what they have learned about language teaching and learning from the two pillar courses they have already completed as well as other graduate courses and experiences they have had as part of the MA TESL program. The teaching philosophy is shared at several points in the semester with other practicum teachers and the Practicum Supervisor and revised to reflect their emerging understanding of language teaching and learning. Not surprisingly, the final assignment for the practicum experience is a reflective narrative in which novice teachers are asked to trace their learning and development in the practicum and placement classes.

Placement Class

In addition to the twice-weekly practicum class, practicum teachers engage in the activity of teaching in one of three ESL programs run by the Department of Applied Linguistics: the first-year academic writing program for L2 students, the program for ITAs, or the intensive English program. Practicum teachers are asked to choose the program they would like to participate in, and often their choices are based on their future teaching goals. First choices are usually granted, and practicum teachers remain in their placement courses for the entire semester. In general, the practicum teacher's placement class meets two to three times each week for a total of three hours, and the practicum teachers are expected to attend each class for the entire semester.

A unique and important aspect of the practicum experience is that practicum teachers are mentored by the teacher of record for the placement class. Mentor teachers are full or part-time instructors in the Applied Linguistics department or graduate students in our PhD program. On rare occasion, an MA TESL student who is on a graduate teaching assistantship and has significant prior English language teaching experience may mentor a practicum teacher. Instructors usually volunteer to mentor, although periodically, the Practicum Supervisor has to recruit mentor teachers. The Practicum Supervisor supports the mentor teachers in several ways, the first of which is by hosting an initial meeting at the beginning of the semester to share goals, expectations, and mentoring strategies. She continues to support the mentors through regular meetings throughout the semester both as a group and individually, and through weekly contact with the mentors via email to monitor the practicum teacher's progress and get a sense of how the relationship between the mentor and practicum teacher is developing. The mentor teachers do not receive any official training.

The mentor teacher is always present in the classroom with the practicum teacher, making this experience a critical learning space for each practicum teacher. To prepare for each class, the practicum teacher and mentor teacher have weekly planning meetings, and the practicum teacher spends a good deal of time planning and preparing on their own. All activities and instructional materials developed by the practicum teacher are approved by the mentor teacher prior to being implemented in the classroom. Each opportunity to plan, discuss, and revise activities with their mentor teachers is an opportunity for practicum teachers to co-construct their learning and internalize their understanding of what it means to teach. Each opportunity to engage in the activity of teaching in their placement classes is an opportunity to externalize that understanding.

The Practicum Supervisor visits each practicum teacher at least three times throughout the semester, and the practicum teacher is expected to provide a detailed lesson plan and instructional materials prior to each visit. Following each visit, the practicum teacher and Practicum Supervisor meet to discuss the practicum teacher's teaching, and the mentor teacher is invited to be a part of that discussion. Digital recordings are made of each visit and uploaded to the practicum teacher's individual web-based file to view again before writing the reflective teaching journal for that visit. The Practicum Supervisor provides detailed notes at the end of each visit and shares them with the practicum teacher and the mentor teacher; she encourages them to use the notes as springboards for discussion and reflection. Important to note is that the word 'visits' rather than 'observations' is used to encourage a more collaborative, dialogic space for sharing and learning.

Another dialogic space is opened up for the practicum teacher and mentor teacher through an additional requirement, five self-video recordings based on the practicum teacher's self-determined professional goals. Using the weekly goals from their reflective teaching journals and dialogues with their mentor teachers, the practicum teachers are required to select five times throughout the semester to film themselves leading an activity in which they focus on one of their professional goals. They work with their mentor teacher to choose the activities they would like to record, upload the recording to their web-based file, and share the recording and the following information with the practicum supervisor:

- The learning objective(s) for the students and how they know whether or not the students met the objective(s)
- Their professional teaching goal for the activity and how well they believe they met it and why
- What they will do to continue working toward that professional teaching goal

The Practicum Supervisor watches and responds to each novice teacher's video. The opportunity to have these brief moments to see the practicum teacher in action without being there gives the Practicum Supervisor a better sense of the practicum teacher's learning and development over time.

Mediation in the Teaching Practicum

By providing multiple and varied mediational spaces, the practicum course encourages practicum teachers to internalize and make sense of what they have learned in their MA TESL program, specifically through the three pillar courses, as they gain more and more control over their ability to self-regulate their thinking in their teaching activity. These mediational spaces include the reflective writing activities and discussions with their peers and the Practicum Supervisor in the weekly practicum classes, the planning meetings and emails with their mentor teachers, and the actual instructional activity they participate in each week in their practicum placement classes. Practicum teachers learn to reason their teaching for the students in their practicum placement class but also begin to see how the pedagogical concepts and principles learned in the pillar courses can be applied to other teaching contexts.

References

Freeman, D., & Johnson, K. E. (1998). Reconceptualizing the knowledge-base of language teacher education. *TESOL Quarterly, 32*(3), 397–417. https://doi.org/10.2307/3588114.

Freeman, D., Johnson, K. E., & Peercy, M. M. (Eds.). (2020). Reframing the knowledge-base of language teacher education. [Special Issue]. *Language Teaching Research, 24*(1).

Gee, J. P. (2004). Learning language as a matter of learning social languages within discourses. In M. Hawkins (Ed.), *Language learning and teacher education: A sociocultural approach* (pp. 13–31). Clevedon, England: Multilingual Matters.

Graves, K. (1999). *Teachers as course developers*. New York: Cambridge University Press.

Johnson, K. E. (1999). *Understanding language teaching: Reasoning in action*. Boston, MA: Heinle, Cengage Learning.

Johnson, K. E. (2009). *Second language teacher education: A sociocultural perspective*. New York: Routledge.

Kumaravadivelu, B. (2006). TESOL methods: Changing tracks, challenging trends. *TESOL Quarterly, 40*(1), 59–81. https://doi.org/10.2307/40264511.

Verity, D. P. (2018). Coming around: Tutors, orientation & prolepsis. *Journal of Academic Writing, 8*(2), 114–123. https://doi.org/10.18552/joaw.v8i2.466.

4
THE MA TESL CAPSTONE PROJECTS

The MA Paper

As with any graduate program that exists as part of a larger institution, our MA TESL program must conform to various institutional requirements and expectations. One dimension of the MA TESL program that is to some extent imposed upon, rather than initiated by, the program, is the existence of two capstone projects required of all our MA TESL graduates: an MA Paper and a professional e-Portfolio. Our MA TESL program, categorized as an academic program rather than a professional program, has the option of assigning either a credit-bearing thesis or a non-credit-bearing MA Paper. For many years in the history of our MA TESL program, we required neither (the capstone paper was optional), but over the past decade, the university has interpreted the guidelines more strictly, and we now require all MA TESL graduates to produce an MA Paper. This is a written text of at least 30 pages (but often exceeding 200 pages in the case of a curriculum project), prepared according to academic conventions, and typically stemming from a higher-level course paper that was written in a previous semester. It does not earn credit, but the title of the paper is noted on the official university transcript. Along with the second capstone project described below (a professional e-Portfolio), the MA Paper is typically completed during the fourth semester often at the same time as the Teaching Practicum class. As a result, we have come to actively support both projects in ways that are consonant with the principles that shape the curriculum, namely VSCT principles of learning and development. While the writing of an MA Paper can hardly be said to represent praxis, we do attempt to embed the preparation of the paper into the larger framework of mediated instructional spaces that characterize the pillar courses where praxis-oriented pedagogy lies at the core of the activity.

This means providing ongoing support for writing, such as setting up structured mediational workshop spaces for collaboration on topic development, writing skills, library research strategies, and research presentations. Not surprisingly, the MA paper is a major undertaking for novice L2 teachers, as it would be in any graduate-level TESL program. Unlike a thesis, which is taken for academic credit and typically takes the form of an individually initiated research project, the MA paper is something of an expansion of an existing work rather than an original project. Normally, we encourage students to choose an academic paper or project they have already written for one of their MA courses and extend it, either by adding a literature review section or by adding more examples and analysis. Thus, the novice teachers do not 'start from scratch' but instead select a previously written paper or project that they are particularly interested in or proud of and continue to work on it beyond the level of the original coursework. This approach valorizes the VSCT-informed principle that more expert knowledge is different in quality than novice knowledge; the fourth-semester novice L2 teacher, though perhaps not a credentialed expert yet, brings more practical teaching experience, more theoretical understanding, and a broader base of professional development achievement to the topic when it is reworked as an MA Paper.

Establishing an Authorial Voice

A primary challenge for our novice teachers, who are at the same time novice academics, is establishing an authorial voice. This phrase refers to the complex business of establishing and representing a certain level of authority over the topic under investigation, a task that goes beyond simply summarizing what others have written. Yet, because they are for the most part not doing primary research, the MA TESL students find it challenging to take ownership of how they frame previous work in support of the claims or investigations they undertake for their MA Paper. Learning to wield an authorial voice also requires that the MA TESL students understand how the discursive and non-discursive choices they make in creating written texts come to represent multiple identities, just as the choices they make in the classroom do: who they are and how they wish to portray themselves in a public, conventionalized arena. Another way in which the MA Paper project is infused with VSCT principles is that, from our perspective, it involves the construction, and inhabiting, of a new identity. Seen in this way, the challenge of writing an MA paper is another form of material and theoretical engagement that contributes to the professionalization of the novice L2 teachers.

Because our MA TESL students bring a variety of backgrounds and writing expertise, not to mention individual interests, with them to the program, we allow several options for the MA Paper, including these three broad categories:

Critical Literature Review: In this option, the novice teacher selects a contemporary academic topic that is of particular interest and is often a topic they have already written a course paper about in one of their graduate courses. Using the course paper as a starting point, they review a wider selection of the pertinent literature (primary and secondary sources) that lay out the central issues and claims about this topic. They normally conclude the paper with a section that outlines their own personal stance on the topic and discuss the implications this stance has for the field of TESOL/Applied Linguistics and for their professional work in the future. Occasionally, they create pedagogical materials to illustrate how this stance might be instantiated in the classroom with learners.

Curriculum Development: In this option, the novice teachers develop a full semester's worth of a curriculum for a particular group of language learners or for a specific language teaching context. In addition to lesson materials and lesson plans, the project includes a literature-based rationale section (about 10–15 pages) explaining the theoretical stance and basis for the content and the skills covered in the course. The project typically includes, as well, a complete course syllabus and suggestions for assessments and projects where appropriate.

Data-driven Project: In this option, the novice teachers develop an analytic empirical research paper based on oral, written, and/or computer mediated discourse. Again, typically stemming from a course paper, the research is grounded in a relevant theoretical perspective and represents original, if limited, data and analysis. As well as the data itself, a critical review of the most relevant literature is included. The paper requires analysis and not description or paraphrases of the data. Because of the requirements of research oversight and the relatively limited timeframe for the MA Paper, this option tends to be chosen by students who have already received Institutional Review Board (IRB) approval in a previous semester and who are already working on a research project under the guidance of a faculty member.

Besides producing an impressive final project that captures a serious academic or research interest, the MA Paper capstone project provides an opportunity for social engagement in one of the department's major annual events. Historically limited to the doctoral students who are graduating, in recent years, the MA Paper projects have been included in the culminating poster session at the end of the spring semester, with every novice teacher preparing a brief oral presentation and a visually interesting and professional-looking conference-style poster. For many MA TESL students, this is the closest they get to doing a public presentation of their work, and the poster session has become a major event in the MA TESL timeline, and faculty, friends, family, and colleagues regularly attend. In addition to providing the novice teachers with a culminating academic experience to their studies, this event brings them further into the departmental and university community and positions their research in a new way. Indeed, some MA TESL capstone projects are now entered into the university Graduate Research Exhibition, a juried event that has a broad footprint at our large research institution.

The e-Portfolio

The second required capstone project that all the MA TESL students must complete is a professional e-Portfolio, typically prepared on a free online platform such as Wix or Weebly. This kind of personal website is widely accepted within the profession as a supplement to a curriculum vitae when searching for jobs and we encourage the novice teachers to continue updating their e-Portfolios as they move into the next stages of their career.

As an interactive website, the e-Portfolio allows the novice teachers to demonstrate the depth and breadth of their learning and to document their accomplishments throughout their two years in the MA TESL program. In line with the VSCT notion that "the method is simultaneously prerequisite and product, the tool and the result of the study" (Vygotsky, 1978, p. 65), the e-Portfolio functions as a tool that is constructed and used to display the results of the work. In VSCT terms, the e-portfolio as a representational tool has a dual function: first, it functions as a tool-*for*-result activity (see Chapter 2 for another discussion of this phrase) because the novice teachers compile the portfolio in order to showcase their learning. In addition, the e-Portfolio also functions as a tool-*and*-result activity; that is, the very process of creating the portfolio (tool *for* learning) is at the same time a result of the learning experience itself (tool *and* learning) (see also Newman & Holzman, 1993). Thus, the design features of the e-Portfolio are fundamentally aligned with our praxis-oriented pedagogy.

As a representation of personal achievement, the e-Portfolios are organized around the seven program objectives, introduced at the beginning of this chapter, and as described in Chapter 3, introduced to the new cohort of MA TESL students every year during their first orientation meeting. This allows for each portfolio to have a similar focus, but also provides maximum freedom for individual interpretation and illustration. The e-Portfolio then is an artful compilation of evidence that the graduating novice teacher has fulfilled each of those goals. Evidence includes (but is not limited to) such items as:

- Documents they produced in their courses. These may include seminar papers, reaction papers, exams, assignments, and/or completed projects
- Documents they produced outside of any specific course that analyze and synthesize their various experiences in the program
- Documents they produced in their field experience courses, including handouts, exams, journal entries about your teaching experiences, reflections on tutoring interactions, interviews with students or teachers
- Documents about their participation in the program written by someone else, including written observations/evaluations completed by a supervisor, a cooperating teacher, or a peer observer, formal course evaluations

To make the e-Portfolio visually compelling, the novice teachers are strongly encouraged to incorporate thoughtful visual design elements, such as color, fonts, and layout; photographs and videos with consideration given to privacy; most portfolios use face-blurring technology for people who are not faculty members or fellow MA TESL students; and decorative items (as appropriate). Many portfolios include pictures and logos from other educational experiences, such as undergraduate universities, summer study programs, language schools, workplaces, and so on. We encourage this kind of inclusion, because it demonstrates that the novice teacher has begun to consolidate a professional identity that reflects all of their relevant experiences.

Given that we conceive the e-Portfolio as a professional job-searching resource, as well as an individual portfolio of achievement, we encourage the novice teachers to prepare portfolios that are not only visually attractive, highly readable, and cohesive but also designed to incorporate a thematically consistent tone, such as a guiding metaphor (My Journey or Building Experience). Creative choices range from using thematic photographs and images to applying the metaphorical lens to every item on the website. For example, one novice L2 teacher, who had worked as an engineer before going into education, developed an architectural metaphor that reflected her interest in structures and the relationships between parts and wholes.

Similar to the MA Paper, the e-Portfolio is not a credit-bearing project. It is evaluated on how well the evidence selected illustrates the requirement that the portfolio preparer has fulfilled each of the seven objectives of the MA TESL Program. We encourage the novice L2 teachers to write clear and concise commentary relating to each objective, and to include easy-to-navigate links between a list of the objectives and each sub-page on the website.

Supporting the Capstone Projects: The MA Workshop Series

When the MA Paper was an option, only novice teachers who were considering further graduate work tended to choose it, and among that group, only the stronger writers. When the paper became required of all MA TESL students, we soon realized that we needed to set up a support system so that every student in the program could successfully complete this challenging assignment. Coupled with a second requirement, the e-Portfolio, graduation requirements brought a burden that tended to overshadow the professional development dimensions of the projects.

Thus, to help our MA TESL students finish these culminating projects, and to help them understand the importance of consolidating their own professional and academic identities and achievements through the completion of the capstone projects, we have established a series of workshops that focus on various elements of academic and professional preparation. Some of the workshops are tied very specifically to the capstone projects; others are more general. But all of the workshops (and we continue to make changes to the format and the topic list every semester) are designed to give the MA TESL students an opportunity to understand the *reasoning* behind the capstone requirements. In other words, we have carried over the pedagogical concepts of REASONING TEACHING and ENGINEER PARTICIPATION into these extra-curricular (but required) elements of the program.

Setting up a required series of MA Workshops made immediate sense, both to us as teacher educators and to the students, as novice teachers and novice academics. Indeed, initiating a series of support workshops may be the easiest feature of our MA TESL program to adapt to a different context: we looked at the needs of our students and at the demands of the academic context and developed workshops to align the two sets of demands.

One semester, for example, when a larger-than-usual cohort of MA TESL students expressed frustration with the demands of writing longer course papers in an acceptable academic register of English, the workshops focused on academic literacy and what we call TESL literacy—the specific kinds of writing that language teachers engage in, tying academic conventions of citation, formatting, rhetorical organization, and so on to the tasks of writing lesson plans, reflective posts, and teaching philosophies. Many of these documents are prepared within the specific confines of the three pillar courses, but by extracting them and studying them in more detail in a workshop format, we were able to highlight for the students how much they already knew how to do and help them identify areas of weakness.

In many of our workshops, we emphasize modeling and referring to sample texts as two particularly rich writing strategies. This led to us developing a workshop designed specifically to introduce examples of one of the capstone projects, the professional e-Portfolio, drawing upon previous graduates' projects, of course after having asked for and received written permission. In recent years, as more and more MA TESL students entered the program with webpage design experience, we focused more on orienting the students to the benefits and drawbacks of various online platforms. Sometimes, we invite a graduate to come back and talk about her own process of developing her e-Portfolio or ask an IT specialist from the university to address the MA TESL students about university resources for web-based design. In other words, we have come to use the workshops as a channel for reiterating our belief in the use of collaboration and resource-sharing as important professional strategies that mirror the kinds of pedagogical approaches we favor in instructional settings.

A workshop that has become a regular feature every year is the MA Paper Topic Development workshop. This session introduces the various options for the MA Paper, as outlined earlier in this chapter, but it also—again—reiterates the importance of dialogue and discussion as crucial for the development of understanding: second-year MA students, who are at the brink of settling on their topics, present and explain their choices to first-year MA students, who are still in their first semester of study and who see the capstone projects as impossibly advanced and far away from their immediate academic life.

One way we structure the MA Paper Topic workshop is by using the Elevator Speech template, an appropriately adaptable tool that pushes the student writer into an organizational and conceptual level of preparedness that is perhaps beyond their actual level: by filling in the blanks of the template with relevant information about their own potential topic, they not only have an easily digestible version of their proposed paper to share with a first-year student, but they also are ORIENTED to see their MA Paper as a finite, doable project with a clear focus and certain conventional parameters. Novice writers, like novice teachers, often do not know where to put their energies; the Elevator Speech exercise creates a useful proleptic moment of clarity for them.

Now that the MA Paper requirement has become fully embedded within the MA TESL program, we ask students to attend 'writing sessions' at which they work on their MA Papers, albeit with a teacher educator or two in the room for immediate and individual consultation. We use these sessions for both motivation and monitoring and encourage the students to bring drafts for review and development. Of course, as we do in every aspect of the MA TESL

Data-Driven Project & Critical Literature Review

My MA paper focuses on _____ (central topic(s)) in/with _____ (setting/context/subjects) because I am interested in _____ (research questions, instructional context, etc.).

My MA paper is important for _____ (audience(s)) because it _____ (rationale) and I expect it to have _____ (implications) for _____ (intended audience(s)).

In order to conduct my project, I collected/read _____ (type of data) from/on _____ (people/context/issue) and analyzed it according to _____ (theoretical orientation/data analysis) in order to understand _____ (project outcomes).

The final format of my MA paper will be _____ (project type) and it will highlight _____ (project findings/outcomes) in order to inform _____ (implications) for _____ (intended audience(s)).

Curriculum Development

I am developing a course for _____ (students) who want to/are expected to know and/or do _____ (needs assessment) in _____ (instructional setting) so that they can _____ (course goals).

I will be using/have selected/created _____ (curricular content) to teach _____ (skills, knowledge, concepts) so that the students will know and/or be able to do _____ (course objectives).

I have created _____ (activities, assignments, tasks, etc.) that will be organized around _____ (conceptualizing content) so as to create opportunities for the students to _____ (course objectives).

At the completion of this course, I expect the students to be able to _____ (learning outcomes). They will demonstrate _____ (learning outcomes) by _____ (assessments).

FIGURE 4.1 Elevator Speech for MA Paper Workshop

program, we build collaboration and mentorship into the MA Paper sequence. Besides being asked to discuss and present their topics to their peers, students choose an academic advisor from the faculty, along with a second reader, and consult regularly with those two scholars throughout the process of writing.

Similarly, the e-Portfolio capstone project is overseen by a faculty member, typically the second reader on the MA Paper or the student's academic advisor. We encourage students to begin working on their e-Portfolio from the first day of study, literally at the new MA TESL student orientation meeting, reminding them to take plenty of photographs, save documents and handouts, and generally start compiling materials that reflect everything they do during their two-year program. More formally, at the Portfolio Development workshop, we introduce the Portfolio Planning tool, a worksheet that we have developed to help the novice teachers think about their activity in the program in ways that will translate easily to the web-based design of the e-Portfolio. This tool, which is essentially a chart with various open-ended categories, serves as both a digest of the required information that needs to be included in the e-Portfolio, and, like the Elevator Speech, a kind of preview of the completed project.

Website design is no longer the unfamiliar specialism that it was a decade ago. Many of the novice teachers in our program are comfortable with online design work. Even so, we find that offering specific work sessions, sometimes under the guidance of a more experienced recent MA TESL graduate or a member of the IT staff, can be helpful.

Your e-portfolio should contain a variety of documentation materials and represent *you* as a professional. Use this list to help you remember, gather, create, and organize the important features and items that you want to include. Make notes to help you organize what you already have and to remind you what more you need to seek out.

e-Portfolio feature	*What I could include*
MA TESL Program Objectives	*Evidence from classes and teaching/tutoring experiences*
1. the ability to design and evaluate instructional materials, technology, media, and other resources that meet the specific instructional and language related needs and abilities of students	
2. the ability to reflect on, critically analyze, and evaluate your own teaching practices	
3. the ability to articulate a philosophy of language teaching grounded in current language and learning theories	
4. an understanding of the complex social, cultural, political, and institutional factors that affect language teaching and students' language learning	
5. knowledge of research and research methods for studying language teaching and learning	
6. knowledge of the teaching field (ESL)	
7. participation in collaborative projects with others	

FIGURE 4.2 Preparing Your MA TESL e-Portfolio: Planning Tool *(Continued)*

e-Portfolio feature	What I could include

Webpage Headings:
What pages do I need/want to represent myself and my learning?

Personal Statement:
An effective statement is both *personal* and *analytical*. Consider these points:

a. personal characteristics
b. what I have learned about the field/about myself
c. what I have learned about myself
d. my long-term objectives & career goals

Photos, images & videos:
What do I have/need that will help demonstrate how I have fulfilled the goals of the program and represent me?

Themes & Colors:
What choices best represent me?

Thematic metaphor:
A theme makes the e-Portfolio coherent. What metaphor could I use throughout the portfolio to help a reader understand me and my activity in the MA TESL program?

Special skills, interests, and accomplishments:
What would I consider my "special expertise" and/or unique accomplishments that reflect who I am as a professional?

Quotations to support your beliefs:
What quotes would highlight my accomplishments and represent my principled beliefs?

FIGURE 4.2 *(Continued)*

Conclusion

Educating novice L2 teachers from a stance of theoretical commitment does not mean that we want, or try, to produce professionals who do not think and explore the activity of teaching for themselves. In this chapter, we lay out the framework of the two capstone projects required in our program, where creativity, individual voice, and the consolidation of personal as well as professional identity are valued. The MA Paper provides the novice teachers with the opportunity to hone their research and academic writing skills, to contribute to the scholarly and professional conversation around topics of interest, and to learn how to receive and incorporate feedback in ways that will be useful throughout their career. The professional e-Portfolio allows each novice teacher to construct a multimodal representation of their goals, their achievements, and their identity as credentialed, reasoning teachers. In both of these capstone projects, as well as in all the courses and extra-curricular activities that we offer, we consistently and coherently encourage our novice teachers to explore and reason their choices with the same care they give to their instructional roles.

References

Newman, F., & Holzman, L. (1993). *Lev Vygotsky: Revolutionary scientist*. London: Routledge.

Vygotsky, L. S. (1978). *Mind in society*. Cambridge, MA: Harvard University Press.

PART III
TRACING THE DEVELOPMENTAL TRAJECTORY OF L2 NOVICE TEACHER REASONING

5
WHY PEDAGOGICAL CONCEPTS MATTER

Introduction

In Part III, we make more concrete and visible connections to the principles of Vygotskian Sociocultural Theory (VSCT) and praxis-oriented pedagogy. We present data in ways that illuminate our commitment to the core pedagogical concepts that have appeared in various mentions throughout the book. As complex theoretical concepts 'packaged for novices,' these concepts play a practical role in our teacher education courses, but they also have helped us understand what VSCT means in teacher education in general. Like all psychological tools, they shape us even as we, in our work, shape them to our purposes.

The aim of Part III is to document and analyze evidence for what we recognize as observable development and transformation in the way our novice teachers understand and instantiate praxis-oriented pedagogy in their instructional activity. The trajectory of this development can be seen not as an unvariegated whole but rather through changes in various internal structures of the activity. We begin with an exploration into why we believe pedagogical concepts matter, how they are infused in praxis-oriented pedagogy, and how they come to function as psychological tools as our novice teachers begin to engage in more agentive, dialogic, and reasoned language teaching. We also identify three core thematic elements—responsive mediation and instructional stance; emotion and cognition; and engineering participation—that help to trace the complex and variable developmental trajectories that our novice teachers experience over the two-year MA TESL program. Each chapter highlights evidence that supports and illustrates our claim that praxis-oriented pedagogy drives change over time in observable and significant ways.

As will be discussed in Part IV, we believe that understanding our work on a thematic level will help other program designers and teacher educators, whose institutional contexts may not lend themselves to wholesale program reform, recognize what may be adoptable and adaptable to their own institutional circumstances.

A Brief History of Pedagogical Concepts

Every teacher education program intends its interventions, its programs, and its initiatives to produce graduates who are prepared for life in the classroom and for engagement with the profession. To the extent that we are a typical teacher education program located within a North American research university, we share this goal. However, as an unusually coherent and theoretically informed program, we actively engage with teacher education as a functional system, an arena of activity that both provides context for existing meanings and creates context for new meanings. There is educational value in what we do with our novice L2 teachers regardless of their future trajectories and whether or not they ever end up teaching English (or any language) in a classroom.

This chapter focuses on why, for us, and potentially other programs and other teacher education initiatives, pedagogical concepts matter. Our goal is not for novice teachers to talk about the pedagogical concepts for their own sake. Instead, we want novice teachers to develop in a direction that results in their understanding and expertise of teaching being similar enough to ours that their use of the pedagogical concepts resembles ours: as accessible nuggets of theoretical insight that can help clarify or illuminate a pedagogical choice, before, during, or after an instructional episode. In general, the way we include pedagogical concepts in our mediational interactions is fluid and adaptive. Several of the examples presented in this chapter do not involve a teacher educator 'giving' or reciting a pedagogical concept to a novice teacher. Rather, we tend to recall and implicitly invoke pedagogical concepts in general ways in our mediation. As the semesters go by, we see the novice teachers adopting this practice themselves in their reflections, discussions, and teaching.

Over the years, pedagogical concepts have become for us what Vygotsky called 'microcosms' of our expert knowledge and consciousness, expert knowledge deliberately and carefully phrased and packaged for novice teachers. As one translation has it, *"the meaningful word is a microcosm of human consciousness"* (Vygotsky, 1987, p. 285). As collections of meaningful words, pedagogical concepts are not merely accessible and user-friendly sayings; we do not reach for them in order to reduce teaching to aphorisms, even though they are, intentionally, compact and concise in form. They are instead mnemonic and conceptual touchstones for everyone who works in our program, from the novice teachers to the most experienced teacher educator. The pedagogical concepts give us a shared vocabulary, a shared focus to our work, and a set of shared meanings that both signal, and shape, our understanding of what teacher education can and should be. As lapidary chunks of instructional language, pedagogical concepts are in a way the currency of our intellectual work with novice teachers: tokens of our theoretical commitment, tokens of reasoned teaching, and tokens of novice development.

There are essentially three levels or dimensions on which pedagogical concepts can be said to 'matter' for teacher education:

- They matter to the theoretical framework of VSCT
- They matter to the practical activity of teaching
- They matter to the conceptual development of novice teachers

Where Did the Notion of Pedagogical Concepts Come From?

The authors' personal histories with pedagogical concepts may be of interest here. In the case of the lead author, Karen E. Johnson, understanding first began to take root back in graduate school (1987–1989), when she read a book by Douglas Barnes (*From Communication to Curriculum*, 1976) at the same time she was being introduced to the ideas of Vygotsky. An early scholar of Vygotsky's initial translations (*Mind in Society*, 1978, *Thought & Language*, 1988) that emerged in the West during the mid-1970s, Barnes only invokes Vygotsky twice; once to recognize the notion that we use language to plan what we will do (to move beyond the here and now) and second to conceptualize language:

> language both as a means by which we learn to take part in the life of the communities we belong to, and a means by which we can actively reinterpret the world around us, including that life itself. Through language we both receive a meaningful world from others, and at the same time make meanings by re-interpreting that world to our own ends.
> (Barnes, 1976, p. 101)

Karen sent Barnes a copy of her 1995 book (*Understanding Communication in the Language Classrooms*), noting some of their parallels of thought. He responded with a gracious and supportive letter (typed; after all, it was 1995) in which he mentions specifically the very Vygotskian distinction between personal sense and conventionalized meaning: "I like Donald Freeman's point about the need to reflect on the relationship between the public and the private in classroom meanings—between social events and cognition, I suppose" (Barnes, *personal communication*, 1995). He follows that comment with what can only be called a highly condensed portmanteau of the pedagogical concepts of ORIENT STUDENTS, PROVIDE RELEVANCE, and TEACHING AS CONNECTING: "I suspect that at times we all fall into the trap of assuming that what was said overtly in lessons means the same to the learners as it does to us teachers" (Barnes, *personal communication*, 1995).

Barnes' ideas on how teacher language plays a crucial role in shaping student experience in the classroom had been published in various outlets in the 1970s, including in a conference proceedings volume in 1974. Karen chooses this paragraph particularly to highlight how his approach to understanding the crucial role of language is a sign of how his idea resonates with VSCT:

> Speech unites the cognitive and the social. The actual (as opposed to the intended) curriculum consists in the meanings enacted or realized by a particular teacher and class. In order to learn, students must use what they already know so as to give meaning to what the teacher presents to them. Speech makes available the processes by which they relate new knowledge to old. But this possibility depends on the social relationship, the communication system, which the teacher sets up.
>
> (Gage, 1974, p. 10)

In this excerpt, we can see an *ur*-form of the pedagogical concept TEACH OFF YOUR STUDENTS, NOT AT THEM: in order to learn, students must use what they already know so as to give meaning to what the teacher presents to them – speech makes available the processes by which they relate new knowledge to old. This seed of understanding blossomed in Karen's subsequent writing and thinking over the next decades, as traced through her book publications (Johnson, 1995, 2009; Johnson & Golombek, 2011a, 2016).

The second author, Deryn Verity, was more familiar with the outlines of VSCT, having written her doctoral dissertation under the guidance of James Lantolf, than with pedagogical concepts themselves, when she joined the faculty in the MA TESL program. She brought many years of language teacher education and language teaching in several countries to the MA TESL program. Being assigned to teach the first pillar course (Teaching ESL) early on and creating and shaping the Tutoring Internship in light of the larger MA TESL program goals and structures helped her understand how powerful these pithy-but-profound insights could be for novice teachers as they struggle to make sense of the many dimensions of teaching/tutoring activity.

For the third author, Sharon Childs, the connection to pedagogical concepts started when she was Karen's academic advisee in the PhD program in Linguistics and Applied Language Studies with an emphasis in English language teacher education. Engaging with VSCT helped Sharon realize (much like our MA TESL alumni do in the follow-up interviews we conducted, see Chapter 10) that her years of experience in the classroom with high school learners prior to entering graduate work had helped her develop similar insights into the importance of *reasoning her teaching*, of making explicit to students what was already automatic and deeply known to her as an expert practitioner.

We recount these rather personal details in order to encourage our readers to understand that knowledge, understanding, and application of VSCT-inspired pedagogical concepts can take root at any stage in one's education or professional trajectory. Pedagogical concepts are compact, condensed, expert knowledge, but they are neither opaque nor intentionally abstruse. By gaining some fluency in the VSCT principles that underlie pedagogical concepts, teacher educators at any stage of their career can become more skilled at representing, engaging with, and providing support for novice teacher understanding of the internal structure of teaching activity.

Pedagogical Concepts Matter to the Theoretical Framework of VSCT

As the data and discussions in this volume abundantly illustrate, there is an ongoing conversation among us about how VSCT illuminates the connection (a word we prefer to 'gap') between practice and theory. By formulating and making pedagogical concepts central to our practice, we believe that we are not only providing more principled instruction to novice teachers, but also providing new lenses for ourselves to study the theoretical structures that those principles rest upon.

Development is open-ended: there is always interaction between the changes we make—in our curriculum; in our instruction; in how we set up contexts of mediation for our novice teachers—and the knowledge those practices generate. So, while this volume represents a robust set of understandings, based on observation, data analysis, and interpretation that represent several decades of study, we are comfortable with the idea that this book would look different if we wrote it ten years hence. As Lantolf (*personal communication*, 2021) expressed it during one of our departmental reading group discussions of praxis and VSCT: "Doubt yourself and be self-reflective; it's key to being a true SCTer."

Pedagogical Concepts Are Tools for Creating, Maintaining, and Engaging in ZPD Activity

Perhaps the most well-known (and well-worn) of Vygotsky's ideas is the Zone of Proximal Development (ZPD), a term and a theoretical construct that—it has often been noted—he did not fully develop in his writings and lectures before his early death. Since then, scholars of many stripes have investigated and expanded his original ideas in several directions on this topic, and there is much disagreement and divergence that continues today on how best to interpret his ideas, and how to apply them to current educational contexts.

In our context, we accept that the ZPD is a construct that can always be further interrogated and explored, but it is fair to say that we accept the following basic outline:

The ZPD is a way of characterizing, and making conditions possible for, potential future development. Such development occurs as a result of meaningful semiotic (symbolic) mediation, that is, mediation primarily through language but also using signs, icons, visuals, and other symbolic systems. Thus, development is future-oriented; though mediation happens 'in the now,' the focus is on what can/should/will happen later: first, the activity is executed only with some kind of external help. Later, ideally, it is carried out independently, as the external mediation is internalized and appropriated by the novice.

The ZPD is a mediational space where other-regulated activity (the now) is transformed into self-regulated activity (the future). It is created in the process of doing mediational activity. For this reason, the ZPD is ephemeral, in that it does not have an independent existence outside of the specific activity in which it arises. Rather, any given ZPD activity is contextually bound to the task, the goals, the participants, and the specific actions and mediating tools used in that interaction; we have evidence of ZPD activity only in relation to a specific learner being in engagement with specific mediating sign systems. In other words, learners do not walk around with ZPDs waiting to be awoken, and ZPD activity cannot be automatically or predictably 'triggered' through even the most skillful instruction or lesson design. And ZPD activity does not exist as an implied or actual limit; the teleological open-endedness of human development is a design feature, and not an epiphenomenon, of VSCT-informed pedagogy.

So, one fundamental question confronting an expert who wants to mediate the development of a novice by creating a productive ZPD activity with them is where to start? We believe that pedagogical concepts serve as excellent tools, both diagnostic and instructional, for those initial stages of development, when novice teachers are by definition unable to function particularly well on their own while learning to TEACH OFF YOUR STUDENTS, NOT AT THEM. As we wrote in 2020, pedagogical concepts "initially function as semiotic devices that novice teachers meet and engage with as they carry out the activities of planning, teaching and reflecting" (Johnson, et al., 2020, p. 22). They are, to use Lantolf and Poehner's words (2006, p. 62ff.), "artifacts," tools which work on both material and conceptual levels for mediating goal-directed activity.

There is no formula for what makes a good or successful mediational choice. VSCT theorists are still debating the specific relationship between mediation and the processes of internalization. Indeed, one recurring question is how this theoretical paradigm positions innovation and creativity. For example, if ZPD activity is about internalizing somebody else's words and skills so that the novice can reproduce them appropriately and independently, then what room is left for individual creativity and innovation, in other words, for individual agency? Do our novice teachers simply 'ventriloquize' what we have taught them, or do they actually transform their understandings, concepts, and activity? How can a novice teacher develop an individual identity if mediation is directly appropriated from the expert source?

Without getting too entangled in the theoretical details, let us focus on this suggestion, as expressed in Poehner and Lantolf (2021):

> the answer lies in understanding the dialectical relationship between the two processes.... reproduction is in conflict with the creative use of language in that creativity undermines yet depends on reproduction, for without the latter process there would be nothing to transform. On the other hand, creativity produces new possibilities of use that are potentially appropriated and reproduced by others in a constant developmental cycle.
>
> (p. 39)

This brief quote encapsulates our belief, as supported by VSCT and by the evidence in the data we have collected and analyzed, that in order for novice L2 teachers to develop their own individual identities, we must first help them engage with, and reproduce, the concepts and principles that guide our praxis-oriented pedagogy. Rather than being hampered by it, our teacher education program actually serves this dialectical tension. Novice L2 teachers who go through our program become enmeshed in this dialectic by being asked to watch and listen, to read and talk, to make sense of, to interpret, to embody, and to imitate (thoughtfully) the concepts and actions we provide. At the same time, we expect them also to appropriate, interpret, experiment with, and adapt the concepts and ideas they encounter. We do not claim that every novice teacher leaves our program with the same level of expertise (a claim that VSCT with its focus on individual histories and trajectories would not permit in any case). Rather, we believe that our data provide powerful evidence for the *ongoing* and *open-ended, continuing* transformation of novice teachers in areas ranging from instructional stance to the skillful use of questions to lesson design, transformations which are initiated during the program, but which develop in ways that are not entirely linear or predictable.

We have consciously shaped the mediational spaces for those transformations to happen, which means that we continually try to animate new ZPD activity into existence and work inside them. We try to coherently mediate novice teachers in ways that not only leaves space for individual agency but actually encourages it. There would be no point in asking students to REASON TEACHING if we did not believe that they were developing the reasoning skills to do so.

Pedagogical Concepts Matter to the Practical Activity of Teaching

Pedagogical Concepts Are Handy Tools for Meaningful Imitation

Real-world teaching is messy, challenging, and sometimes confusing and contradictory: Should I attend to classroom management or to the topic on the lesson plan? Should I elicit questions from the learners or show a PowerPoint slide to make this point clear? Pedagogical concepts are ways of invoking VSCT principles in contexts where they might be obscured by the distracting details of a real-world instructional space. They are mnemonic devices useful not only to the novice teachers, who are able to keep them in mind due to their conciseness, but also to us, the experienced teacher educators who continuously seek to identify moments that will serve to instruct, model, and capture VSCT 'in action' for our MA TESL students.

One powerful effect of giving pedagogical concepts to novice teachers is that the simplicity of the pedagogical concept formulation allows the novice teachers to immediately 'sound like' an expert. Although of course just 'talking the talk' is not the same as mastering the underlying conceptual basis for each pedagogical concept, the theoretical perspective that VSCT takes prioritizes mindful, goal-directed imitation as an important step toward autonomous functioning. One of the easiest ways to see if a novice teacher has some mastery of the meaning of a pedagogical concept is to look for instances when they (re)produce it accurately, either verbally, or, even better, in combination with actions that match the words. Repetition without understanding is not the goal; it is what Vygotsky (1962) called "empty verbalism" (p. 150) – in other words, parrot-like repetition instead of meaningful imitation. But as VSCT reminds us, tool use, even with limited understanding, is the first symbolic step toward self-regulated activity: being concise and easy to remember, the pedagogical concepts can rise to consciousness as a kind of life-saving device, allowing for more-expert activity even when they are not fully in control of the task:

> …rather than waiting for learners to be developmentally ready, the very activity of teaching creates the conditions for development to occur. Moreover, the approach empowers students to explore the possibilities provided by the new conceptual knowledge to engage with and transform their environments (Stetsenko & Vianna, 2009, p. 44) rather than to see things through the lens of right and wrong answers.
>
> (Lantolf, 2020, pp. 5–6)

In the following example, we see imitated words as leading development in the case of a very novice tutor who channels an analogy (a kind of mini-pedagogical concept) provided by the Tutoring Supervisor in the seminar class.

In this case, Qing channels the Tutoring Supervisor' words exactly *tutors should dole out grammar like candy, a treat not the main part of the diet* to her tutee. In doing this, she not only ORIENTS her tutee to the expectations of the tutoring program (strong focus on content and organization, weak focus on grammar and sentence structure), but also strengthens her own commitment to understanding and instantiating those guidelines. As Lantolf and Poehner (2014) explain, "Reliance on verbal support in order to appropriately use a concept in practical activity is an important step in transferring the knowledge and how to use it from the material to the mental plane" (p. 66), and we can see Qing giving herself verbal support while also supplying it to her tutee:

Excerpt 1

We had a brief introduction and luckily this Korean girl's hometown is not far from my hometown in China! Then, I told her attendance requirement, **grammar posteriority** and so on. I said what I learned a few days ago, **"'Grammar is always a candy', and we can share this candy in our last session in this semester".** My tutee laughed and said, "oh! It's a candy?" I confirmedly said, "yes, we need to have more vegetables and meats first." Jiyun said she knew what I mean and agreed with me.

(Qing, Tutoring Internship, Session 1 Post, with Jiyun)

The fact that this happens in her very first session with this tutee suggests that Qing is using the Tutoring Supervisor's words to connect her own formal instruction (as a tutoring intern) with her material work as a teacher (as an actual tutor having instructional responsibilities for a learner). Her use of the word *confirmedly* suggests that she was trying to 'sound like' an expert even though the analogy itself sounds a bit childish. In the Tutoring Internship class, the Tutoring Supervisor uses this analogy in service of the pedagogical concept ORIENT STUDENTS, making explicit the attitude we take toward the role of grammar correction, it should be given limited attention, a position Qing expresses with the word 'posteriority' here. Even as a very new tutor, Qing realizes that *grammar=candy* can be a useful, and simple, analogy.

In this second example, the imitation is less exact. Layla describes a tutoring session with a rather recalcitrant tutee. She is not sure which pedagogical concept to invoke, explicit explanation (PROVIDE RELEVANCE) or indirect guidance (BE DIRECT, NOT DIRECTIVE) and indicates that she understands there is some tension between the two choices of action:

Excerpt 2

...it seems to me that Whan needed to focus more and maybe repeating the steps again can help her develop awareness that writing is a process and she should not write in a hurry. **I did not know if I should tell her that explicitly or indirectly because while discussing her draft**, every time I ask her about something from last session, she said that she didn't remember or forgot to do it in her draft.

(Layla, Tutoring Internship, Session 5 Post, with Whan)

The Tutoring Supervisor decides to foreground the pedagogical concept that most closely matches Layla's own choice of words:

Excerpt 3

In a case like this I might encourage you to be strongly directive— not to tell her 'what to write' but to tell her 'what she is expected to write'—she may not be good at reading and interpreting instructions.

(Supervisor, Tutoring Internship, Session 5 Response)

While verbalism is never a final goal, it is a useful sub-goal on the journey toward mastery. The novice teacher is informed through mediation about the meaning of the sign (for example, a pedagogical concept), and then personally realizes that it encodes something relevant in the situation and identifies its utility in the immediate context (teacher educators typically PROVIDE RELEVANCE which is mirrored by the novice teachers), so they produce that same sign in order to regulate their own activity, in the best case. In the worst case, they produce the sign in an empty way because they cannot think of anything else to say. Uttering something, even if it is not your own thought, is a sign of slightly higher development than not knowing that an utterance is needed at all.

In this final example, we hear Chen's thoughts about how imitation both served her and disadvantaged her in the Teaching Practicum. She recounts how she tried at first to just literally mimic her mentor teacher's personal style. She then goes on to recall that this initial attempt at mimicry actually added a burden, distracting her from her true goal, to develop her own teaching self. This experience, short-lived but in the intense situation of being her first-time teaching English in a university classroom, illuminated for her the importance of REASONING TEACHING, though in an indirect way.

Excerpt 4

I like this teaching style and from student's reaction, I believe they also like it. So, **I tried to mimic. I tried to used jokes in class and pretended to be relaxed and natural. But pretending to be someone else made me feel uncomfortable. And I just realized that this kind of mimicking made me more nervous because I was** actually taking more work that I was not good at while I was teaching. I could not totally focus on teaching itself.

(Chen, Teaching Practicum, Final paper)

She could not, she realizes upon reflection, reason like the expert she was imitating, so her activity remained superficial and unexamined. Although she does not quite make this connection in that section of her final paper, it is no coincidence that in the next paragraph she goes on to write in detail about learning how to reason her teaching.

Recognizing and Evaluating the Success of Mediation ZPD Activity

One outcome of helping the novice teachers see teaching through the VSCT lens is that they learn to recognize when their mediation has been successful not in final grades or 'output' but in more subtle and relevant ways, identifying clues that they have created successful ZPD activity.

In this example, we can see Layla's reaction, after tutoring Munwah in academic writing for two months, when she realizes that her mediation of him has succeeded on this particular task: using a concept map to plan out a written text. Thanks to her mediation, including both demonstration and engagement, the tutee is now able to independently apply the semiotic tool she introduced him to. Layla's reflection is noteworthy for how striking she finds this moment of transformation:

> **Excerpt 5**
>
> While we were talking excitingly, surprisingly Munwah stood up and said I think we need a paper. **He brought a paper and started drawing a concept map. In all the previous sessions, I was the one who brought out the paper to map our ideas. So, it was an astonishing for me to see him doing this.** I am happy because he found it useful and it actually helped us a lot in breaking down his topic.
>
> (Layla, Tutoring Internship, Session 8 Post, with Munwah)

As experienced teacher educators, we are not 'astonished' when our mediation succeeds at transforming novice thinking and activity. But moments of insight like this help us trace the novice teachers' deepening understanding of what teaching activity can be. Although she is a teacher with four years of classroom experience, Layla is still consolidating her understanding of the effects of responsive, contingent mediation and praxis-oriented pedagogy.

It is of course impossible for us to claim that creating and using pedagogical concepts in our teacher education work in any way changes what Vygotsky wrote 100 years ago. It is not even clear that it influences in any significant way many of the debates that scholars hold today about correct interpretations of the original Russian-language texts. But we believe that exploring our understanding of how we use pedagogical concepts as psychological tools can contribute to the discussions that surround teacher education and the role of theoretical commitments in that field. At the same time, pedagogical concepts are simply useful mediating devices; they serve as invaluable 'entrance tokens' for our novice teachers. As a result, our mediation can become more accurately graduated (to use Aljaafreh's & Lantolf's, 1994, term) and individualized to what we perceive is the need of any specific novice teachers in a specific instructional context. In other words, the pedagogical concepts are useful for both initiating ZPD activity and for working successfully within it.

Pedagogical Concepts and Reasoning Goals

Although to the expert teacher educator, it is second nature to offer responsive mediation, such mediation is not always obvious or easy for a novice teacher to take in, or, at times, even to recognize. Our data suggest that novice teachers find it easier to keep certain guiding principles in mind when they can recall those principles in the form of concise pedagogical concepts. For example, in the Tutoring Internship class, the Tutoring Supervisor always begins the semester by emphasizing the fundamental goal of the Internship: to learn how to help tutees become better writers rather than make their essays better texts. This goal is reflected in the frequently repeated guidance that tutors should avoid taking over authorial duties for their tutees, while at the same time, they should be explicit in focusing tutee attention. The Tutoring Supervisor encodes this message in several different ways, but the basic message is always a paraphrase of the guiding pedagogical concept of the Internship, BE DIRECT, NOT DIRECTIVE, that is, it is acceptable to identify explicitly what you think needs attention in the text, but not to do the actual revision for the tutee.

Many of our novice teachers come from cultural and educational backgrounds where the activity of 'tutoring' is explicitly associated with fixing grammatical errors in texts, telling tutees what to say or write and, ultimately, helping tutees earn better grades. So, we are not surprised that it often takes quite a bit of time for the message (i.e., the mediation) embodied in the pedagogical concept to sink in. Especially because the very first time many novice teachers find themselves faced with the responsibility of running an instructional interaction occurs during a tutoring session, the Tutoring Internship provides particularly striking insights into novices attempting to appropriate and internalize the pedagogical concepts.

Goal-directed activity is at the center of VSCT. In a way, the list of pedagogical concepts is a kind of rhetorical representation of ZPD activity. We, as teacher educators, do not invoke the pedagogical concepts rigidly or predictably, because exactly as VSCT says, it is impossible to know exactly what form of mediation will work best at any given moment. This gives the pedagogical concepts, as conceptual tools, an interesting characteristic: they are not, strictly speaking, formally necessary, but they are conceptually necessary. It is not the phraseology of the pedagogical concept that matters, though it is precisely that phraseology that endows them with mediational power; it's the way they help novice teachers enter the sometimes-intimidating theoretical conversation around pedagogy and praxis that matters.

In this example we see Ai, in her second tutoring session, making sense of her emerging understanding of the larger goal of the tutoring program (to develop novice academic writers); she is working with a tutee who really wants to be told what to write. In her post, Ai reflects on how she responded to the tutee's desire for directive tutoring (a term she does not know yet but a dynamic she clearly recognizes). Her post suggests that she has both heard and to some extent understood the Tutoring Supervisor's injunction not to give the tutees too much specific language for their assignments, but also that her ability to carry out this request is still emerging. It is hard for her to separate her empathy with the tutee's 'longing' for directive guidance from her desire to tutor in an acceptable and appropriate way in this new instructional context:

Excerpt 6

Obviously, Mang was frustrated with his instructor's comments, and he wanted me to "just tell him how to write". **I felt that he was longing for the most specific, straight-forward, and explicit instruction from mine [sic] because he kept asking me, "What should I write after this part?"**

(Ai, Tutoring Internship, Session 2 Post, with Mang)

Although she does not invoke the pedagogical concept exactly, it is clear that Ai is recalling a pedagogical concept (REASON TEACHING) from the previous semester's Teaching ESL course:

Excerpt 7

Of course, I didn't want to just "give" him the content to write ... It's interesting to see him making himself to think about the importance and value of his contents ... **My intention was to enforce him to find some reason behind his writing...**

(Ai, Tutoring Internship, Session 2, Post, with Mang)

She describes her direct (and possibly sometimes directive) actions, again trying to balance her commitment to applying the pedagogical concepts with her sense of the tutee as dependent upon her for filling his academic gaps:

Excerpt 8

During the rest of this tutoring session, I always found myself talking directly to him about what he needs to write in each paragraph, which was not delightful because I don't want to limit his thinking or force him to think and write in "my way". However, if I don't give him the "certain answers", he would be confused and lost himself in his own words. **I really hope that I can find other ways to inspire him rather than just tell him everything in our future tutoring, maybe I need to read more of his paper and figure out his "style" of thinking and writing.**

(Ai, Tutoring Internship, Session 2 Post, with Mang)

The Tutoring Supervisor responds by highlighting her gratification at Ai's attempt to put the pedagogical concept REASON TEACHING into action. She also reiterates BE DIRECT, NOT DIRECTIVE by picking up on Ai's use of the word in her reflective post:

Excerpt 9

Ai, I think this is a very insightful post! **You realized... that the most important thing ... is that he is learning how to THINK about his writing and how to REVISE & IMPROVE its coherence and unity.** Don't be too hard on yourself; it's hard to NOT give advice when the tutee clearly wants you to and the time is ticking away. **One strategy you can always use is to explain to the tutee that in fact... he needs to learn how to write in a way that HELPS his readers!** That's an important lesson for him as a novice writer and he may benefit from a direct comment about it.

(Supervisor, Tutoring Internship, Session 2 Response)

In this example, both the Tutoring Supervisor and the novice teacher recognize the relevance of the pedagogical concept REASONING TEACHING that Ai was richly exposed to in the Teaching ESL course. At the same time, the Tutoring Supervisor takes the opportunity to underscore a second pedagogical concept that provides more specific guidance about how to reason toward the program's established goals in this specific context: BE DIRECT, NOT DIRECTIVE.

The influence of the mediation provided in the form of pedagogical concept can rise to the surface of novice teacher's reasoning during the first few weeks of the Teaching Practicum experience as well. During these fraught first days in the classroom, feeling overwhelmed is normal: not only does she have to face a large group of actual learners in an actual classroom, but the novice L2 teacher also has to juggle many new details of an unfamiliar curriculum, daily announcements, in-class tasks, homework, and communication with her mentor teacher.

In this Week 2 Reflective Teaching Journal, we can see Fen drawing actively on the mediation given by her professors in earlier semesters; she specifically recalls the mediation she received in Teaching ESL (the first pillar course) to

Excerpt 10

...**think of how Karen taught us, Karen always used activities to guide us to think** [ENGINEER PARTICIPATION; PROVIDE RELEVANCE]. **And then she would take what we gave to her to teach us** [TEACH OFF YOUR STUDENTS, NOT AT THEM]. Given this information, I reflected my presentation, and I remembered the students listened carefully but they seemed to be tired after my presentation [REASONING TEACHING; TEACHING AS CONNECTING]. **Now I know it is because there is not much space for them to think, and this is my main focus for next activity.**

(Fen, Teaching Practicum, Week 2 Journal)

The Practicum Supervisor responds by validating Fen's efforts to make use of those resources for her own development and by articulating the implied insight that Fen hints at but does not quite say in so many words: Expert behavior is incredibly compact; each minute is full of meanings and decisions. The Practicum Supervisor writes in response: *You learned so much in just one moment of teaching, Fen.* (Supervisor, Teaching Practicum, Week 1 Response).

Yet it is also interesting to see how Fen's multifarious concerns disappear into something of a hazy memory by the end of the Practicum semester. In her final reflective paper, Fen puts some distance between her newly expert self and that rather frantic first-week novice. As VSCT predicts, she can no longer actually access the full range of emotions and thoughts she had at that earlier level of development; they have been internalized into her new level of expertise and have lost their immediacy and specificity:

Excerpt 11

However, in the first week of my practicum teaching, I realized that the real teaching context is much more complex than the imagined community of learners I had envisioned. **I thought I was prepared with my many strengths and my creativity, but the truth was that I could barely find my position and authority in the classroom.**

(Fen, Teaching Practicum, Final Paper)

ZPD activity is a way of mapping progress toward a goal, and, at the same time, of demonstrating the ephemerality of goals when it comes to human learning. Just as you achieve a goal, it disappears. A pedagogical concept has, essentially, a double function: it is simultaneously a label for an *'ideal'* teaching activity (a reachable goal) and a kind of *abstraction*, a phrase that exists as a linguistic entity, separate from real world activity (a sign). Like the goal in ZPD activity, the pedagogical concept is both concrete and immanent. While a pedagogical concept can be literally invoked as a reminder or a suggestion, it can also, as a philosophical statement, represent an aspirational level of understanding. As teacher educators, we always look for moments to link pedagogical concepts-in-current-activity and future goals.

In this example, Zeina interrogates the challenge of CREATING PREDICTABILITY when her best choice, at first, appeared (at least to herself) to be using 'random' strategies. To her tutees, she was a responsible, authoritative tutor; to herself, she was a novice who needed to figure out what it meant to be a writing tutor, something that become clearer to her when she realized that the only way she could learn to teach 'off' her tutees was by getting to know them individually (TEACHING AS CONNECTING but growing out of REASON TEACHING):

Excerpt 12

Understanding tutees. Among the things I developed throughout this journey is some effective strategies to tutor. It started by exploring randomly, as I was not sure about work more with each ....**Hence, one of the first thing that I needed to learn and which helped me a lot through the sessions is understanding my tutees.** My tutees come from different countries, and this is my time working closely with international students. **Through noticing closely and using my tutees answers to my questions writers, I started to learn more about them as students and more importantly as writers.**

(Zeina, Tutoring Internship, Final Paper)

Another tutor, Lai, expresses her recognition of this duality even more explicitly by invoking a Confucian adage to illuminate an episode in which she confronts the material reality of being able to benefit from being simultaneously a student and a teacher/tutor. The classroom instructor of her tutee happened to be sitting at the next table during her tutoring session, so he offered extra (and presumably more-expert) information on the topic of how to find online library sources. Lai is grateful for the help, but more importantly, she seems to be aware that as a novice tutor, she can always productively maintain the mantle of learner and take advantage of resources in the environment:

Excerpt 13

There is a rational knowledge that I have learned long before— teaching process benefits teachers as well as students, from an

ancient Chinese educator Confucius. **In this session with Ethan, I completely get Confucius's words in a perceptual way. Ethan came earlier today, and he waited at the next table so he heard what me and Jin discussed concerning the database.** Thus, he kindly shared with us the Try These First LionSearch service that contains the Opposing Viewpoints in Context category, which may help their comparison and contrast essays a lot.

(Lai, Tutoring Internship, Session 4 Post, with Jin)

Pedagogical Concepts Matter for the Conceptual Development of Novice Teachers

Pedagogical Concepts Are Tokens of Shared Meanings

Many scholars who study socialization of academics and other discourse group contexts have written about how becoming a functioning and accepted member of a group typically involves learning the shared meanings of the established members of the group. Pedagogical concepts can spur the consolidation of these shared, expert meanings, allowing novice teachers first to speak like and ultimately to think like the expert language teachers who comprise the new discourse community they are joining.

To be a full-fledged member of a group, it is not enough to 'know what the words are'—what is crucial is to be able to use them in the same ways that other members of the group do, with an understanding of how they fit into the network of formal and informal understandings that more-expert members have already mastered. We see the pedagogical concepts as being a first-level tool for giving the 'words' to the novice teachers. These words (short phrases) act as a kind of 'beginner's telescope' allowing them to peer into the way expert teachers think, act, and organize their beliefs and expectations about teaching, learners, and the classroom, a telescope that, in other words, can see *behind* the words. Being able to see how the teacher educator "means" is the first step toward intersubjectivity, the sense of shared meaning—often highly incomplete and partial—that allows ZPD activity to be constructed and meaningful mediation to begin.

Of course, we know that the novice teachers already "know the meaning" of the words (and therefore, to some extent, of the pedagogical concepts) that they encounter. As adults, they bring not only dictionary knowledge of words, but also lived experiences, some of which have occurred in instructional settings. What they do NOT bring, however, is context-specific knowledge that is structured the way our VSCT expertise is structured. Instead, they bring meanings that are more informal and experientially—what Lantolf and Poehner (2006, p. 72) call "personally relevant meaning" and described by another scholar as "more hermetic, idiomatic, and individual than [expert] meaning is… more closely connected to motives and the core of the personality" (Engeness, 2021, p. xliii).

We see this every year when novice teachers arrive on campus with very 'personally relevant' meanings attached, for example, to the word 'teaching' or the word 'language.' Through the strategic and reiterative use of pedagogical concepts, we can help them reformulate not just their formal definitions, but also their lived understandings of the expert meanings that are represented by the deceptively simple words.

As noted frequently in this volume, many novice L2 teachers arrive at our program genuinely believing that a teacher's 'job' is to give information and knowledge 'to' the students. They conceptualize this job as having various predictable and inherent characteristics, such as being expected to talk more than anybody else in the room, controlling who else talks and when, choosing and initiating all topics, and being continuously 'on the spot' to provide a perfectly developed, fully informed answer upon request. Novice L2 teachers do not arrive to the MA TESL program without goals, but their goals, as derived from these strongly held beliefs, often align poorly or not at all with those of our program.

We see evidence for development in understanding, and thus for shared expert meanings, when the novice teachers talk or write about their changing ideas about what teaching 'means.' In this sample reflective post, written near the beginning of the semester, Chul makes it clear that he defines the job of the tutor to be evaluating tutee's texts, fixing textual problems, and helping tutees achieve getting an A in the writing class. Although he confesses that he may have pushed his tutee too hard on one detail, indicating that a teacher should be kind, there is no sense of the tutoring work involving CONNECTING, RELEVANCE, or PREDICTABILITY. Indeed, Chul notes his gratitude for the fact that with so many 'problems' in his writing, sessions with this tutee will never lack for topics of discussion, making it clear that he conceptualizes tutoring as 'fixing problems':

Excerpt 14

Because he has no specific examples, his thesis sentence is usually weak. I'm actually pretty thankful that we have something to work on for the rest of the semester. But what I recently think is that I focused too much on weaknesses. His main points are usually very pursuasive [sic]. His class recently learned how to cite sources in MLA style, and as a matter of fact, his citation skills are pretty good. He seemed to hold a good grasp of it. I'm aware that ESL 015 does have a certain expectation from students to follow the 'conventions', **but I think I tried too much to make Jaareh fit into that convention too early.** I used "hedging" words to sound more polite and kind, but from deep within my mind, I might have wanted him to take those suggestions seriously and fix his problematic features. **I'm happy to help him with his works in** class, but I think there is something more to just help him get an A for his 4 credit class.

(Chul, Tutoring Internship, Session 3 Post, with Jaareh)

By the end of the semester, Chul has clearly begun to reformulate the meaning of what 'good teaching' can be. He does not cite the pedagogical concept exactly, but he expresses an emerging understanding of the relevance of at least one pedagogical concept (TEACHING AS CONNECTING) by formulating it in his own words, with both literal and figurative language. Rather poetically, Chul compares himself in his final tutoring paper to a plover bird removing food scraps from the mouths of crocodiles:

Excerpt 15

Despite of my various tutoring experience in Korea, I did not realize how important it is to approach each tutee differently at first. **I think I was so immersed in the role of an instructor that I focused too much on 'correcting' my tutees' mistakes. It was almost near spring break when I realized that my tutoring is not efficient. My tutees were making the same mistakes over and over again.**

I could also see them opening their mouths, and that is when I realized that each crocodile wants its food scraps removed in a different way.

(Chul, Tutoring Internship, Final Paper)

He also concedes that without CONNECTING, his tutoring work would not have succeeded to the extent that it did:

Excerpt 16

But I believe that it must have been impossible to get her comfortably talk about her ideas in front of me if I had not built a personal bond with her.

(Chul, Tutoring Internship, Final Paper)

Sometimes the novice L2 teachers signal their emerging expertise by invoking the pedagogical concepts explicitly, signaling a more-expert use of these signs. In this next example, Pavel writes in his final reflection paper for the Teaching Practicum class about how the practicum experience was an arena of consolidation for him: the formal instruction he had received in the MA TESL program and the material activity of teaching in the Practicum classroom have merged with his previous experience and transformed him from the person he was when he first arrived to a newly aware, educated practitioner. As an already relatively experienced teacher, Pavel came to the program with a relatively expansive understanding of how to teach in his own context. Over his two years in the program, he changed much of what he understood teaching to be. The pedagogical concepts are obviously touchstones for his new understanding:

Excerpt 17

Practicum also served as a place to practice the concepts that had been already acquired in the previous MA courses. **For example, I learned a couple of valuable strategies, such as "teaching off the students not at them", "justification of what is being taught to students" in Teaching ESL. I realized how important it was "to lead a student to the answer, not just give the answer myself" in Tutoring**... I tried to do my best in taking advantage of all those mentioned concepts and applying them to Practicum course where it was possible. I think they worked well together. Of course, I learned some useful teaching strategies from Practicum as well. **I was taught how it was important to make my content relevant and meaningful to students and how to connect the activities and the lessons within each other.**

(Pavel, Teaching Practicum, Final Paper)

The pedagogical concepts are, thus, conceptual tools that allow us to create intersubjectivity with the novice L2 teachers, provide meaningful and productive mediation to them, and usher them into the discourse community of expert language teachers who recognize the unity of *obuchenie*, the productive tension between teaching and learning.

Creativity and Innovation in ZPD Activity

In a brief example of a novice teacher creatively interpreting the choices available to her, let us look at Ai, a tutoring intern. At about mid-semester, she decides to try something experimental with her tutee: she shifts from praising (TEACHING AS CONNECTING) to asking her tutee to spend some time in the session actually writing text (ENGINEER PARTICIPATION). When she realizes that the tutee is reluctant to sit and write while she watches, she makes the innovative decision to 'walk away' and leave him alone for a few minutes. While this is a minor moment in the bigger picture of a teaching career, for this novice teacher, it represents a kind of insight into the pedagogical concept that teaching sometimes involves specific and even creative choices about physical movement (EMBODIMENT IN TEACHING).

Excerpt 18

So I changed my mind on "praising" him like the last time I did and asked him to start writing on our tutoring session. He seemed a bit reluctant, saying that, "I felt Laird when writing under teacher's watching." "Alright. I'll walk away for a while so that you could write on your own. But I need to see your 'production' of evaluation this time." I said to him. **It's actually fun to be asked "walk away" for a while. I understand that for many writers, it could be embarrassed when writing under others', especially tutors' watch because they don't want to make any mistake with others' noticing.**

(Ai, Tutoring Internship, Session 7 Post)

Continuing with her reflection, Ai goes on to describe her actions, but even more important, she ties this creative choice to her thinking about all the choices she has made up to this moment (i.e., she inhabits more fully the identity of a reasoning teacher). She concludes by accepting that an unusual (and in some contexts, certainly impermissible) choice was appropriate for this tutee and this situation.

Excerpt 19

Also, at this point, I began to think about all the tutoring sessions I've been working on with my tutees. **Are they feeling uncomfortable and therefore unable to write very well because I'm "watching" all the time? Maybe sometimes I should stop staring at their computer screen and giving them the intense attention when they're writing.** With this thought on mind, I "hid" for a while and showed up when Bin finished everything. **This time, he seemed to finally be able write an evaluation that meets the requirement, and it's also interesting for me to find a strategy ("walk away") which was useful for working with him.**

(Ai, Tutoring Internship, Session 7 Post, with Bin)

Ai has never been told, taught, or encouraged to walk away from her tutee during a tutoring session. It is not a typical or even a permissible choice on its surface. But she reasons through it, drawing upon a set of interconnecting and accessible principles (as stored in her mind in the form of pedagogical concepts), which allows her to reason through her decision to carry out her mini-experiment and, importantly, to justify it and evaluate it in a productive way.

In response, the Tutoring Supervisor acknowledges this creativity:

Excerpt 20

Ai, you took a creative step because you could see that something 'new' was necessary **to push this tutee forward, from the stage** of 'talking to think' to the stage of 'writing to think'–it's a hard step for many novice writers because writing is more laborious than talking and it goes more slowly. So I applaud your choice here!

(Supervisor, Tutoring Internship, Session 7 Response)

Here we see a tutor confronting the power of the pedagogical concept CREATE RELEVANCE, not only for her own tutoring *I am a learner* [of tutoring] but for learners in general *I am a teacher* [with responsibilities toward my learners]. In this reflection post about a late semester tutoring session, Ai clearly demonstrates that she has developed in her ability to REASON her teaching, though she does not cite any specific pedagogical concept in so many words. The tutor and the Tutoring Supervisor agree that relevance and reasoning lie at the heart of successful instruction, though the appropriate pedagogical concepts (CREATE RELEVANCE; ORIENT STUDENTS) are not specifically invoked. In this reflection, Ai shows that she now aligns herself with the goals of the tutoring program; she is much more aware, through her own learning, of the big picture that contextualizes what she has learned:

Excerpt 21

By looking back this "journey" with him, it's delightful to see Bin gradually become a motivated and "responsible" writer, and his motivation are actually "growing" during the whole semester. **I think Bin's performance interestingly reveals that, when students can understand teachers' purpose behind each assignments and to really think about the relationship between every in or after class activity and his writing, it will be effective for them to become a more advanced writer and also for teacher to adjust their pedagogy and methodology in teaching.**

(Ai, Tutoring Internship, Session 12 Post, with Bin)

The Tutoring Supervisor responds with her own paraphrase of REASONING TEACHING:

Excerpt 22

I agree strongly with you that giving students more chances to UNDERSTAND and not just 'do' the assignments provides them with more motivation and more autonomy because they have a sense of both purpose and goal.

(Supervisor, Tutoring Internship, Session 12 Response)

Charts and Visuals: Supplementing Verbal Mediation

One of the first supplementary forms of mediation that most of our novice teachers encounter is the drawing of a concept map or visual depiction of a concept or activity early in the first-semester pillar course. One week prior to the start of the semester, students enrolled in Teaching ESL are asked to complete a Visual Depiction assignment (see Figure 5.1). This assignment serves a multitude of purposes in the Teaching ESL course. Since it is assigned for the first session and students do not know one another, sitting in small groups and describing their visual depictions gets them immediately involved in a non-threatening, simple but engaging collective activity. Additionally, they exchange groupings at least three times, so they are able to interact with almost every one of their classmates. The experience of moving about the classroom, engaging in shared laughter, and describing information about themselves and their classroom language learning experiences creates an immediate sense of shared community. Just as important, this activity exposes both their past 'apprenticeship of observation' (Lortie, 1975) in language classrooms and also their future-oriented imagined teacher selves. Upon returning to a whole group discussion, they are then asked to

Before creating your visual depictions, consider the following:

a) Think about your most memorable language teacher (positive or negative). What was memorable about him or her and why? b) Think about your most memorable classroom language learning experience (positive or negative). What was memorable about it and why? c) Think about what has influenced you the most as a language learner/ teacher?

Based on these reflections (you don't need to write anything, just think about a), b), and c)) draw or construct two visual depictions.

1) The typical language teacher you have had.
2) The type of language teacher you aspire to be.

We will be working with these visual depictions on the first night of class, so make sure you complete them, or you will feel left out!

FIGURE 5.1 Reaction Paper #1 Visual Depictions

highlight similarities and differences they found in these depictions and/or to characterize images that stand out as unique. This typically encourages extended description and dialogue around their shared experiences as language students and their ideals as future language teachers. For the teacher educator, this activity enables her to gain easy access to their prior classroom language learning experiences and relevant episodes of *perezhivanie* surrounding those experiences.

Based on decades of completing this activity, regardless of the country of origin, age, gender, or prior teaching experiences, we can say that there is tremendous consistency in these drawings. As is clear from the sample drawings in Figure 5.1, the typical language teacher is depicted as teacher-fronted, students are faceless and identical, communication is unidirectional, and the subject matter content is stored in the head of the teacher. In an ideal setting, however, the language teacher is depicted as friendly, the students typically have individual identities, the chairs are arranged in a circle, and the students seem attentive and comfortable. In fact, in the idealized image in Figure 5.1, it is unclear who the teacher is.

Overall, we find that the novice teachers frequently borrow and adapt this visual style of mediation in the Extended Team-Teaching Project and in their tutoring sessions. In this example, Yan comments on the writing teacher's use of a chart to help the tutee prepare one of the major writing assignments, an Annotated Bibliography. She also reflects on how she herself, also a learner in her graduate program, could have used it for a similar assignment in one of her MA TESL classes. This conscious triangulation happens quite often in the Tutoring Internship; it is common for the tutors to point out that they are learning a great deal about academic writing by tutoring. Specifically, mediation through non-linguistic modalities seem to resonate particularly strongly with the tutors, just as they do—not surprisingly—with the even more-novice writing students they are tutoring.

In this reflective post, Yan identifies the (physically distant) writing teacher as a valuable source of mediation, for both her tutee and for herself, inhabiting as she does the teacher role and the student role simultaneously:

Excerpt 23

And another good thing I learned this time was a method Emine used to make them clear what they should do with A.B. It's a small assignment before they are really getting into their A.B, in which they were asked to use two sources they found to fill up a chart. The chart is called Annotated Bibliography Organizer. …. **I asked his opinions about this assignment and he said that he found it really useful. Since he could know very clearly what he should write in an Annotated Bibliography.** What they wrote in this chart are exactly what an A.B should contain, they only need to use some transitions between each part to make it complete and fluent. **I thought that if I used this strategy when I first time writing an A.B, I could save lots of time to figure out what I should write and how I should organize my words. And if I knew this method earlier, maybe I could help the tutee I met yesterday better.**

(Yan, Tutoring Internship, Session 8 Post)

Novice teachers are exposed to forms of mediation that go beyond verbal explanation in their own classes with the teacher educators and other faculty and in their tutees' writing classrooms; they also observe their mentor teachers use such artifacts during the Practicum Teaching experience. By experimenting with various modes of mediation themselves in their teaching, the novice teachers broaden their understanding of the nature of mediation: when the form of mediation changes (no longer just oral explanations), they are pushed to pay attention to its functionality. They also begin to recognize that not all helpful mediation is received directly from the mediating 'other.' In another example, Qiao introduces the Venn diagram as a mediating visual tool, though it is not clear whether her previous use of this kind of visual occurred in the MA TESL context:

Excerpt 24

Then I grabbed a paper, draw a Venn Diagram to help Zian open her minds. The Venn Diagram worked for me when I was writing my CC essay. The overlapping section stood for the similarity, and the two separate sections stood for the difference. I shared my feelings when I stepped into Berkey Creamery and Beaver Stadium. Since they differed in their inner structure and decorations, the atmosphere they conveyed to me was also in two different ways.

(Qiao, Tutoring Internship, Session 2 Post, with Zian)

Audio and Video Recordings

As Karen Johnson's previously published work clearly illustrates, narrative lies at the heart of our praxis-oriented pedagogy (e.g., Johnson & Golombek, 2011b). Creating stories from experiences gives the novice teacher something material to focus on and creates a small but powerful arena for development. Each time a teacher educator or a novice teacher makes an audio or video recording of novice teacher activity, an 'episode' has been captured, providing rich data for analysis, discussion, and recall.

Novice teacher Fen notes that *reflection is just a magical process, there are no new things coming in but many new thoughts and connections coming out* (Fen, Teaching Practicum, Week 2 Journal). Though we do not make any claims for its magical properties, there is no doubt that using reflection in conjunction with electronic recordings makes memory much more solid and material. In this example, Shu recounts in her final tutoring paper how her stance has changed toward instructional activity, an insight she probably could not have gained such clarity on without the use of the audio recordings she made of her two tutoring sessions:

> **Excerpt 25**
>
> **Instead of looking at the miscommunications in the writings as something that I need to 'fix', questions help me look at those as chances to understand what my tutees were trying to convey and why they decided to express themselves this way.** I realized how much my tutees and I grew when listening to the two recorded tutoring sessions. **In the fourth session, I 'lectured' a lot, that I was not good at asking questions, and that the tutee did not have many chances to express herself.** However, in the tenth session with the same tutee, **the tutee took the responsibility of deciding the direction of the tutoring session, and she talked much more about how she could solve some writing problems.**
>
> (Shu, Tutoring Internship, Final Paper)

Oral Presentations: Engineering Not Only Thinking but Writing

The Tutoring Internship is connected to the first-year academic writing program, and at the end of the semester, writing students prepare a brief oral presentation of their research essay topic. Besides giving the L2 writing students a chance to practice English presentation and speaking skills, most writing teachers in the program also emphasize that organizing one's ideas to share orally with others can have a very positive effect on the final written draft. So, while the tutors often share their tutees' initial understanding of this assignment, at first, as just another item on a checklist of assignments, they just as often express their surprise and pleasure when they discover the 'hidden agenda' of supporting better written texts.

In this example from a late-semester session, Layla expresses her insight into the pedagogical reasoning (SEQUENCE ACTIVITY; PROVIDE RELEVANCE) of the writing teacher's goals

> **Excerpt 26**
>
> **I liked how helping Huan in preparing for this activity actually helped us also in the process of writing for the final essay which I believe this is what the teacher designed the activity for.**
>
> (Layla, Tutoring Internship, Session 10 Post, with Huan)

Conclusion

Through contingent, creative, and *responsive mediation*, the novice L2 teachers who join us with their 'hermetic' and 'personally relevant' understandings of teaching and learning transform into junior scholars, more-expert teaching practitioners, and independent decision-makers who demonstrate increased and greatly transformed mastery over their practice and understanding of pedagogy by the end of two years. While we cannot give all the credit to a list of simple phrases, the pedagogical concepts serve us, and our novice teachers, in a myriad of ways. They matter to us, to the teachers we educate, to the learners who are directly affected by the education we provide to those teachers, and to our program.

References

Aljaafreh, A., & Lantolf, J. P. (1994). Negative feedback as regulation and second language learning in the zone of proximal development. *The Modern Language Journal*, 78, 465–483.

Barnes, D. (1976). *From communication to curriculum*. London: Penguin Books.

Gage, N. L. (Ed.). (1974). NIL conference on studies in teaching; panel 5, teaching-as a linguistic process in a cultural setting. *National Institute of Education* (DHEW), Washington, D.C., 10.

Engeness, I. (2021). *P. Y. Galperin's development of human mental activity. Lectures in educational psychology*. Switzerland: Springer.

Johnson, K. E. (1995). *Understanding communication in second language classrooms*. New York: Cambridge University Press.

Johnson, K. E. (2009). *Second language teacher education: A sociocultural perspective*. New York: Routledge.

Johnson, K. E., & Golombek, P. R. (Eds.) (2011a). *Research on second language teacher education: A sociocultural perspective on professional development*. New York: Routledge.

Johnson, K. E., & Golombek, P. R. (2011b). The transformative power of narrative in L2 teacher education. *TESOL Quarterly*, 45(3), 1–24. https://doi.org/10.5054/tq.2011.256797.

Johnson, K. E., & Golombek, P. R. (2016). *Mindful L2 teacher education: A sociocultural perspective on cultivating teachers' professional development*. New York: Routledge.

Johnson, K. E., Verity, D. P., & Childs, S. S. (2020). Praxis-oriented pedagogy and the development of L2 novice teacher expertise. *The European Journal of Applied Linguistics and TEFL*, 9(2), 3–23.

Lantolf, J. P. (2020). World language education and the pedagogical imperative. In L. Zhang (Ed.), *The Oxford encyclopedia of educational psychology*. Oxford: Oxford University Press.

Lantolf, J. P., & Poehner, M. E. (2006). *Dynamic assessment in the foreign language classroom: A teachers guide*. University Park, PA: Center for Advanced Language Proficiency Education and Research, the Pennsylvania State University.

Lantolf, J. P., & Poehner, M. E. (2014). *Sociocultural theory and the pedagogical imperative in L2 education*. New York: Routledge.

Poehner, M. E., & Lantolf, J. P. (2021). The ZPD, second language learning and the transposition – transformation dialectic. *Cultural Historical Psychology, 17*(3), 31–41. https://doi.org/10.17759/chp.2021170306.

Lortie, D. (1975). *Schoolteacher: A sociological study*. Chicago: University of Chicago Press.

Stetsenko, A., & Vianna, E. (2009). Bridging developmental theory and educational practice. Lessons from the Vygotskian project. In O. A. Barbarin & B. H. Wasik (Eds.), *Handbook of child development and early education* (pp. 38–54). New York: Guilford Press.

Vygotsky, L. S. (1962). *Thought and language* (E. Hanfmann, & G. Vakar, Eds.). Cambridge, MA: MIT Press.

Vygotsky, L. S. (1987). Thinking and speech. In *The collected works of L.S. Vygotsky. Problems of general psychology* (Vol. 1, pp. 37–285) (translated by Norris Minick). New York: Plenum Press.

6
RESPONSIVE MEDIATION AND TEACHER INSTRUCTIONAL STANCE

Introduction

This chapter focuses on the role of *responsive mediation* and its effect upon teacher instructional stance. The data illustrate how being the recipient of contingent, targeted mediation themselves helps novice teachers learn how and why to provide responsive mediation to the learners they work with in various instructional roles. Simply put, this means that they shift their understanding of what teaching is from being something like a 'dispenser of information' toward being something more like 'mediator of knowing.' This change is documented in the ways that their instructional stance moves; it swings away from being centered on the self, on the lesson plan, and on the individual's internal monologue to being outwardly and other-directed, that is, toward engagement with learners rather than simply engagement with the content of the lesson. This shift can be seen in the way they articulate their understanding of their teaching activity (how they discuss and describe their instructional stance as teachers) and in the way they engage with their learners and the lesson materials.

Engagement in *responsive mediation* is not a one-way street: it includes both the mediation offered by teacher educators (and mentor teachers) and also the ways in which novice teachers respond to that mediation, how they experience it, what they take up, and how it comes to shape their reasoning over time. While we engage in *responsive mediation* in different ways and for different purposes throughout the three pillar courses, our data suggest that during the Teaching ESL course, our novice teachers become consciously aware of what engagement in *responsive mediation* entails and its pedagogical value in creating quality instructional dialogues. However, their ability to engage in

DOI: 10.4324/9781003268987-9

responsive mediation with their learners begins to emerge during the Tutoring Internship as they build dialogic instructional relationships with their tutees, which then becomes internalized during the Teaching Practicum when they engage in *responsive mediation* with their learners.

This transformation is initiated through extensive and intensive reflection and dialogue about their tutoring/teaching experiences, as mediated by teacher educators and mentor teachers; it gradually shifts for the novice teachers to being a new way of conceptualizing language teaching and engagement with their learners during tutoring and teaching activities. In other words, over time and with extensive and intensive mediation from expert others, our novice teachers become increasingly self-regulated in their ability to engage in *responsive mediation* with the learners they teach.

Using data collected from the three pillar courses, this chapter presents illustrative evidence to show that teacher instructional stance changes as teacher reasoning develops and principles of responsiveness become internalized. The data represent both 'in-flight' or real-time data collected through digital and audio recordings, and reflective written and oral data collected through stimulated recall sessions, reflective journals, reflective papers, and teaching journals.

We strive to make *responsive mediation* as a principle of praxis-oriented teacher education pedagogy reflected in both the mediation that we as teacher educators provide and in the ways that our novice teachers engage with their own learners in practice settings. The data presented in this chapter lay out the ways in which we help novice teachers learn to make thoughtful and reasoned choices about mediating their learners through modeling *responsive mediation* and through reflective activity. Because of our commitment to an instructional stance that focuses on the teacher-learner interaction rather than on the preplanned contributions that we make as educators, we focus much more on *how* to teach (how to think like a teacher, how to react like a teacher, how to interpret learner activity like a teacher) than on *what* to teach (content, techniques, and tasks). As experienced, expert teachers and teacher educators, we find that this stance is second nature to us. Our work with novice teachers, as illustrated by the range of data presented in this chapter, demonstrates how we can help them develop a more automatic focus on *responsive mediation* when teaching.

Instructional Paraphrasing: Learning to Create Instructional Dialogues

Core to the principles of VSCT, the interdependent unity of teaching/learning (*obuchenie*) is a form of dialogic mediation. An initial step in taking on a *teaching as dialogic mediation instructional stance* is being able to create instructional dialogues with learners. This requires creating comfortable and open spaces for learners to contribute their understandings, ideas, and experiences. And since learners are often 'working out' what they think while they are speaking (e.g., exploratory talk), novice teachers need to listen carefully to what learners are saying and establish a sense of how their learners are experiencing the content/ activities in which they are engaged. Once they think they have understood a learner's contributions, they need to explicitly link that to what they are teaching. Decades ago, Barnes (1976), an early follower of Vygotsky's work, argued that talk and interaction in classrooms unites the cognitive and the social, that there is no such thing as curriculum on the one hand and the communication used to deliver the curriculum on the other. Instead, he argued that communication *is* the curriculum. This being the case, the quality of teacher/learner interaction, or instructional dialogues, is paramount.

In our praxis-oriented pedagogy, the pedagogical concept INSTRUCTIONAL PARAPHRASING functions as a psychological tool in assisting novice teachers in their initial attempts at creating productive instructional dialogues. We insert it here for ease of reference (see also Appendix 1).

INSTRUCTIONAL PARAPHRASING
Whatever learners say, rephrase or paraphrase it out loud so that you

a. acknowledge the learner's contribution
b. make it comprehensible to everyone
c. provide appropriate language input/model
d. relate it to what you are teaching (i.e., take learners from where they are to where you want them to be)
e. establish a pattern that any and all learner contributions are welcome (i.e., lessen face-saving threats)
f. give yourself an opportunity to 'comprehend' it

During the first pillar course, Teaching ESL, novice teachers are exposed to this pedagogical concept, and it is repeatedly modeled by the Team-Teach Supervisor. However, to fully grasp its meaning-potential in creating instructional dialogues, novice teachers need to experience it directly, in the activities of teaching, with targeted mediation directed at ZPD activity by an expert other (e.g., teacher educator, mentor). To illustrate the developmental trajectory of novice teacher reasoning and how the pedagogical concept of INSTRUCTIONAL PARAPHRASING moves novice teachers toward a *teaching as dialogic mediation instructional stance*, we begin with a series of data sets that took place throughout the Extended Team-Teaching Project. The team, Natalie, Qing, and Qiao, was assigned to teach the use of hedging and boosting as rhetorical devices to demonstrate author stance in a graduate-level disciplinary writing class for L2/multilingual research students. The class instructor had given the team sample research articles from different academic disciplines representative of the research backgrounds of the graduate students enrolled in the class. During the *practice teach*, the team asked small groups of their classmates (fellow novice teachers) to read the discussion and conclusion sections of their articles to see if they could determine the author's stance, a concept that had been covered in the previous composition course session. Specifically, they were told to judge the author's stance, to say if it 'exudes confidence' or 'shows the author's attitude.'

In Excerpt 1, Qing asks members of the small groups to *share their opinions with us*. The person who contributes first offers a long-winded and somewhat convoluted monologue followed by a long pause, leaving Qing speechless with a blank expression on her face. The Team-Teach Supervisor (TE) notices this as an expression of cognitive/emotional dissonance and breaks the silence by opening up a space for Qing to verbalize what she is thinking.

Excerpt 1

TE: **Qing what is going on in your head?**
SS: ((laughter))
TE: This is something, just a sidebar. This is something I noticed in a lot of the videos that I watched so far. **You get a student who gives you this really long explanation and I can see the wheels turning like, what am I gonna do with this?** What am I gonna do with this? What am I gonna do with this? Right? so, you have to, sort of, **listen, because you kind of wanna know what he's saying, you have to think about, ok, how can I summarize that concisely, make it clear to the group, but link it to what I'm trying to teach?** And that's a hard skill. That's a hard skill, that's sort of, you know **expertise in terms of teaching**, but, you gotta be, sort of, ready for that.

TE: **Now, it doesn't mean you have to repeat everything he says, but you can say,** "so, then, the essential comment you just made was x." And then you link it to something that you're trying to teach, ok? And I, I'm, I'm sort of, calling out Qing here, but all of us, have to work on this. This is a skill that, that, all of us, and I saw it in all the videos, **that it's something that you, you have to sort of learn to process and learn to deal with, as part of teaching, ok?**

TE: So, you don't have to answer my question (Qing), what was going on in your head, but maybe you can ask another one.
QING: Oh, someone else?
SS: ((laughter))
TE: No, that was perfect, because what Jason, what you did was exactly what happens in classrooms. **And teachers need to know how to deal with that. You need to know how to summarize it, connect it to what you're trying to teach.** It was perfect! (.)

(Extended Team-Teaching Project, Teaching ESL, Practice Teach)

The mediation offered by the Team-Teach Supervisor is directed at the entire class, although it was initiated in response to Qing's immediate experience of being unable to respond to a classmate's comment. Without explicitly mentioning the pedagogical concept, the Team-Teach Supervisor focuses on the reasoning behind INSTRUCTIONAL PARAPHRASING, emphasizing how it can be used to link what learners say to what is being taught. She also revoices how a teacher might respond, qualifying that INSTRUCTIONAL PARAPHRASING is not necessary or even appropriate at every turn, but she emphasizes that this is a common occurrence in language classrooms and that, as teachers, they will need to learn how to make connections between what their students may say and what they are trying to teach.

Immediately following this exchange, another class member makes a comment about what their group found in their research article, mentioning two adverbs (*clearly* & *definitely*) as evidence of author stance. It is apparent that the Team-Teach Supervisor's mediation in Excerpt 1 has not been immediately taken up by Qing, as she fails to use INSTRUCTIONAL PARAPHRASING in response to this contribution and instead answers with a simple, *Ok!*

Excerpt 2

QING: Ok!

TE: **No, you gotta say more than ok**. Not gonna get by with that. So, you gotta say: **So, you think that the con-, that, uhm, confidence is shown by the words "definitely" and "clearly"?** And you have this wonderful teammate who put it on the board for you, so you can reference back to that, ok? As you're responding to her, so she's helping you here, she's giving you a way to sort of respond back, ok?

QING: **So (we point out) "definitively" and "clearly" to show how, how certain the author is, right?** for us (.) Uhm, so, here are two important, (.) here are two important definitions of hedging and boosting. So, ((reads)) **hedges are phrases that display uncertainty, deference, modesty or respect for colleagues' views. It can show a lack of confidence. And boosts are phrases that show confidence in the author's claims or results** ((ends reading)). **So, here are the two important definitions that we should pay attention to them.**

(Extended Team-Teaching Project, Teaching ESL, Practice Teach)

Not letting this mediational moment slip by without comment, the Team-Teach Supervisor models how Qing could have used INSTRUCTIONAL PARAPHRASING, noting also that her teammate had written both adverbs on the board, as a reference for her response. This interaction seems to help Qing become consciously aware of the need to take up what learners say and link it to the content of the lesson. However, unable to act autonomously at this point in her development, she essentially imitates the Team-Teach Supervisor and just reads the definitions of hedging and boosting on the PowerPoint slide. Yet, VSCT would characterize her engagement in conscious imitation as a leading activity of development, since learners imitate that which they are in the process of developing. Therefore, these quick and seemingly innocuous moments during the *practice teach* set the stage for how Qing begins to shift her reasoning and her instructional stance more toward *teaching as dialogic mediation*.

Within a VSCT orientation, concept development is never a linear process, described for instance by Smagorinsky, Cook, and Johnson (2003) as following a long and *"twisting path"* (p. 1432). Thus, it is not surprising that a similar occurrence happens to Qing during the *actual teach* of this lesson. In fact, it occurs at almost the same juncture in the lesson, after the small groups have discussed the readings and have been asked to share their findings.

Excerpt 3

QING: You all had a great discussion, and someone want to share with us about the discussion? (.)

S: In our group I can explain. In our group, uhm my article uhm and his article is really mild. The author is not confident while mention about mentioning his results, uhm because there is so many words like "may", "perhaps", "possible". So, we can say the author makes his sentences more softer by using these modals.

QING: **And what, what, what is your paper uhm talking about?**

S: My paper is talking about "Trans Siberia in East Asia".

QING: Uhum. (.) Somebody else? (.) (0.7) You two had a big discussion just ()

((QING IS LOOKING AT A GROUP OF TWO STUDENTS)).

S: So my paper is about (bio) engineering where you use (first) student modal and then use the modal to explain some experimental results, so some things about a phenomenon. So, they also use a lot of "mays" and "potentially" to soften their opinion, and the reason is (kind of kind of) is very new. So they are not sure. It's a modal, is one hundred percent sure or uhm there is something missing in the model. In the second paragraph there is also uhm a claim that their model has some possible correlation with the experimental result. So it's kind of like strengthen their, their, like, opinion.

QING: **Ok, so you mentioned in your paper you find out "may" and some, other modals to show, to weaken other statement, right?**

QING: Ok! Somebody else?

S5: Ok, in my paper, it talks about uhm, this is a quantitative work so this is a so there's use of very strong words like "significantly", "definitely", "clearly", so the author is very confident of the claims in his work, so this is very strong.

QING: Yes! **You mentioned uhm "significantly", and "definitely", "clearly". These are all adverbs to strengthen your state- to strengthen all the statement, right?** (.) So actually there are two professional terms describing this phenomenon. **They are hedging and boosting. So, we can see their definitions.** ((reads)) **Hedges are phrases that display uncertainty, deference, modesty or respect for colleagues' views. It can show a lack of confidence. And Boosts are phrases that show confidence in the authors' claims or results** ((ends reading)).

(Extended Team-Teaching project, Teaching ESL, Actual Teach)

In the first half of this exchange, Qing does respond to the learner's contribution, although not through INSTRUCTIONAL PARAPHRASING. Instead, she asks the student what her paper was about, and then moves on without comment. In the second half of this exchange, Qing does take up the learner's identification of certain modal verbs that soften the author's claims, but, again, moves on to the next group without comment. In the final portion of the exchange, Qing repeats isolated words (*modals*) offered by the learner, links them to their rhetorical function (*strengthen your stance*) and then orients the class to the formal definitions of hedging and boosting on the PowerPoint slide. Clearly, Qing can be seen as attempting to use INSTRUCTIONAL PARAPHRASING to respond to the ESL learners' contributions, each attempt with a bit more success. It is only during the *stimulated recall session* that we gain insights into how and why Qing struggled to take up and respond to learner contributions. However, the Team-Teach Supervisor recognizes this as a struggle since she begins the session by saying, *I almost read in your faces as they were giving their long, long, long explanations and I could see you thinking, ok! What do I do? What do I do?* as the team members laugh. The Team-Teach Supervisor then pauses the digital recording at the exact point when Qing is attempting to respond to the small group report and again, recognizing this as a dramatic moment, opens up a mediational space for Qing to verbalize her thinking:

Excerpt 4

TE: So what was going on in your head there when she was talking?
QING: **I want- actually I wanted to paraphrase, and maybe-**
TE: I thought you did ((laughter))-
QING: But I didn't see (.) 'cause **I'm not sure I was fully understanding what she-**

TE: She was saying, yeah, yeah. It's hard I mean, what she brought up and what Natalie was writing on the board was the idea of modals. So, even if you couldn't really understand what she was saying, **you could link and say, "so, you found modals were an indicator that uhm of the author's stance."** But I think on the very next turn, you do instruc- you do paraphrase the student. You didn't in the first one, but I think for the ones that follow, all of them, you did, so, again, **it's a technique to acknowledge student comments, give yourself some time to think about it, connect it to what you're trying to teach, make it relevant for everybody, because, I don't know if I understood what she was saying,** I mean it's-

NATALIE: Yeah! I heard, like, I was writing- I wrote modals, but you know what I was thinking: "did she say models?"- I hope she didn't say models-

TE: Right, yeah, so again, it's just a, **it's a technique for doing that, and I think the strength of the technique is linking whatever the student said to the thing you're trying to teach.** But sometimes it is hard to figure that out, right?

(Extended Team-Teaching Project, Teaching ESL, Stimulated Recall)

Qing now seems consciously aware of the pedagogical concept of INSTRUCTIONAL PARAPHRASING when she says, *Actually I wanted to paraphrase...*, but notes that she could not implement it because she was struggling to understand what the learner had said. Empathizing with Qing, the Team-Teach Supervisor revoices what she could have said, even if she had not fully understood the learner's comment. When Natalie, a teammate, expresses her own struggle to understand the same learner, this creates an additional mediational space for the Team-Teach Supervisor to reiterate the pedagogical value of INSTRUCTIONAL PARAPHRASING for linking learner contributions to what is being taught.

In her final reflection paper, we find evidence of Qing's cognitive/emotional dissonance over engaging with learners' contributions throughout the various stages of the Extended Team-Teaching Project. Yet by this point she is able to recognize why she is struggling, in other words, she can name the source of her dissonance. She also reaches several new realizations; that teaching is about CONNECTING learners' ideas to *the topic of our class* and *use what we listened from students* and *guide students to talk*. In describing the *practice teach* as *a terrible night* she claims:

Excerpt 5

Until that day, **I didn't realize that I need to make a connection between students' ideas and the topic of our class.** It was hard for me because I even could not clearly understand students' main idea sometimes.... **I learned that we teachers could use what we listened from students into our next part of our lesson, in which is also a good link between different parts, to guide students to talk.**

(Qing, Teaching ESL, Final Paper)

Qing concludes her reflection paper by referencing her range of emotions and realizing that teachers, like students, can feel emotions during class. She notes the seemingly novel feeling of being a 'real' teacher and restates, in her own words, the pedagogical value of INSTRUCTIONAL PARAPHRASING: *without students' reaction, teachers could not achieve their class goals.*

Excerpt 6

I had an indescribable feeling when teaching an actual ESL class, the change of role gave me many inspirations. As a student before, I had seldom thought a teacher standing in the front of our classroom could be nervous or worried. Before teaching in real class, I thought a successful class all depends on teacher's capacity. However, combining with some articles I read recently, **I realized that teaching process is like a two-way channel, in which need both teachers and students cooperate** together. To be specific, in my real teaching class, **after students' speech, teachers should make a conclude of that speech to make sure all students understand, and then link what students said to the main topic, not just let students say and others listen.** Similarly, without students' reaction, teachers could not achieve their class goals.

(Qing, Teaching ESL, Final Paper)

At the end of the Teaching ESL course, we begin to see a transformation in how Qing reasons about her teaching (REASONING TEACHING), describing teaching as a *two-way channel* and we hear how Qing has taken up the pedagogical concept of INSTRUCTIONAL PARAPHRASING and made it her own. While at this point in her development she may not be able to create productive instructional dialogues, she is consciously aware of their pedagogical value and now sees teaching not just as depending on *teacher's capacity* but as an activity in which *both teachers and students cooperate together.*

Be Direct, Not Directive: Building a Dialogic Instructional Relationship

Whether engaged in teaching or tutoring, the tendency of most novice teachers is often to display their own knowledge rather than to guide and support their learners to engage with ideas. In our praxis-oriented pedagogy, the pedagogical concept BE DIRECT, NOT DIRECTIVE asks novice teachers to make their instructional goals, expectations, and instructions explicit while at the same time asking them to refrain from giving specific answers or detailed suggestions for new language or structures to learners. This pedagogical concept is designed to help novice teachers understand that their task is to offer targeted mediation that guides learners to new understandings and contextually appropriate uses of language. We insert it here for ease of reference (see also Appendix 1).

BE DIRECT, NOT DIRECTIVE

a. Be explicit about what language point you are focusing on
b. Do not tell the learner what to write or say in place of their own contribution
c. Use targeted mediation to support the learner's use of language

In short, we expect our novice teachers to BE DIRECT, i.e., to be explicit about what feature of the text or aspect of the language they want students to pay attention to, but NOT DIRECTIVE, i.e., to tell students what to say or what to write. This pedagogical concept serves as a highly relevant psychological tool for the Tutoring Internship because the goal of this tutoring program is not to get higher grades for the tutees, or just to produce better written texts for their own sake, but to develop into more autonomous, self-aware, versatile academic writers. A central goal of the Tutoring Internship for the tutors is to build a dialogic instructional relationship with each tutee, to encourage tutees to think through and work over their ideas alongside the tutor, and to discuss and engage with the drafting, revising, and rewriting process that is foundational to the first-year academic writing course. However, learning to engage dialogically with tutees requires a conceptual shift in how tutors position themselves and how they reason about the tutor-tutee roles and relationship. *Responsive mediation* provided by the Tutoring Supervisor plays a critical role in assisting and supporting tutors as they first recognize the need to take up a more dialogic stance and then in their multiple (and not always successful) attempts to enact this instructional stance with their tutees over time. Writing reflective posts about every tutoring session while engaging with the Tutoring Supervisor through her written commentary creates a safe mediational space for tutors to express their struggles, to work over new ways of thinking about their role as tutors, and to become skilled at more productive ways of engaging with their tutees, all of which supports the building of a dialogic instructional relationship with their tutees.

It can be destabilizing for the novice teachers to realize that there is no specific or single formula that they can use to establish the long-term instructional relationships they must build with their tutees. Tutoring is a context where, at first glance, CREATE PREDICTABILITY and PROVIDE RELEVANCE can feel hopelessly out of reach; a tutor must wait until the tutee enters the room before they even know what the topic of the tutoring session will be. It is for this reason that the Tutoring Supervisor encourages the novice teachers to use their first tutoring session to create some personal rapport (TEACHING AS CONNECTING) with each tutee, since the tutee will be more likely to raise questions and bring topics for consideration if a trusting relationship has been established.

In the following discussion, we draw on Gan's Tutoring Internship final reflection paper which is interspersed with quotes (in italics) that he inserted from his weekly reflective posts. This reflective strategy, which we strongly encourage, allows us to hear him in the process of working out how not to be a *teller* (NOT DIRECTIVE) during his tutoring sessions as well as his emerging realization of what it means to be *a qualified tutor* (BE DIRECT, NOT DIRECTIVE). In addition to Gan's writing, we have culled from the written responses of the Tutoring Supervisor to illustrate how this tutor is supported as he comes to understand, and then starts to build, a dialogic instructional relationship with his tutees.

Initially, Gan recalls, he thought that his role as a tutor was to offer *informative and productive* words and to *make the students learn new knowledge*. Looking back at his activity in one tutoring session, he realized that he felt unable to do this because he was unfamiliar with the topic of the tutee's paper. Looking forward, he proposes that if he let the tutee *express more ideas* he might be able to offer *more effective feedback*.

Excerpt 7

Besides, another thing I realized later is that it is better not to be a teller in the tutoring task. At the early phase of the tutoring session, I thought my words should be informative and productive, and I need to make the students learn some new knowledge from our meeting sessions.

> "Based on this meeting, I thought that I am already accustomed to give some thought-provoking ideas to stimulate tutee's thought. However, I did not figure out what should I react when I have no idea about the topic. **Maybe, I need to encourage tutee to express more ideas so that I could give more effective feedback according to their ideas.**" (Tutee 1 Session #7)
>
> (Gan Tutoring Internship, Final Reflection Paper)

In her response to the excerpt (in italics) from his original reflective post, the Tutoring Supervisor had indicated that offering *thought-provoking ideas* is not really the *job* of a tutor. She went on to suggest that asking questions about the topic the tutee is writing about may be a more productive means of helping her *know how important it is to focus and develop a topic carefully.*

Excerpt 8

I don't think, in any case, that it is your job to give thought-provoking ideas all the time. Just asking questions: **WHO is affected by this problem? WHO cares about solving this problem? WHAT causes this problem? WHAT is the problem that most interests you in this topic?** etc etc etc is more the tutor's job than being brilliant with ideas! That's why instructors provide assignment sheets, concept maps, brainstorming exercises, etc. to help students develop their topics because novice writers do NOT really know how important it is to focus and develop a topic carefully.

(Supervisor, Tutoring Internship, Session 7 Response)

Gan continues his final paper by articulating what *a qualified tutor* should be: *a facilitator who encourages my tutees to express their own opinions* and someone who listens to *their concerns, needs, and problems.* He is beginning to realize that this instructional stance will enable him to *give more specific feedback.* To support this new realization, he inserts a concrete example from a reflective post written early in the semester where he did not *just give direct answers* (BE DIRECT, NOT DIRECTIVE) but instead successfully *induced his tutees to find the answers by themselves.*

Excerpt 9

I gradually knew that I cannot equate a good teller to a qualified tutor. **As a tutor, I am supposed to be a facilitator who encourage my tutees to express their own opinions.** Compared with instructing something that they do not know, it is more important to enable them to internalize what they seemingly know. **Additionally, by listening to the tutees, I can also know their concerns, needs and problems, which help me to give more specific feedback helping them to solve their problems.** For example,

> "......*I can sense this paragraph is incongruous in this essay.* **Then I talked with Tutee 2 and asked him to explain his purpose of writing this paragraph. When he explained his idea, he suddenly figured out that maybe this paragraph is irrelevant to his essay.**" (Tutee 2, Session 3).

I gradually knew that I should not just give the direct answers to my tutees. **It is best if I can induce my tutees to find the answers by themselves.**

(Gan, Tutoring Internship Final Paper)

In response to his reflective post (in italics), the Tutoring Supervisor originally had complimented him on helping his tutee *discover certain weaknesses*, while also giving him credit for offering *helpful mediation*.

Excerpt 10

It sounds like the student really worked hard to improve his 'second chance' draft and **I'm glad that you felt he was also able to discover certain weaknesses mostly by himself (with your helpful mediation, of course!)**

(Supervisor, Tutoring Internship, Session 3 Response)

She also had asked several clarification questions about references he made (not included in the excerpt above) to *organize his* [the tutee's] *resources* and his tutee's divergent *thinking style*. This opened an extended dialogue between them in which Gan clarified that he meant the organization of the essay (cohesion) rather than outside resources and offered a rationale for why his tutee's essay lacked clear support for the arguments he was attempting to make.

Excerpt 11

When you say 'organize his resources' I'm not exactly sure what you mean: do you mean find useful information in outside sources like articles or websites? Or do you mean organize the examples and information that he put into the essay (i.e., his "own" information)? **Also, it would be interesting to hear more about your comment that this tutee's 'thinking style is divergent'–I'm not sure what you mean or what implications that has for his writing.**

(Supervisor, Tutoring Internship, Session 3 Response)

When I say 'organize his resources', I mean organize the examples and information that he put into the essay. He cited a story and analyzed it from different perspectives, and he used these different analyzed outcomes to support his argument. However, I found he cannot capitalize on these outcomes very well, because I could see the story and his comments everywhere in his essay, but I could not easily figure out which one support which argument of his essay.

(Gan, Tutoring Internship, Session 3 Post)

Thanks for this explanation. I was confused whether you meant 'outside source information' or just 'examples' when you said 'resources'. **I can see how you helped him organize the connections inside the text (cohesion)!**

(Supervisor, Tutoring Internship, Session 3 Response)

The dialogic nature of these reflective posts creates a safe mediational space where Gan is able to further articulate his reasoning for how and why he engaged with his tutee; at the same time the Tutoring Supervisor takes the opportunity to remind him that 'cohesion' is an academic concept which functions as a rhetorical strategy for organizing connections inside a text, and which may give him a useful term to use in future reflective writing and future tutoring sessions.

Since tutees often begin their tutoring sessions with similar assumptions about fixing grammar errors and wanting to be told what to write, building a dialogic instructional relationship can take time to develop; some tutors struggle more than others. In another exchange with Gan, after he expresses his frustration with his inability to get his tutee to engage in dialogue with him, the Tutoring Supervisor offers concrete examples of how he might create more comfortable spaces for his tutee to respond.

Excerpt 12

It's true that not every tutee is talkative and this can feel frustrating. Even though you are using questions to try to open her up, maybe you can also try using "statements" in the sense that it may be easier for her to react to a statement rather than formulate a good answer to a direct question.

Here's an example: you see that there is no good transition between Paragraph 1 and Paragraph 2. If you ask, "What do you think you could add here?" she might feel pressure to find the single, one answer that you have in your mind.

If you say, on the other hand, "I don't see any transition between P1 and P2" and then wait for her to respond, she doesn't feel that she has to come up with an answer, just a comment. You can try that; it may work.

(Supervisor, Tutoring Internship, Session 5 Response)

As the semester moves along, we find evidence of Gan's emerging ability to work more dialogically with his tutees. To illustrate this development in his final reflective paper for the Tutoring Internship, he includes a short excerpt from an interaction he had with one of his tutees, which he offers as evidence of his development as a more dialogic tutor. By positioning himself as the *question asker*, Gan was able let his tutee *be the giver and teller in our conversation*.

Excerpt 13

TUTOR: *Maybe, I think the grammar is no longer the biggest challenge for you, right? Maybe, word choice? getting ideas? Paragraph development?*
TUTEE 2: *Yes, I always have trouble to choose proper words when I write.*

TUTOR: So, maybe, we can focus on the word choice this time? How do you think the "area" you use here? What you want to express when you use this word?

TUTEE 2: I want to say that even though the policy of American government is generally friendly to the immigrants. But, I want to say that there are also some policy that constrain the development of international students in America.

TUTOR: In other words, you use "area" to refer to the policy which constrain the international students in America?

TUTEE 2: Y...es. Except this, the "area" here can also be divided into the policy of education for international students and policy of job opportunities for international students.

TUTOR: Oh....yes. Now I know what you mean. Maybe, it is not a word choice issue. You just need to give some explanation for this word. In this way, the reader can understand what you mean.

TUTEE 2: Yes, I know that. I will add some information to explain the "area" here.

The reason why **I think it is an achievement of the tutoring meeting is that I made Tutee 2 to be the giver and teller in our conversation.** Tutee 2, a Korean girl, who is a little introverted, does not like to be the teller in a conversation. She prefers to ask me question and then wait for my answer. Before this meeting session, hardly can I engage Tutee 2 into our talking. There was a lot of pause and silence in our meeting sessions. Therefore, in this meeting, **I tried to encourage her to talk and induce her to share her own ideas. I became the question asker in this meeting session. As a result, Tutee 2 started to know how our tutoring sessions work.**

(Gan, Tutoring Internship, Final Paper)

In this comment, we hear how this exchange helped to shift this tutor-tutee relationship to be more productive for both participants; up to this point, Gan has been unable to get his tutee to engage with him in dialogue. When he takes on a questioning stance and gives her space to respond genuinely, it marks the beginning of a more dialogic instructional relationship for future tutoring sessions, as he notes in his reflection.

In the introduction to his final reflection paper for the Tutoring Internship, Gan acknowledges his own conceptual shift as a tutor. Recognizing the need to change his instructional stance, he positions himself no longer as an ESL learner but as an ESL tutor, as someone *who needs to assist, to consolidate, to help them internalize knowledge.* While he recognizes the need to be direct when tutees have specific questions, Gan credits this shift in his instructional stance as enabling him to *gradually know who I am and what should I do* as a writing tutor.

Excerpt 14

Then, I gradually found that the first thing I need to do is to change my stance. I am no more an ESL learner in our tutoring meeting. I am the person who needs to assist my tutees to consolidate what they have learned in classroom and try to help them to internalize the knowledge. Also, sometimes, **I need to give clear answers for solving my tutees' questions.** In hindsight, **I totally changed my stance from an ESL learner to an ESL tutor until near the middle of the semester. As time goes by, I gradually know who I am and what should I do in the tutoring meeting sessions.**

(Gan Tutoring Internship, Final Paper)

Interestingly, at the conclusion of his final reflection paper, Gan characterizes himself as a strategic mediator. His comments embody the pedagogical concept of BE DIRECT, NOT DIRECTIVE and how it seems to encapsulate both his reasoning and how he proposes to engage with his tutees in the future.

Excerpt 15

By listening to the tutees, I can also know their concerns, needs and problems, which help me to give more specific feedback helping them to solve their problems…**the strategy I use is arousing the awareness first, and then … discuss … the problems and finally reach an agreement… rather than pointing out the issues directly, I always encourage them to analyze the issues…after that, I will ask the tutees to find a way to solve the problems on their own. If they cannot find a proper way to solve the problems, I will offer them hints supporting them to find the answers. Under the other circumstance, if I do not know how to solve the problems too, I will express my opinions first, and start a discussion with my tutees. In this way, we will end up with reaching an agreement.**

(Gan, Tutoring Internship, Final Paper)

Ultimately, the pedagogical concept BE DIRECT, NOT DIRECTIVE offers a reasoned way for tutors to navigate between directly addressing tutees' questions and concerns while also guiding their thinking, creating space for them to work out their ideas, and supporting them as they become more agentive, resourceful, and independent academic writers. Implied in this pedagogical concept is the notion that tutors are not expected to know all the answers or fix grammar errors but to engage with their tutees' ideas and various forms of oral and written expression by building and sustaining a dialogic instructional relationship.

Teach off Your Students, Not at Them: Learning to Engage in Responsive Mediation

The pedagogical concept TEACH OFF YOUR STUDENTS, NOT AT THEM has come, over the years, to encompass all the other pedagogical concepts we have integrated into our praxis-oriented pedagogy (see Appendix 1). Yet at its core, its simplicity makes it a powerful tool that enables novice teachers to instantiate a *teaching as dialogic mediation instructional stance*. This stance shifts novice L2 teachers' attention toward their learners' histories, sense-making, engagement, episodes of *perezhivanie*, and most importantly, productive engagement in language learning. It encourages more dialogic, collaborative, and co-constructed interactions between teachers and learners. It requires that teachers create spaces for learners to make their understandings explicit, to listen carefully to those understandings, and to create links to new concepts or new ways of thinking about the content they are teaching. Not surprisingly, we find that our novice teachers come to understand and take up this pedagogical concept in different ways, but it enables them to develop a conceptual understanding of the value of and how to take on a *teaching as dialogic mediation instructional stance*.

By the time our novice teachers begin teaching during the Teaching Practicum, the pedagogical concept TEACH OFF YOUR STUDENTS, NOT AT THEM has not only permeated how they talk about their teaching, but it also functions as a psychological tool that drives the way they organize their instruction and how they orient to and interact with their learners.

During a lesson on the rhetorical triangle (*ethos, pathos, logos*) in her Teaching Practicum class, the first-year academic writing course for L2 speakers, Fang TEACHES OFF a student (S1) when he offers the correct answer, which she follows by requesting that he *be more specific*. By giving him the floor, he can elaborate his answer, even locating evidence of pathos in the reading and the rhetorical effect of using an exclamation point. Fang PARAPHRASES his response and links it to the notions of persuasion and taking action. This interactional pattern is repeated when she reads the second sentence and asks what rhetorical strategy the author is using.

Excerpt 16

FANG: So have you finished? Right, okay, so how about number one number one.
S1: Pathos.
FANG: Pathos, right, **can you be more specific?**
S1: I mean so if we look at the last, like the last part of the sentence it says ((*reads*)) "we don't want to be a laughingstock in the community."
FANG: Right.

S: **Exclamation point.**
FANG: Right.
S1: Kinda like directly talk to you and use the personal like connection and like gave the bracket or the parenthesis at the top it says ((reads)) "invokes an emotional response" feel bad this time especially with **the exclamation mark at the end** directing it towards them that make him feel a certain way.
FANG: RIGHT exactly **so the sequence here there is an exclamation mark in this sentence and this sentence is trying to persua:de the audience to take action** so we put pathos here and second one ((reads)) "by doing decades of experience in public service, my talents compliment to the people of this community, and willingness to reach across the aisle and cooperate with the opposition makes me the ideal candidate for mayor" **what kind of rhetorical device does this sentence use here?**
S2: Ethos and pathos.
FANG: **Ethos and pathos, correct, could you be more specific?**
S2: Oh because that's about the commitment, willingness ((inaudible))
S3: He also says that any time about his commitment ((inaudible))
FANG: Right, so, in this sentence **like what he said this speaker's using his or her three decades of experience and also prior commitment** and also the willingness to prove to prove what? (1.0) the credibility so as to convince people, right, okay, how bout number three? (3.0) logos? any other answer?
S4: I think it's pathos.
FANG: Pathos?
S3: Ethos.
FANG &SS: ((laughter))
FANG: RIGHT **the answer is ethos (.) wh:y? Paul.**
S1: Ah because ah **doctors' authority, authorities, the authority of his position.**
FANG: Right, **and also the doctor says** ((reads)) "I am qualified to tell you" why? because he's a doctor so he has such professional knowledge to tell the audience what the audience should do, right? Okay, number four.

(Fang, Teaching Practicum, Week 10)

Toward the end of this excerpt, when the learners give Fang conflicting answers, she TEACHES OFF by asking a learner, Paul, to explain *why?* Fang then PARAPHRASES his explanation and links it to the rhetorical effect of ethos in academic writing. Clearly, Fang is in control of this large group discussion, but there is a generous amount of learner participation and engagement illustrating how she has begun to take on a *teaching as dialogic mediation instructional stance*. And she is highly aware of this shift, even using the pedagogical concept TEACHING OFF YOUR STUDENTS, NOT AT THEM in her final reflection paper to describe how much she enjoyed hearing what her learners were thinking and how she used their ideas to make the content clear, and how much she valued the mentoring she received throughout the Teaching Practicum.

Excerpt 17

Being a practicum teacher this semester was like a **treasure hunt, with surprises around every choice I made**... I encountered many difficulties, but I really enjoyed the process... **hearing what the students were thinking, using their ideas to make my content clear, teaching off them, not at them feels like treasure to me now**. I didn't do it alone... my mentor, my professional partner, my supervisor, even my students **guided me on my treasure hunt to become a real teacher**.

(Fang, Teaching Practicum, Final Paper)

Often engagement in *responsive mediation* with mentor teachers prompts novice L2 teachers to consider ways of TEACHING OFF their students instead of lecturing at them. Writing about an exchange she had with her mentor teacher in her practicum class, Lin reflects on his questioning her about why she planned to review the content of the previous lesson by lecturing from a title slide she had designed.

Excerpt 18

"Teach off students, not at them": When I designed the review part, I simply put the title of slide—review. Jack asked me the reason why I just planned to talk about that. I said that I did this because I thought this part was so small and we could go over quickly. **Then, Jack said, "how about ask them?", which I never thought about that asking students to provide where they are can tell us how much they have learned from the last class.**

(Lin, Teaching Practicum, Week 8 Journal)

His question, *how about ask them?*, prompted her to ORIENT toward the learners and assess from them what they learned from the previous lesson. This reorientation in stance creates a mediational space where she can TEACH OFF what her learners recall from the previous lesson, rather than telling what they may already know. Lin even invokes the pedagogical concept itself, evidence that it is aiding her in making a shift toward a more *teaching as dialogic mediation instructional stance*.

With a heightened awareness of this pedagogical concept, our novice L2 teachers often recall closely observing more experienced teachers TEACH OFF

STUDENTS, perhaps at first simply noticing how a mentor teacher or teacher educator responds to students' contributions. For example, recognizing her inability to make smooth transitions from one instructional activity to the next, Qing recalls observing how her mentor teacher and the Practicum Supervisor create transitions between activities. In response to this journal entry, the Practicum Supervisor encourages her to think about and even write down what she might say as a way to begin *thinking in the moment and as a teacher*.

Excerpt 19

In next several lessons, on the one side, I am interested to observe how my mentor responds students' speaking including her body language and emotions. I would observe my mentor's transitions between two activities. Sharon's great transitions in [Teaching Practicum] class inspired me a lot and made me start to notice the importance of transitions. I have faced this problem when I did my intern before. But I didn't pay attention to this point. **Transition is the part that I ignored in the past. So I really want to see how professionals deal with this issue.**

(Qing, Teaching Practicum, Week 2 Journal)

I would also suggest that you start to think about and maybe even write down what YOU would say if you were leading an activity or transition from one to the next. For example, if a student asks Ellen a question, take a moment to think about how you would respond – and compare that with what Ellen says. This will help you start thinking in the moment and as a teacher!

(Supervisor, Teaching Practicum Week 2 Response)

The Practicum Supervisor asks her to imitate the mentor teacher as an initial step in reasoning like a teacher, but also encourages her to craft her own responses as a (future) autonomous instructor.

In their reflective teaching journals, our novice teachers sometimes script out their debriefing conversations after having taught a lesson. Because Hannah was teaching in two sections of the same course a few hours apart, she describes how debriefing with her mentor teacher over lunch pushed her to speculate on the reasoning behind her mentor's instructional choices.

Excerpt 20

Between the morning and afternoon section, Emine and I ate our lunches and debriefed a little bit – **she said I did a better job of situating the lesson in the context of the course and the compare/ contrast essay assignment, but the smaller transitions, like** between the two parts of the activity, I could still think through some more.

> EMINE: Oh, so for example, why did we start with source-related language instead of compare/contrast language? Maybe that wasn't arbitrary? **Mm, yes, I did have a reason. What do you think?**
> HANNAH: **Ah! Because it fits with the flow of how we've been doing this assignment** – *there's been a major focus on using sources, so this feels connected to the past week's work, and then from there, we can move to genre-specific language.*
> EMINE: **Exactly. And also because they need more help with the source language, and this way we can spend a little more time on it.**
> (Hannah, Teaching Practicum, Week 6 Journal)

Likewise, Hannah describes how her mentor teacher pressed her to articulate the intentions behind her own instructional choices, even when those choices seemed *trivial or arbitrary*.

Excerpt 21

> **One of the things I've been picking up on from Emine is the intentionality involved in aspects of lessons that I might originally overlook as trivial or arbitrary.** For instance, she asked me later about the four articles I had chosen, and why I had chosen those ones in particular. Well…I had been looking for one article from a traditionally more liberal newspaper, one from a more conservative newspaper, one from an international newspaper, and one source that was blatantly unreliable. But Emine pressed further: once these sources were selected, why these articles in particular? **I didn't have a good reason, other than the fact that they were not too long, and I found them personally interesting.**
> (Hannah, Teaching Practicum, Week 9 Journal)

Not surprisingly, our novice teachers often recognize the conceptual interconnectedness between the pedagogical concepts that infuse our praxis-oriented pedagogy. In Shu's final reflection paper, she combines the notions of INSTRUCTIONAL PARAPHRASING with TEACH OFF as a means of helping learners not only make connections to new concepts (TEACHING AS CONNECTING) but also to help them *become independent problem solvers*.

Excerpt 22

> **… I realized that when teachers paraphrased students' answers and taught off of them, they were able to guide them to the goal**

of the discussion instead of 'lecturing' at them, it is this engaging teaching process of connecting the knowledge that students have to the new concepts that they are learning and helping them to become independent problem solvers. I could help them with their struggles.

(Shu, Teaching Practicum, Final Paper)

Again, these pedagogical concepts come to function as psychological tools that drive novice teachers' reasoning and shape their teaching activities.

One outcome of *a teaching as dialogic mediation instructional stance* is a shift from a focus on oneself to a focus on learners. In her final reflection paper, Lin recognizes her own shift from focusing on herself as a teacher at the start of the Teaching Practicum to now focusing on *the needs of the students* and *regarding her students as individuals*.

Excerpt 23

I began to shift my focus from myself as a teacher to the needs of students. At the beginning of the teaching practicum, I focused on was my own teaching in order to meet all the requirements of the practicum, instead of regrading students as individuals.

(Lin, Teaching Practicum, Final Paper)

In case the point needs to be clarified any further, the pedagogical concept TEACH OFF YOUR STUDENTS, NOT AT THEM does not suggest that novice teachers have no plan or that their instruction is driven by the whims of their learners. On the contrary, it requires that teachers have clear instructional goals and a coherent plan for how to achieve those goals. But it also requires that teachers be flexible in the enactment of their lessons, and sensitive to learners' understanding (or misunderstandings), consistently and continually balancing what they are trying to accomplish with how the learners are responding to and experiencing their instruction. In the next example, Hannah recognizes that in order to TEACH OFF her students, she needs to be fully prepared and comfortable with the content of the lesson, because if she is, she will be more likely to deviate from her lesson plan, and thus TEACH OFF her students. She projects that in future lessons, she will spend more time *mapping out my ideas* and *practice what I wanted to say* so that in the activity of teaching she can *align with how the students are making sense of things as they happen*.

Excerpt 24

If I had it to do over (creating a PowerPoint and using it for the lesson), maybe **I would spend more time mapping out my ideas on paper beforehand, and also I might practice more what I wanted to**

say, not because I need to get it perfect, but because if I'm more familiar with it, I think I would be better able to deviate from it and align with how the students are making sense of things as they happen.

(Hannah, Teaching Practicum, Week 5 Journal)

Ultimately, the pedagogical concept TEACH OFF YOUR STUDENTS, NOT AT THEM is a simple, memorable phrase that is easily understood by novice teachers but in fact very difficult to enact in teaching activity. As novice teachers begin to adopt this concept as a psychological tool, it permeates all levels of their activity: reasoning, planning, interactions with their learners, and teaching activities. As a result, the approach to instruction that we see developing is neither teacher-fronted nor student-centered, but instead goal-directed, a major part of that goal being to engage learners in dialogic, co-constructed, collaborative activities of teaching/learning. As we have seen here, the process of shifting this pedagogical concept from inter-psychological (external) to intra-psychological (internal) emerges out of extensive and intensive engagement in *responsive mediation* and direct experiences in teaching activity.

Engaging in Responsive Mediation with Learners

Our goal in taking *a teaching as dialogic mediation instructional stance* is that our novice teachers will ultimately be able to engage in responsive mediation with the learners they teach. Opportunities to engage in responsive mediation with learners are built into the Extended Team-Teaching Project at two levels.

The first is during the *practice teach*, where they practice various ways of responding to learner contributions. These practice sessions are playful and exploratory, yet at the same time highly structured, featuring constant mediation from the Team-Teach Supervisor, mediation which pushes them to take whatever the students give and try to link that to what they are teaching (INSTRUCTIONAL PARAPHRASING).

The second comes during the *actual teach*, when the novice teachers again have the chance to engage in *responsive mediation* with their learners, but this time without the immediate support of the Team-Teach Supervisor. During the stimulated recall session afterwards, however, the Team-Teach Supervisor often points out moments in the lesson to remind the novice teachers of how and when they could have engaged in *responsive mediation*, particularly at moments when the learners did offer contributions or ask questions. In Ai's final reflection paper, she mentions her struggle to *take whatever the students give me* and imagines why this instructional stance may have developmental value for her students.

Excerpt 25

Besides, the art of "take whatever the students give me" is still a major difficulty for me. I've tried to think about developing this ability during and after the team-teaching project. ... I think that sometimes we need to push our students to "think out loud", that is, when they are giving us unexpected answers, instead of interrupting them and just forcing them to think in our way, we could just ask them to explain how and why they've come up with those answers. **Especially in advanced level, most of the time there are no exactly "incorrect answers" but just simplified or incomplete ones. The point is that students didn't just come up with a simple idea without further consideration and critical thinking. When being asked to explain or defend their statements, they can offer organized and logical reasons maybe with strong evidence, which is also one of the main goals of teaching English academic writing.**

(Ai, Teaching ESL, Final Paper)

In their progress through the Tutoring Internship, the novice teachers have frequent opportunities to engage in *responsive mediation* with their tutees. As we saw earlier in this chapter, tutoring sessions require tutors to reorient their instructional stance, to ask questions, to guide tutees' thinking, to allow tutees to clarify their own thoughts, and to talk through what the tutees want to express in their writing. Chen uses the phrase *asking before telling* to describe how she is now able to engage in responsive mediation with her tutees. By encouraging her tutees to express *how well they know about it, how they think* and *what their problem is*, based on this knowledge she can guide them but *they need to try to walk on their own feet.*

Excerpt 26

Another impressive point for me is leading students to think instead of giving them answer directly. I call it "asking before telling". At the beginning, when I heard students' problems, I was eager to give answer and I think they really get help in this way. However, the feedback for my session reflection made me realized that I should ask them first. According to their answer, I can get information about how well they know about it, how they think about it and what their problem is. **I reminded myself to use this technique in the later sessions and I discovered that it is very helpful for my tutees. The most obvious change is that tutees became the one who talked most. My role is more and more like a guider. I give them a direction and they need to try to walk on their own feet.**

(Chen Tutoring Internship, Final Paper)

In her final reflection paper, Chen (C) compares a transcript from an early tutoring session (Session 3) to a later session (Session 13) in which she is clearly able to prompt her tutee Wei (W) with questions that encourage him to articulate what he had done since their last tutoring session and articulate a rationale for his argument.

Excerpt 27

This change is also reflected in two transcripts. **I used to read their papers by myself instead of letting them introduce it.** Actually, the latter method is obviously better for tutees recalling and retelling and also better for me to know their situation.

C: *Is it (assignment) going well?*
W: *Good.*
C: *Is this the reflection for peer review?*
W: *Yeah.*
C: *OK. How many students gave peer review to you?*
W: *Two in total.* **Silence** *(reading first draft of Comparison & Contrast and peer review) (from Session 3)*
C: *What is your new assignment?*
W: *Uh… What do you mean by that?*
C: *I mean what else you did after we met last time.*
W: *Oh, I wrote an argument of solutions to talk about what the best solution is.*
C: ***Can you introduce your argument?***
W: *Yeah. First I introduced the serious desertification in China and the nature reasons and human reasons of this problem … This is the best because it won't influence residence life and make full use of ground. (from Session 13)*

One of my tutees mentioned this change at the last class. She said with these questions, she is pushed to recall what the teacher said in class, what requirements are in assignment sheet and what kind of problem is in her paper.

(Chen, Tutoring Internship, Final Paper)

Clearly, the second excerpt demonstrates a more dialogic stance and features greater engagement by the tutee. Additionally, Chen's concluding comment indicates that she is aware of the pedagogical value of this instructional stance because her tutee found this kind of questioning to be helpful while working on the paper.

As our novice teachers gain more teaching experience during the Teaching Practicum, they continue to have multiple opportunities to engage in responsive mediation, both in dialogue with individual learners and during whole class instruction. In Excerpt 24, recorded during the second half of the semester, Hannah is now managing the majority of the instructional work for her first-year academic writing course. In this exchange, she is leading a whole class discussion after the learners had worked in small groups analyzing writing examples to determine if citations were needed, and if so, if they were written correctly. Hannah begins by ORIENTING the learners to the fact that the written sample they are about to discuss may be a bit more challenging than the sample they previously analyzed (ACTIVITY BUILDING). We see her use INSTRUCTIONAL PARAPHRASING as she recasts learners' responses and asks them to expand their answers by explaining why as well as by providing an example.

Excerpt 28

> HANNAH: Alright (.) **sample two, this one is a little bit harder,** a little bit harder to fix, what do you think about sample two? Wh- you guys had sample two, you ((Hannah points to two Ss groups)) alright, what do you see as being a problem?
> S1: There's no in-text citations.
> HANNAH: **Okay, so there needs to be an in-text citation, why?** (4.0)
> S1: So that we can look for the main ().
> HANNAH: Good, so you see a quote from somebody, so it needs to be cited. Okay, what about cohesion? How does it, how does it flow with the rest of that paragraph? (2.0) **If you looked at sample one, you can also turn over the page and look at sample two (.) (1.0)**
> S2: **The writer doesn't really explain the quote.**
> HANNAH: Okay, the writer doesn't really explain the quote, so how do you fix that?
> S2: Uh, some explanation.
> HANNAH: **Okay, can you give us, make up an example (.) for, for this person** (.) How would you incorporate this ()?
> S2: Um, (10.0) use his own words to paraphrase.
>
> (Hannah, Teaching Practicum, Week 10)

Throughout this and the following excerpt, Hannah is TEACHING OFF HER STUDENTS, that is, she is asking questions, seeking additional information, and fielding their responses. A salient example of this comes at the end of this excerpt when she acknowledges that the questions she has asked are tricky and suggests that the learners talk with a classmate before sharing their ideas with the whole class. Given the length of the pauses following her questions (8.0 & 6.0), this instructional move not only gives learners time to prepare to answer her questions, but it also gives the learners a chance to re-ORIENT to the topic and thus be more likely to engage in the large group discussion.

Excerpt 29

Hannah: Okay, s:o, **I think here is where this part becomes tricky**, because if you look at the sample, he does introduce it, he says, "according to this professor and here's who this professor is", and that's a good set-up for a quote, you say, "here's why you should listen to this person, here's why they're important, and here's what they have to say" (.) Then what? (1.0) And if you look at this sample, he does say something (.) There are some words after, but how do we make it, how do we make sure it's connected? (8.0) What would be an example of something you could put after this quote? (6.0) **This is a tricky question? So take, take one minute, talk to the person next to you, and come up with something that could follow, follow or proceed this quote, that would help it feel more connected.**

(Hannah, Teaching Practicum, Week 10)

Hannah's examples of *responsive mediation* occurred during actual classroom instruction, and our novice teachers often describe multiple incidents where they intentionally engage in *responsive mediation* with their learners. In the next excerpt, Lin recalls listening in on small group discussions and identifies the moment she realized that the entire class could benefit from considering a learner's question, which she recalls as an effective way of incorporating the concern into the whole group discussion (INSTRUCTIONAL PARAPHRASING).

Excerpt 30

I also listened carefully to students as they were working in groups and incorporated their responses into the lesson when we came together. For instance, a student asked a question about citation, "Does it count as plagiarism if I cite a whole paragraph?". **I felt that the whole class had the same question, so I brought this question to the class and let them discuss, which worked very well.**

(Lin, Teaching Practicum, Week 5 Journal)

Likewise, in Excerpt 31, Mei recognizes that engagement in *responsive mediation* increases the level of learner participation, with evidence of *both giving and receiving ideas/suggestions/inspirations*. Employing plot diagrams to enable writers to talk through and expand their story ideas, Mei recognizes the value of engagement in *responsive mediation* for garnering greater levels of learner engagement and participation.

Excerpt 31

With this activity, **every student is engaged in both giving and receiving ideas/suggestions/inspirations**. I finished two plot diagrams and talked to the authors, and **we had some great discussions about how to further develop their stories**. This actually took quite a long time, but I think it's worth it.

(Mei, Teaching Practicum, Week 10 Journal)

Conclusion

As the data presented in this chapter clearly illustrate, we value a *teaching as dialogic mediation instructional stance*, both for ourselves as teacher educators and for the novice L2 teachers we work with. This stance represents a core value in VSCT-oriented praxis: it provides a context in which both teacher goals and students goals are considered and given value in the instructional setting, that is, to see *teaching as dialogic mediation* is to accept the inextricable unity of teaching and learning (*obuchenie*).

By engaging with our novice teachers through *responsive mediation*, we gain a clearer picture of their development. First, we share our own understandings of teaching, through our use of pedagogical concepts, structured mediational spaces, and frequent, rich responsive dialogue. Second, we hear (and read), in recordings, transcripts, reflective comments, and recall sessions, their own accounts of their personal, emerging conceptualizations of what teaching can be. Dialogue is, by definition, a collaborative activity; *responsive mediation* gives space to novice teachers to verbalize their intentions and provides accessible language that helps them to frame their conceptual understandings. As teacher educators, we work to help our novice teachers develop stronger and more robust rationales, which they can clearly and coherently articulate, for their pedagogical choices.

References

Barnes, D. (1976). *From communication to curriculum*. Middlesex: Penguin.

Smagorinsky, P., Cook, L. S., & Johnson, T. S. (2003). The twisting path of concept development in learning to teach. *Teachers College Record, 105*(8), 1399–1436.

7
ORIENTING TO EMOTION
The centrality of *perezhivanie* in teacher development

Vygotskian Sociocultural Theory (VSCT) embraces the notion of the dialectic, the tension that gives apparently opposing concepts complexly interdependent meanings. From the VSCT perspective, just as theory and practice are in dialectical opposition to each other, so are cognition and emotion. Humans do not learn in an emotional vacuum; motivation, excitement, anxiety, and other emotions are always involved, and the emotional dimension of an experience may affect the cognitive uptake.

A realization that nearly all our novice teachers share, as they participate in the activity of teaching, is that teaching is not as simple as it looks on the surface. It is more than just standing in a particular place in the classroom or speaking for a particular amount of time or in a particular way. Thus, the many ways in which we ask them to engage with teaching activity in our praxis-oriented courses—practical, theoretical, observational, dialogical, reflective, and so on—bring varied, and sometimes strong, emotions to the surface. Just as we 'preach' that there is no way to pre-script or totally pre-plan a lesson, we 'practice' a continuing understanding of the effects of our educational work on novice teachers.

Our theoretical stance means that we engage with our novice teachers knowing they are agents, with full histories, bringing specific and individual emotional connections to, and orientations toward, teaching activity. We expect them to have different reactions to praxis-oriented pedagogy, and throughout each course we see that they react to, and focus on, different personal, professional, and pedagogical issues. This is consistent with the principles of VSCT; their histories are shaped not only by their lived experiences but also by the ways in which those experiences are refracted in the new social situation of development of the program (and, especially, the pillar courses).

DOI: 10.4324/9781003268987-10

Recognizing these varied histories is crucial to understanding how they are experiencing our praxis-oriented pedagogy.

Therefore, in our practice, we attend to both their learning and their reactions to the interactions we ask them to participate in. As might be expected, gaining access to this combination of cognitive learning and emotional processing is not easy or straightforward, neither for us nor for the novice teachers. To understand the way emotions and cognition interact, we invoke the VSCT term *perezhivanie*, which might be loosely translated as 'the living through' of an event. Briefly put, this word means that the way we feel about an experience or an encounter is a kind of prism through which we interpret it. To take a simple example, think of a novice teacher who has been asked to engage learners in active discussion during a lesson. The emotions that are aroused in one individual when attempting to do this may be quite different from those felt by another. A history of studying in classrooms where learners are not encouraged to speak up may cause a novice teacher to feel extremely uncomfortable with that kind of interaction, no matter how well it is logically understood or how well it has been theoretically justified, while a novice teacher who comes from a culture where being outspoken and verbal is valued may feel quite different, even if learners are not frequently encouraged to speak up in class. What looks like resistance on the part of the first novice teacher might be an unexamined emotional response to a teacher relinquishing 'control' of the classroom. What might look like enthusiasm for classroom discussion on the part of the second teacher might be an emotional level of comfort with active, loud conversations based on cultural norms familiar to the teacher. No matter how well the two teachers understand the theory and justification for reducing teacher talk and encouraging learner talk, they may not be able to help having very different emotional responses to the activity of leading a discussion. As Johnson and Golombek (2016) explain it, "since individuals will most certainly experience the same event quite differently, one's *perezhivanie* is not the experience itself, but how that experience is interpreted and understood by the individual" (pp. 42–43). Through *responsive mediation*, novice teachers learn how to cope not only with initial emotional reactions, but also with the more challenging task of using those emotions to shape a thoughtful response. In this brief excerpt from a much longer reflective post in the Tutoring Internship, for example, Azadeh notes both her initial reaction—*embarrassing*—and her ability to move past it: *how you can react to this surprise that your student has brought to you is what actually matters*:

Excerpt 1

There is always that **embarrassing** moment for every (let's say inexperienced) teacher when you have no idea what your student is talking about but **how you can react to this surprise that your student has**

brought to you is what actually matters. I assume a key to handle this overwhelming moment is to accept the fact that a teacher is not a know-it-all and does not have to be one.

(Azadeh, Tutoring Internship, Session 8 Post)

In her reflection, Azadeh demonstrates her emerging ability to apply the new instructional stance, an understanding clarified by her strong initial emotion: the teacher must be ready to provide *responsive mediation* rather than expert knowledge. The Tutoring Supervisor's response is a simple but clear example of how we recognize and accept such emotions, and support the novice teachers in their attempts to engage with both affective and cognitive elements in the situation:

Excerpt 2

Azadeh, **you eloquently describe the feelings that arose when your tutee brought up an apparently opaque topic… you asked questions and then you asked more questions.**

(Supervisor, Tutoring Internship, Session 8 Response)

As teacher educators demonstrating praxis-oriented pedagogy, we try to accept the responsibility of being aware of—to an appropriate and reasonable degree—the emotional and sometimes visceral responses of our novice teachers to the situations we place our novice teachers in, and to the mediation and engagement that we offer them. This responsibility starts with giving novice teachers 'permission' to experience their emotions, and, just as importantly, providing spaces for them to reflect on their emotional responses to their teaching. By recognizing the importance of the emotional dimension of activity, we find that novice teachers become more willing to acknowledge and share their emotional orientations and begin to understand them as potential spaces for growth and learning.

Teaching has long been considered an *emotional practice* (Denzin, 1984), in which the familiar activities of lesson planning, leading class activities, and interacting with students and other people such as administrators, fellow teachers, and parents are infused with emotional meanings and influences (Hargreaves, 2000). Yet the emotional dimension of teacher reasoning and expertise is perhaps the most ignored aspect of teacher education; in many teacher education programs, expressions of emotion are, as Johnson and Golombek (2016) put it, "at best recognized as normal and either ignored or glossed over, or at worst seen as serious a character flaw" (p. 43). Yet surely teaching, particularly teaching language, is one of the most deeply personal, and therefore, emotionally engaging, activities of all. To ignore the emotional aspects of learning, especially learning how to teach language, a subject which already involves issues of identity, culture, and context, seems, from a VSCT perspective, unreasonably narrow and even self-defeating.

It is true that novice teacher emotions do tend to be intense. Our data suggests that novice teachers often express their emotions with terms that fall at the extreme ends of the emotional spectrum. Not surprisingly, these 'highs and lows' frequently emerge when the novice teacher is asked to perform as a self-directed teacher/tutor before having developed the necessary competence to do so. But they also appear when there is a moment of 'collision' (emotions collide with intellect, ignorance collides with knowledge, expectations collide with reality) that are far from uncommon in all teaching contexts, even among experts. The data in this chapter make visible our novice teachers' *perezhivanie*, the 'lived experiences' that happen at the intersection of their emotions, cognition, and teaching activity. In the discussion, you will see how we, as teacher educators but also as fellow humans with our emotional matrix of experience, engage with and mediate these moments of 'collision' as spaces for learning.

Emotions in the Extended Team-Teaching Project: First Encounters

Emotions come to the surface in the first pillar course, Teaching ESL, as might be expected when for many novice teachers, they step in front of a classroom full of real learners for the first time. In this excerpt, however, the novice teacher we look at is, in light of her relatively extensive professional teaching experience, not as new to teaching as many of her peers. Indeed, it seems to be her previous experience that lies at the root of the negative emotions that Ana expresses, as she struggles to locate a familiar identity, her 'teacher self,' while working with her team members as they teach their lesson. In the stimulated recall session following the *actual teach*, the Team-Teach Supervisor tries to help Ana express her *perezhivanie* about the *actual teach* experience, to help her articulate why she felt that she was "not herself" in that event:

Excerpt 3

TE: Ana you ()?

ANA: They- they really liked () comfortable um because they felt comfortable with um with all of them um both of you because you're here ((laughter)) um working. And I think that um I mean the problem that we had at the beginning planning because first we did not know how to go about it but then when we found the video and we started working that looked kind of cool. **I personally (.) felt a little bit fear and not in the- in our class um-**

TE: The practice teach.

ANA: **Yes um (4.0) a different.** I mean I because maybe because it was my students and I felt (.) as if- as if I would be like (think). You know?
TE: Oh. With a- with the class or here?
ANA: There.
TE: Oh really!?
ANA: Yes.
TE: **Why? Explain us.**
ANA: **I don't know what- because um I-**
LEO: Because we were there.
((laughter))
ANA: **I cannot- I think- and now I'm freaking out because now every time I meet the class every (day) right?**
TE: (The call of good) ((laughter))
ANA: Yes, but if () people complain I cannot put in words what I mean- I felt great but there **was something that I wasn't being myself and now I('ve been thinking) about identity. Right. And I have no idea why.**

(Extended Team-Teaching Project, Teaching ESL, Stimulated Recall)

Through mediation with the Team-Teach Supervisor, Ana finally becomes able to verbalize the emotion she is experiencing, namely that she feels she could not be herself with her learners. The Team-Teach Supervisor carefully engages with Ana's emotions, first by helping Ana justify her feelings:

Excerpt 4

TE: Ok. Well. **Team teaching is not something that we normally do. It happens really rare.** And we do that because think of how you guys came up with the ideas and you worked them out and you held that sort of, you know, collaboration and three heads are better than one kind of thing (.) in that sense it was really productive but the enactment of it is difficult because there are three people and who talks when and, you know, do you interact. **Perhaps it was more of that but you know Aisha had a particular role, and Leo had a particular role and you had a particular role. And it was not (.) normally the role you have cause normally you always hold that role. So maybe that is why you were feeling- feeling that way.**

(Supervisor, Teaching ESL, Stimulated Recall)

The Team-Teach Supervisor next helps Ana locate additional reasons for her 'loss of teacher self' including the fact that she is not able to be as spontaneous with her learners as she might normally be (as her true teacher self) because she has to stay *on script* for the team:

> **Excerpt 5**
>
> ANA: **I realize now** like because I- I () but now you see that I turn to the screen because I was thinking about what I wanna say and we prepared it in a team. So I need to go back to um yeah-
>
> TE: **Right. And that's the difference between having experience as a teacher and being comfortable with going off script** and being a novice teacher and not going off script. **And so (.) because you're the teacher of the classroom, you probably go off script all the time.** It's possible that you don't have a script but you have a general idea of where you gonna go. **This probably felt more scripted to you than normal. Right?**
>
> ANA: **And maybe that is the thing. That's why I also felt that I wasn't being myself because I usually ()**
>
> (Teaching ESL, Stimulated Recall)

As the stimulated recall session comes to a close, Ana's *perezhivanie*, her emotion-infused understanding of the episode and her response to it, shifts as she comes to terms with the reasons behind the emotional response she experienced. The mediation provided by the Team-Teach Supervisor guides Ana from a 'collision' between emotions, cognition, and teaching activity and the feeling of loss around her teacher self to a newly understood level of understanding so that Ana can reclaim her teacher identity and her sense of self in her classroom, while also learning something new about herself and about teaching.

For other novice teachers, with much less teaching experience, the prevailing emotion can be closer to fear than the confusion that Ana experiences. *I thought I was not qualified to be their teacher* (Ai, Teaching ESL, Final Paper), an emotionally laden statement, is one we hear quite frequently from our novice teachers, an emotion probably intensified by the fact that they are, frequently, English L2 speakers themselves.

For Mei, a novice teacher from China, fear of being qualified to teach other English learners as part of the Extended Team-Teaching Project is quite real. She recounts her initial fear, confusion, and lack of confidence in her final reflection paper:

> **Excerpt 6**
>
> When I first get the topic of our group teach, **actually I was totally confused because I knew nothing about Annotated Bibliography.** Another thing is that **my writing is not good and I'm afraid that I**

don't have the quality to teach an academic writing course for undergraduate freshman who are quite high-level in English. What's more, **I have little teaching experiences so I lack of confidence and experience to deal with all the situations in class.**

(Mei, Teaching ESL, Final Paper)

Mei remembers that her lack of self-confidence grew when she visited the class she was scheduled to teach and found the learners sitting silently and choosing not to participate, even in response to their regular teacher. The silent learners reinforce her fear of being able to teach the class, and she recalls her emotions clearly, *stressed out, afraid*, and anticipating how *super awkward* it would be if no learners participated:

Excerpt 7

The second observation class **really stressed me out because I found that students were very silent during the whole class**... Since I had a pretty good impression of them after the first observation class, I expected them to be more active and talkable. **I was afraid that when we teach the lesson, we throw out a question and no one response. That would be super awkward.**

(Mei, Teaching ESL, Final Paper)

Perhaps because the Team-Teach Supervisor welcomed and engaged with the *perezhivanie* of the novice teachers in the course, fear eventually becomes a fruitful emotion for Mei. It pushes her to carefully and thoroughly prepare to teach her part of the lesson. In fact, because she was able to articulate and then respond to her fear, Mei pre-scripts her language for the *actual teach* and finds that this concrete action settles her nerves in a way she still cannot explain, and she is able to enjoy the experience of the actual teach:

Excerpt 8

Before our actual teach, I was so nervous and I wrote down everything I would say on paper to calm down myself. But when I actually stood before the students and began to talk, all of my nervous flew away somehow. The students were very cooperative and active, what I worried did not happen at all. **We really enjoyed the whole class.**

(Mei, Teaching ESL, Final Paper)

Mei's *perezhivanie* journey in this episode, from the initially fear-inspiring class visit to the enjoyable final actual teach, is shaped by her emotions and her response to those emotions, but also, it is important to note, by the mediation she receives from the Team-Teach Supervisor, her team members, and the instructor of the ESL class, *My teammates and instructors of that class really helped a lot* (Mei, Teaching ESL, Final Paper), making the Extended Team-Teaching Project one they ultimately *enjoyed*.

The Extended Team-Teaching Project is a shared learning experience for our novice teachers, yet, as the two preceding episodes illustrates, the unique histories each novice teacher brings to the program can result in the shared experience feeling *not* so shared at certain points. Consider the case of Layla, another relatively experienced classroom teacher, who describes her situation like this: *suddenly moved from being an experienced teacher in Saudi Arabia to a novice teacher in The United States* (Layla, Teaching ESL, Final Paper). There are certainly elements in this new context that are completely new to her; she gained her education and experience in a country where the genders study separately, and her nervousness about teaching a mixed-gender class conflates with her general concern at being an L2 speaker of English herself and potentially having to face learners who are better in English than she is: *boys and girls whose English is maybe even better than my English*. For her these new conditions, though only potentially threatening, are *terrifying*:

Excerpt 9

Ten minutes after the class: **My body is acting weird. I am excitingly breathless, full of energy and calm at the same time. I thought of this experience at first as unknown terrifying zone but now I think of it as an accomplishment, not only from teaching side but also from personal side.**

(Layla, Teaching ESL, Final Paper)

Layla recounts the EMBODIMENT of this teaching experience and experiencing such incredible fear that it results in a visceral response for her. At the same time she is processing these strange physical sensations, she realizes that her emotional orientation to the entire experience has opened space for both personal and professional growth:

Excerpt 10

I came from a society where genders are segregated strictly. Thus, by teaching this group and dealing with unexpected incidents in a good way made me break stereotypes were built inside me about women and men…It made me see "the teacher me" in a totally different way.

(Layla, Teaching ESL, Final Paper)

Layla's *perezhivanie* in this episode is both validated and resolved by a brief but powerful moment at the end of the class in which a student who shares the same cultural background compliments them on their lesson:

Excerpt 11

I will never forget that one of the students before going out said to us "you did a great job today". **Afterwards, we knew that he is a Saudi student. It was a moment of pride and happiness. Actually, the whole experience is about pride and happiness.**

(Layla, Teaching ESL, Final Paper)

Tutoring Internship: Self-doubt and Goosebumps

The Tutoring Internship is the second of the three pillar courses, but it is typically the very first time for many of the novice teachers to find themselves solely responsible for setting up and working in an instructional space without the immediate support of either a partner teacher or a teacher educator. This solo effort, of course, is quickly complicated by the presence of the other participant, the tutee, and the unpredictable nature of the tutoring sessions that must take into account the tutee's own unique life history and goals. This inherent unpredictability results in many emotions being expressed in the reflective posts written about the tutoring sessions. In response, the Tutoring Supervisor attempts to acknowledge these emotions and to help the tutors integrate them into their developing understanding of tutoring activity in various ways.

In this example, Chul experiences a moment of intense emotion after the first two sessions with a tutee, who shares with Chul a basic feeling of trust and comfort with one another. This feeling of comfort shifts in the third session when Chul learns that his tutee has earned a lower-than-expected grade on an essay, and importantly for Chul's own emotional stance, is upset by the grade. Chul's response to the grade and to his tutee's emotion is compounded by the addition of guilt, which reflects Chul's pre-program understanding of the goal of tutoring, to help tutees earn high grades:

Excerpt 12

It seems like **the grade he got for his last essa[y] shocked him a lot**. Of course, **I'm not really tutoring him just to help him get a good grade, but I was also shocked and felt a little guilty for not giving him enough help**.

(Chul, Tutoring Internship, Session 6 Post, with Jaareh)

This is a challenging emotional and cognitive moment for Chul, who like his tutee comes from a cultural context where tutors are expected to focus on grades rather than, as in our Tutoring Internship, on developing better overall academic writing skills and understanding. He recognizes his emotional response to the grade and tries to distance himself from it with an interesting combination of intellectual insight (he *knows a good grade* may be important to the tutee but is not the responsibility of the tutor) that does not quite erase his emotional response (he *feels* that a grade is an important element of a writing assignment). Cognitively, he understands the final grade is not a primary goal of his tutoring, yet he cannot completely reconcile that knowledge with his feeling that he did not provide adequate support for the tutee's efforts. Chul does not hesitate to use strong emotional words, expressing 'shock' and 'guilt' for his tutee's grade.

The Tutoring Supervisor engages with Chul's *perezhivanie* here by offering another perspective, gently moving Chul's 'collision' of emotion, cognition, and activity to a space of learning by reframing his guilt as empathy; she also normalizes his response to his tutee's emotion as one that is both expected and acceptable:

Excerpt 13

This session sounds interesting and busy for both of you: **don't be guilty about his grades, please, but I understand that you have empathy with your tutees and their emotions do have an effect on yours!**

(Supervisor, Tutoring Internship, Session 6 Response)

Several weeks later in the semester, writing about the same tutee, we can see that Chul's emotional orientation has shifted dramatically when he recounts the moment of excitement he felt when he realized the progress his tutee has made in his journey toward being an independent writer of academic English. It is notable that while the tutoring relationship has been ongoing for nearly three months at this point, Chul expresses his emotions with the word *suddenly*, suggesting that his perception of the tutee's success feels immediate and salient. It is also noteworthy that Chul is able to discuss a rather complex constellation of emotional responses (*pride, enjoyment, thrill*) to his tutee's successful efforts, rather than focusing only on one intense emotion, a sign that he is more able to recognize the value of the emotional dimension of teaching:

Excerpt 14

Again, as usual, I asked him to clarify and elaborate on those. He confidently explained and clarified them with relevant examples. Speaking of examples, **I suddenly realized how much progress he has made**

throughout this semester. Providing examples was one of our goals at the very beginning of our tutoring, but **seeing him giving instances of his topic and main points now just gave me goosebumps. I was even more thrilled when he thanked me** and **told me that he appreciated having me as his tutor.** I'm not sure how much of help I gave him skill wise, but **I am proud of myself for getting that kind of comments from him**. I really enjoyed working with Jaareh and am so happy that he is going to pass with the grade he had expected.

(Chul, Tutoring Internship, Session 10 Post, with Jaareh)

Chul's *perezhivanie* in this episode leads to a salient shift in his instructional stance, from seeing a tutor as someone whose primary role is to guarantee higher grades to recognizing a tutor as a working, responsive partner/mediator in the journey to master the nuances of academic writing. It is interesting to note, even at this stage of his own professional journey, that Chul cannot resist ending with a grade-oriented comment, revealing the persistence of his early apprenticeship in education.

We see a similar expression of self-doubt in early tutoring sessions with Qing as she tries to help her tutee select an appropriate topic for an assignment. Neither Qing nor her tutee is clear about what might constitute an acceptable topic. Qing's frustration leads to a moment of collision between her own self-doubt, her desire to be a helpful tutor, her empathy with her tutee's lack of understanding, and her intellectual ability (as a graduate student) to select a topic for a first-year writing assignment. Perhaps drawing also upon the mediation of the Tutoring Supervisor, who cautions tutors to calibrate their mediation to what the writing class instructor expects, Qing decides to take action (visit the tutee's writing class), and we can see that this determination allows her to maintain a sense of professionalism (it will help her tutor *efficiently*) while acknowledging her own sense of frustration or perhaps confusion about this particular tutoring moment (*why we thought* what was good turned out not to be acceptable):

Excerpt 15

I'm not sure so far whether I'm doing the thing that my tutee really needs, so I **will go to Jinny's ESL015 class next Monday** because she told me on next Monday's class, her teacher will talk about their first draft of this essay. I want to find out the root cause **why we thought such good topics were not what her teacher wants.** Then, **better comprehending my role** and what should I do most **efficiently** in tutoring.

(Qing, Tutoring Internship, Session 3 Post)

While we see in her reflective post an expression of positive commitment to learning more about the writing class and thus more about how to tutor a learner from that class, we can read a few weeks later a slightly veiled, but still clearly emotional, expression of disappointment and mild anxiety about the tutee's apparent lack of commitment. Although she does not use overtly emotional vocabulary, it is clear in this post that Qing feels frustrated and anxious when her tutee chooses to ignore her preferred discussion prompts and instead spends valuable tutoring time looking at Korean-language websites. This post reflects Qing's sense (a *perezhivanie* of inadequacy, at least) that her performance as a tutor is lacking in the face of the tutee's challenge, ignoring prompt questions and paying more attention to her screen than to her tutor. Here it is not adjectives or nouns that describe emotions that the Tutoring Supervisor pays attention to, but the implied emotions behind Qing's confession that she does not 'know how' to respond:

Excerpt 16

In this tutoring, sometimes Jinny was absorbed in her Korean websites, and at that time, **I really didn't know what should I do except keep asking and asking and asking…**However, I suggested her to look for some former sources to have a general view of this technique. For example, I recommended her the book called *The Annuals of Plastic Surgery* to know its development in all ages. **In addition, Jinny didn't count on the tutor to push her to do something but forwardly finished her task by herself and accepted some of my suggestions. The only problem about our tutoring I could come up now is maybe we could have more communications. I didn't know why most of the time, our dialogue was like "I ask and you answer". And I don't know how to change this atmosphere…**

(Qing, Tutoring Internship, Session 6 Post, with Jinny)

The Tutoring Supervisor mediates Qing's *perezhivanie* by first acknowledging her emotional orientation and validating her sense that something is lacking in this session, namely, responsiveness on the part of the tutee, which is complicated by the fact that the tutee *is* demonstrating a certain level of autonomy, which is a stated goal of the tutoring program. She also confirms Qing's suspicion that a tutee who chooses to work alone with a tutor present and does not respond to a tutor's attempts at providing guidance are not ideal examples of the kind of autonomy the program seeks to nurture:

Excerpt 17

Qing, **your question about how to improve communication between yourself and your tutee is a really important one! Even though this tutee clearly has good autonomy about her own research project, if you are not part of the dialogue, then I can understand how you would feel a little bit 'out of the loop' with her!

(Supervisor, Tutoring Internship, Session 6 Response)

After helping Qing come to terms with her emotional response to this moment, the Tutoring Supervisor then offers some practical suggestions to Qing, in the form of questions she could potentially use to create dialogue with the tutee:

Excerpt 18

First, my suggestion would be to get off the internet...perhaps you could focus on ONE source—how to read it? how to summarize it? why is it a good (or poor) source for her particular problem? Try to have a discussion about the source rather than about the process.

(Supervisor Tutoring Internship, Session 6 Response)

These suggestions resonate with a frequent form of mediation in the Tutoring Internship, when the Tutoring Supervisor provides actual language for the tutors to use:

Excerpt 19

Second, as the tutor you have the right to say "I'd like you to talk to me instead of looking at your screen for a few minutes" and then ask her a useful question such as "When you look at a website, how do you judge if it is trustworthy or not? Can you show me?" Then—although she needs to show you the screen—she is doing a task that includes you.

(Supervisor, Tutoring Internship, Session 6 Response)

The Tutoring Supervisor responds to three levels of Qing's post: her emotional orientation, her tutoring activity, and her language choices. These recommendations give Qing concrete steps she can take to ENGINEER PARTICIPATION with her tutee by building on her tutee's strength in finding sources. By having specific activity in which to engage her tutee, Qing's self-doubt and frustration over how to regain her tutee's trust and build a more collaborative tutoring environment are mitigated in ways that give her both emotional and intellectual feedback.

As often happens, however, the tutee does not come around to being a model tutee and three weeks later, Qing interprets an unexplained absence by her tutee as meaning that Jinny actually wants to terminate the tutoring relationship and stop meeting with her. Intellectually, Qing seeks to understand the tutee's possible reasons for this negative turn of events, even resorting to politics as a potential cause, noting that tensions exist between her tutee's country of Korea and her own homeland of China. What is noteworthy in this episode is Qing's burgeoning awareness of the power that emotions can have for the teacher when interpreting learner behavior. Here we see her attempting to make sense of (responding to her own *perezhivanie* about) the emotion-laden moment as a space to understand her tutee, but more importantly, to learn about herself:

Excerpt 20

As a novice tutor, my feelings could be so complicated and **I would reflect myself too much when I found my tutee seems to be a little reluctant to attend tutoring sessions.** So many relevant or irrelevant possibilities I thought of before this tutoring, such as cultural difference, my tutoring style, language barrier, or even....political relation between China and Korea recently???......

(Qing, Tutoring Internship, Session 8 Post, with Jinny)

After exploring possible reasons for why her tutee might be hesitant to attend and actually did not come to one tutoring session, she shares, with implied but obvious relief and even empathy, connecting Jinny's apparent apathy with her own reluctance to confront a difficult class situation, the actual reason for her tutee's absence the previous week:

Excerpt 21

Finally, **it turned out that Jinny forgot her tutoring last week as if nothing happened.... I could understand her because to some extent, I am experiencing the similar thing with her.** I have one class this semester which is too difficult to understand. So initially I didn't have any courage to write an email to tell my group member that I haven't finished my part when it was definitely late and impolite.

(Qing, Tutoring Internship, Session 8 Post, with Jinny)

Clearly, Qing is relieved that her tutee's absence was apparently caused by simple forgetfulness and not by complex emotional reactions to either her 'poor tutoring' or obscure political tensions. She relates a personal story that seems to echo the tutee's experience perhaps to convince herself that the tutee is being honest but also to tie what can be seen as an empathetic response to a cognitively familiar situation. The Tutoring Supervisor supports the tutee's forgetfulness as a legitimate reason by telling her own story of a time she embarrassed herself by forgetting to show up for an important exam at a university in Japan when, as a senior member of the faculty, she was expected to help with proctoring, and it helps:

> **Excerpt 22**
>
> **Thanks for talking me your case in Japan! For me, embarrassing things are happening all the time, and yes, we easily forget them and continue moving on.**
>
> (Qing, Tutoring Internship, Session 8 Post)

Qing gratefully acknowledges her Tutoring Supervisor's experience as evidence that even expert teachers have embarrassing moments and seems to be at peace with the situation with her tutee.

Teaching Practicum: Moving from Focus on Self to Focus on Learners

The final pillar course, the Teaching Practicum, is, not surprisingly, an arena for emotional and cognitive 'collisions' as well. While by this point in the program, the novice teachers are expected to have quite robust ability to articulate their understandings and their emotions, the impact of an unexpected event, and the emotions it sparks, is not necessarily reduced.

One particularly salient moment of insight occurs at the midpoint of Qing's practicum experience, a time in the semester when she confidently prepares instructional activities with the guidance of her mentor teacher but still is able to recognize that she has much to learn:

> **Excerpt 23**
>
> **This week, I did something as usual. More importantly, I did many things that unusual.** Tuesday was the first day that I taught them "purely grammar". It is hard for me to come up with interesting activities to teach them "I am sorry for/to/about/that clause", etc. **First I wanted to do was role play, but my mentor and I both thought we didn't have enough time to do that. Then, my mentor inspired me that we could ask them to come up to the board and write down some apology language which might be useful in the future.**
>
> (Qing, Teaching Practicum, Week 7 Journal)

With her mentor teacher's mediation, Qing develops an engaging activity for the grammar points she is asked to cover, and the class progresses mostly as expected until the activity ends early (that is, before the scheduled time):

Excerpt 24

One unexpected thing happened that day. I thought the time frame would be very tight that I need shorten my reaction time, shorten my speech, shorten everything I could. **However, it turned out that I had 8 minutes left when I finished everything I need to say. I had never thought of a plan B because the tasks and activities were so tense that day. At that time, my speech became incoherently while I was thinking what I am going to do.** Anyway, eight minutes passed.

(Qing, Teaching Practicum, Week 7 Journal)

Her mentor teacher decides to use this anxiety-filled moment as a space for Qing's learning about the importance of knowing her lesson plan so well that she could come up with a *plan B* if necessary:

Excerpt 25

My mentor told me after class that I could do my role play activity during that time, but I didn't think of it when I was standing on the platform. **This gave me a lesson that I should have a plan B to know what I can add/delete based on the time adjustment. I should always keep thinking that when I prepare a lesson plan.**

(Qing, Teaching Practicum, Week 7 Journal)

Upon reading this reflection, the Practicum Supervisor expresses her understanding of Qing's discomfort and uses the opportunity to highlight for Qing the existence of *perezhivanie* in this situation, and how understanding and working with emotions during teaching activity can lead to learning:

Excerpt 26

Qing, **this type of moment is an important learning moment for you – awkward, perhaps, but you now understand what is needed in our planning. I'm sure your language during those 8 minutes was not as incoherent as you think, but I understand why you think it was.** Ellen's idea of the role plays was wonderful, and quite honestly, for just about any context, role plays can be a good Plan B. Of course you would have to be ready to adapt them to whatever you just covered, but that's a good activity to keep in mind.

(Supervisor, Teaching Practicum, Week 7 Response)

By the end of her 15-week practicum experience, Qing displays increased awareness of the complexity of learning to teach and appears to understand how emotions, and the emotional lens of *perezhivanie*, can be crucial to that process. She shares her interpretation of the trajectory her *perezhivanie* has taken in a Teaching Philosophy text that she, like other practicum teachers, has been writing and revising throughout the semester:

Excerpt 27

> Even though I follow my conviction that I am growing to be an excellent teacher, **there may be times along the road to the teaching process that are hard**. For example, my teaching methods may not be effective for some students. At those moments, I put my bad feelings aside. **My beliefs do not change at all and I change my own emotions to positively face those moments**. For instance, **when I encounter problems, I reflect and try to reveal their roots**. However, the heart of being a good teacher never shakes. **I could adjust teaching strategies with empathy and reasoning but never change my beliefs.**
>
> (Qing, Teaching Practicum, Teaching Philosophy)

From this excerpt, we see that at the heart of Qing's experience in the classroom is a nugget of helpful insight mediated by her own *perezhivanie*: beliefs (cognitive commitments) about teaching and learning do not change in response to the immediate situation, but emotions can. Knowing this, she can adjust her emotional response to re-access her beliefs. At this stage of the practicum, she is comfortable with acknowledging her emotions because she realizes that these 'collisions' are a natural part of teaching, moments that she can use for positive change.

Another practicum teacher, Mei, learns to embrace rather than ignore her emotions as she navigates her learning-to-teach process. As we saw in Qing's case, this learning begins at the point in the semester where Mei has more responsibility for developing and leading classroom activities with the learners. In the excerpt below, Mei notes that she has carefully prepared pre-reading questions that ask the learners to think about and share a challenging moment from their early school days. She reasons her choice by explaining that a school-related dilemma from childhood is an issue that the main character of the story is dealing with.

Mei writes that she plans to model what she expects her learners to do by sharing a challenging moment from her own early school experience, and believes she is fully prepared to ENGINEER STUDENT PARTICIPATION:

Excerpt 28

> Before Hailey read them the story, **I prepared some pre-reading questions for them, the questions are about their childhood, I asked them to recall their early school memories and think**

about are there any embarrassed or scared moment in their schooldays.

(Mei, Teaching Practicum, Week 8 Journal)

Unfortunately, her thoughtfully designed pre-reading activity is met with silence, a response which is more intensely negative in her perception of it because these learners are not normally silent or reluctant to speak:

Excerpt 29

However nobody wanted to share this kind of "bad" experiences in front of the class, I asked them are there any volunteers? And they all shook their heads, **this was the first time that nobody wanted to say a thing**.

(Mei, Teaching Practicum, Week 8 Journal)

Mei goes on to write that after reflecting-in-action, she was able to save the activity by having the learners turn to a nearby peer to share their stories in pairs. She writes that they begin to actively engage with one another and seem to be enjoying the task. However, when she reconvened the class, the awkward silence returned. Again, her negative assessment of the silence is intensified because she calls on a learner who can usually be counted on to speak but who declines to do so this time.

Rather than resting with her frustration, she uses the chance to reflect on the episode by creating a more positive view of what felt like a negative experience at the time, a perspective she has learned to take because of the role model of her mentor teacher. In other words, her personal lived experience of the negative, silent, non-responsive learners is mediated by her conscious use of her mentor teacher's modeling combined with her 'second chance' thinking (provided by the reflection task) so that she shifts her *perezhivanie* on this incident. In doing this, she demonstrates an increasingly expert way of reasoning through, and about, a challenge:

Excerpt 30

Thanks to my "wrong" decision which helped me know my students "personal space" and understand why Hailey always has a second choice for them if the blog theme related to some personal experiences or feelings.

(Mei, Teaching Practicum, Week 8 Journal)

In her final reflection paper for the practicum course, Mei looks back at her emotional orientation toward classroom teaching when she started the practicum and traces how it has changed. Although she does not use the term itself, it is clear that she is aware of the *perezhivanie* involved in gaining expertise in reasoning and concrete activity:

Excerpt 31

At the very beginning of the practicum teaching, my mind was filled with such complex feelings mix with excited, curious, nervous, worries, and uncertainty, but one thing I knew for sure was that I determined to take this as a challenge and do my best...I still remembered the first day when I sat in the classroom and observed the class, I was shy and quiet, and I made a stupid mistake when we did an ice break activity which made me feel extremely awkward and that feeling has lingered for such a long time. **I lacked confidence at that time, I was afraid of making mistakes, and I felt like an outsider in the classroom because I was not a teacher, nor a student.** But this situation didn't last long because **I was highly adaptable to different environments, so I immediately adjusted my condition and emotion to make myself fit more into the classroom.**

(Mei, Teaching Practicum, Final Paper)

Mei recalls her emotional orientation as an *outsider*, an identity that is in some ways in limbo, somewhere between a graduate student and a teacher, and notes her pleasure at having moved to a space of knowing, of understanding that emotions, cognition, and the activity of teaching have prepared her to be *highly adaptable to different environments.*

As the third pillar course, the practicum is an arena of activity where it is natural to see a range of different kinds of emotional engagement and orientations among the participants. By this time, just before graduating from the program, the novice teachers have typically begun to consolidate their abilities to plan, reason, mediate, and understand teaching. In this final section of the chapter, we share Hannah's emotional highlights on her journey through the practicum. Unlike the previous two teachers, Hannah is not an international student and English is her first language, and she gained a moderate amount of teaching experience before entering the program. Even so, as we see with the first two novice teachers described in this section, she experiences initial fears about her teaching ability. What is noteworthy about this reflection is that she seems to be aware of the role that the emotional lens of *perezhivanie* may play in the way even an expert teacher might prepare to meet a new class for the first time:

Excerpt 32

Taught today in both of Emine's sections. **I was feeling nervous before the first class even though we had prepared the lesson** about as thoroughly as lessons probably ever get prepared,** but in the last few months **I've started asking other teachers how they feel on the first day of a new class, and it turns out even experienced teachers get a little jumpy.** At any rate, **I went to class anyway and (spoiler alert) am still alive to tell about it.**

(Hannah, Teaching Practicum, Week 3 Journal)

Her writing reflects both actual activity (seeking input from other teachers) and a self-awareness that her emotions are perhaps not quite appropriate, as reflected in her humorous comments about surviving the class. The Practicum Supervisor, as one of the expert teachers she could have confided in, confirms that what she is feeling is quite typical and shares some early career experiences of her own, to both validate and respond to Hannah's emotional openness:

Excerpt 33

Always tough to engage with a new class, and yes, we usually survive! Even after many years of teaching in the high school context, each fall, I would have a particular dream and get a little rash on my wrists – stress! At this level, I don't have either, but I do have concern that I'm doing the right thing for my students – **so yes, it's quite natural!**

(Supervisor, Teaching Practicum, Week 3 Response)

In the second week of teaching, these fears pop up on Hannah's emotional horizon again. She is in the classroom, but her mentor teacher has already left, when a learner brings a question about thesis statements to her attention. Using humor again, Hannah efficiently pokes mild fun at herself as an emotional being—she is slightly embarrassed by her dependence (her mentor teacher is her "go-to source for right answers")—and also at the implication of the very existence of 'right answers,' something only a novice would even admit to:

Excerpt 34

After class, and after Emine (my go-to source for right answers) had already left, **Student C came up and asked how a thesis statement would be written for this kind of essay, as opposed to the extended definition essay from last week.** Wow, what a good question! What a fine student!

(Hannah, Teaching Practicum, Week 4 Journal)

She acknowledges that the learner's question is legitimate, but in that moment, she first goes blank and cannot provide any kind of response and then cobbles together what she knows is an inadequate list of suggestions:

Excerpt 35

Alas, whether because I was still getting over my cold and had entered my afternoon naptime brain fog, or because I was just having a generally incompetent kind of day, **I drew a blank. At that moment I had no idea how to write a thesis statement for a compare/contrast essay. So I tottered around mentally for a bit and gave her some suggestions – which, to be frank, were unimpressive – and said we would discuss it more in class next week.**

(Hannah, Teaching Practicum, Week 4 Journal)

Hannah interprets this brief collision of emotions, cognition, and teaching activity as reason enough to question who she is as a teacher, *Sheesh. What kind of teacher doesn't even know her own content?* (Hannah, Teaching Practicum, Week 4 Journal). In response, the Practicum Supervisor helps Hannah explore her emotions at the moment by expressing compassion for Hannah's perception of herself as inadequate and ill-prepared, which is a logically acceptable condition, given her novice teacher status, but an emotionally unacceptable one, given her identity as a fourth-semester student in the MA TESL program, and providing concrete suggestions for how she might manage a similar situation in the future (again validating emotions as things that can, and will, appear again and again):

Excerpt 36

You are probably being a little tough on yourself given that all of this is new for you…At the same time, this is an important reminder to us…to think about questions, and how we can use questions to help a student (and ourselves!) learn through discovery. **You might have asked her to share what she remembers about the purpose of an extended def paper, about a c/c paper, about a thesis statement. Then help her see what is similar/different and how that can change the way a TS is written.**

(Supervisor, Teaching Practicum, Week 4 Response)

The Practicum Supervisor assures Hannah that her willingness to seek mediation and answers, from her mentor teacher or from other sources, is both acceptable as an emotional orientation to this situation and useful as a platform for further thought. The Practicum Supervisor ends with this admonition:

Excerpt 37

These are important questions, and my general response to each is to be honest, authentic, genuine. Admit that you aren't sure, but then follow up with answers.

(Supervisor, Teaching Practicum, Week 4 Response)

Some weeks later, about halfway through the 15-week teaching practicum, we see that Hannah has shifted her focus away from being concerned primarily about her own emotional responses and now seems to engage with the instructional situation mostly in terms of recognizing, acknowledging, and expressing concern for the affective needs of her learners:

Excerpt 38

One idea that keeps being brought up (expectedly) is meeting the affective and emotional needs of students. (Side note: the feminist in me wonders periodically whether I feel extra pressure, being a woman, to be able to address emotional needs, but the teacher in me keeps arguing back that emotional needs are important, and maybe all teachers, regardless of gender, should be feeling the pressure to meet them. So here we are.)

(Hannah, Teaching Practicum, Week 8 Journal)

Hannah's *perezhivanie* journey is compelling because we see a gradual reorientation of her attention, a shift that marks more expert-like focus: paying more attention to the affective needs of her learners and less to her own. To enact this new stance, Hannah shares small and important pieces, though parenthetically, of her identity and history, and concludes that it is important for all teachers to care for their learners' affective needs. In response, the Practicum Supervisor takes advantage of the space Hannah has opened:

Excerpt 39

I would agree that any teacher can benefit by developing an awareness of his/her emotional responses as a space for learning about themselves, their teaching, etc. I also believe that we have to be aware of the emotional responses of our students, particularly in the types of classes we teach.

(Supervisor, Teaching Practicum, Week 8 Response)

In her final reflection paper for the Teaching Practicum course, Hannah indicates that she and her mentor teacher continue to focus on building relationships with and among their learners, relationships that encourage them to pay attention to their classmates as individuals as well as a class group, and to value each other:

Excerpt 40

Recently **Emine and I were commenting on how unique our group of students is. For all we applied linguists like to talk about the uniqueness of individuals, it can still come as a surprise just** how much variety there can be in a group of seventeen, and my perception of that variety has increased steadily as I have gotten to know the students better.

(Hannah, Teaching Practicum, Final Reflection Paper)

Hannah continues until the end of the Teaching Practicum course to notice, and acknowledge, moments of emotion. In her final paper, she writes warmly about an email she and her mentor teacher received from a learner; though the email was functional (explaining an absence), Hannah notices its many strong points and recognizes the individual as someone with many dimensions, not all of which have been salient in the class work:

Excerpt 41

Today Emine showed me an email from one of our students saying that he was sick and would miss class. **It was an extraordinary email – creative, funny, sentimental, reflective, poetic. It was a work of art in her inbox. The same student, though, has struggled this whole term to make sense of academic writing.**

(Hannah, Teaching Practicum, Final Paper)

Hannah reflects on other students she has come to know and understand through her emotional engagement with them over the course of the semester. Her *perezhivanie*, a lens of appreciation as well as insight, is enriched as she describes the emotional atmosphere her mentor teacher and she created among the members of the class community:

Excerpt 42

Another student sticks to simple argumentation and weak language in his writing, but exudes confidence and charisma in public speaking. A third student sits in the corner and never once has spoken in class without being called on, but consistently has earnest, insightful answers. One student encourages another through depression. Four students become best friends, keep the rest of us laughing, and effectively demonstrate how to push classmates to be their best.

(Hannah, Teaching Practicum, Final Paper)

At the beginning of the semester, Hannah interprets her learning-to-teach journey mostly in terms of her own perspective, focusing on herself, her emotions, and her struggle to find legitimacy as a teacher of her learners. By the end of the semester, Hannah's own sensitivity and self-awareness has changed the way she interprets the practicum teaching experience, a striking example of how *perezhivanie* can function in the development of a novice teacher. From self-doubt to gratitude, she encapsulates this emotional shift with her well-chosen words:

> **Excerpt 43**
>
> **The diversity of backgrounds and personalities exhibited in this group, the conglomeration of skills and weaknesses, and the beauty of seeing all of them meld together have made this class a privilege to teach.**
>
> (Hannah, Teaching Practicum, Final Paper)

Conclusion

Being aware of the emotional dimension of development places greater responsibility on the teacher educator, but it also provides a channel for more complex engagement with the trajectories of development that we oversee. As the data in this chapter clearly illustrate, the novice L2 teachers we work with do not hesitate to express their emotional reactions, and to explore the effects of their own emotions and those of their learners, upon their teaching activity. Accepting that other people live other lives, yet at the same time taking it upon ourselves to share what we know from our own lives with the novice teachers we are privileged to teach, has given us a vivid and "lived" sense of the term *perezhivanie*.

We bring our own histories to the classroom and the mediation we provide the novice teachers in our program has its roots in the unique and specific experiences and encounters of those histories. While helping novice teachers become aware of the power of emotional engagement, we also strive to remain aware of the emotional threads that run through our own expertise. Maturity as teachers and as teacher educators suggests a complexity of emotional development that echoes the cognitive and intellectual complexity that infuses our work.

Although it may be a cliché, we do continue to learn from our teachers, and sometimes it is in the moment of emotional openness, of *perezhivanie* laid bare, that we learn the most. Being good at an activity carries many emotions with it, and perhaps it is easier to be jaded or at least complacent about the joy that expertise can spark. Being there with, and for, a novice teacher who experiences, and writes about, their feelings of *delight, frustration, happiness*, of being *nervous, tense*, and *proud*... is an aspect of our work that is perhaps less fully understood and appreciated in the professional literature than it could be, but definitely one that we want to continue to explore.

References

Denzin, N. (1984). *On understanding emotion*. San Francisco: Jossey-Bass.
Hargreaves, A. (2000). Mixed emotions: Teachers' perceptions of their interactions with students. *Teaching and Teacher Education, 16*, 811–826. https://doi.org/10.1016/S0742-051X(00)00028-7.
Johnson, K. E., & Golombek, P. R. (2016). *Mindful L2 teacher education: A sociocultural perspective on cultivating teachers' professional development*. New York: Routledge.

8
INTERNALIZING PEDAGOGICAL CONCEPTS

The principles of praxis-oriented pedagogy are the foundation of our pillar courses and foster our novice L2 teachers' conceptual development of what it means to teach from a reasoned, dialogic, responsive instructional stance. Essential to their ability to instantiate this positioning in their teaching is their internalization of the pedagogical concepts they learn in our courses and the eventual fluency they develop with using these concepts as psychological tools to mediate their reasoning.

In this chapter, we focus on four interrelated pedagogical concepts, ENGINEERING STUDENT PARTICIPATION, PROVIDE RELEVANCE, CREATE PREDICTIBILITY, and ACTIVITY BUILDING, and provide data that we believe makes visible how our novice teachers come to internalize these concepts, make sense of their interrelatedness, and use them to make reasoned, intentional instructional choices to implement in their classrooms.

Engineering Student Participation

ENGINEERING STUDENT PARTICIPATION focuses on how to intentionally design learning activities that encourage student engagement through thoughtful, intentional instructional design. This seemingly simple pedagogical concept bundles a complex set of meanings, which novice teachers need help unpacking as they learn how to create learning activities that encourage student participation in and out of the classroom. We introduce ENGINEERING STUDENT PARTICIPATION in the first pillar course, Teaching ESL, and reinforce it in the other courses. Each pillar course represents a new teaching context, different material conditions, and gives our novice teachers the opportunity to understand the power of this pedagogical concept for designing instructional activities in a variety of teaching/learning contexts.

We include the pedagogical concept ENGINEERING STUDENT PARTICIPATION here for quick reference, and it is also available in Appendix 1:

> ENGINEERING STUDENT PARTICIPATION
> a. Don't assume students know how to participate
> b. Be explicit about HOW you want them to participate
> c. Arrange the classroom in ways that invite participation
> d. Continue to monitor participation throughout the lesson

In Teaching ESL, novice teachers participate in an intentionally designed, carefully mediated learning-to-teach activity, the Extended Team-Teaching Project (see Chapter 3). For this project, students work in teams to design and teach a lesson for a class of university-level language learners. The Team-Teach Supervisor provides *responsive mediation* at strategic points throughout each phase of the project and helps the novice teachers begin to make sense of what it means to ENGINEER STUDENT PARTICIPATION. One of those strategic points is during the *practice teach*, the phase of the project in which the team teaches their lesson plan to their own classmates and receives immediate feedback from the Team-Teach Supervisor and from the other students in the Teaching ESL class.

In the following data set, the team, which consists of Pavel, Chen, and Mei, has prepared a lesson about how to create an annotated bibliography for a class in the first-year academic writing program for L2 learners, a class in which teams are frequently placed. As part of their lesson, the team has decided to show a short video clip of a movie review and then ask the class to identify the summary and evaluation segments of the review. The mediation by the Team-Teach Supervisor and their classmates focuses on how the team decides to talk about the summary and evaluation in the movie review, both of which are also components of an annotated bibliography entry. For the team members, the relationship between the components of the movie review and an annotated bibliography is obvious, but the Team-Teach Supervisor recognizes that the students in the academic writing class probably will not understand that connection unless the team explicitly draws it for them. Rather than directly telling the team to make that connection for their learners, the Team-Teach Supervisor (referred to in the transcript as TE) engages in *responsive medication* to co-construct an understanding with the team members of what can be helpfully added to their lesson to better ENGINEER PARTICIPATION:

Excerpt 1

TE: Ok so you'll set them up to listen for certain things and then after the video is done what will you do?

CHEN: Should we ask them something like did you hear something about summary? Like uhh was there any sentences summarizing that cartoon?

TE: ((*to Ss*)) What do you think you guys just heard a little bit of that video (.) what would you be able to do after you watched that video?

SS: Exactly this right ok like what is the summary part in the video what's the evaluation or the ()

CHEN: Or we could just ask them to look to look for some sentences or to look for some samples uhhm for summary and some samples for like evaluation.

PAVEL: Um I think we might not mention summary and evaluation before we play the video uhm I think we might ask some questions like uhh what is the structure of this () review and after the the video we ask them can you tell me uhm (.) what are the similarities between this two things.

TE: So you set them up to listen for the structure of this movie review.

CHEN: Yeah.

TE: And then you say (.) tell me what the structure is. And they say well sometimes he was describing what was going on in the movie which is essentially summary and sometimes he was evaluating what was happening in the movie which is essentially evaluation. Now when we look at and then you move on to what an annotated bibliography is.

(Extended Team-Teaching Project, Teaching ESL, Practice Teach)

With the Team-Teach Supervisor's *responsive mediation*, the team realizes they need to make two adjustments to their lesson to better ENGINEER PARTICIPATION and understanding; specifically, they need to make explicit the connection between the structure of the movie review and the annotated bibliography (which will help the learners see the RELEVANCE of the video) and also provide a concrete task for the students to complete as they watch the video. As these data show, learning to REASON TEACHING and to think about how to engage learners in specific lesson activities is a complex cognitive process. Intentionally designed learning-to-teach activities, such as the Extended Team-Teaching Project, and *responsive mediation* within those activities, can jumpstart the shift in stance for the novice teachers, from learner of language teaching to language teacher.

Most novice teachers in our program enroll in the second of the three pillar courses, the Tutoring Internship, during their second or third semester. There, they experience a change in the material conditions of teaching and learning. They learn that the pedagogical concept of ENGINEER PARTICIPATION can inform their instructional decisions even in a one-on-one tutoring context, an awareness that sometimes comes as a surprise to them. In this excerpt, Layla, an experienced English as a Foreign Language (EFL) teacher, discusses the differences in how she ENGINEERED PARTICIPATION previously in her EFL classroom back home and what she has learned about the possibilities of doing so in the Tutoring Internship:

Excerpt 2

On the other hand, being in a classroom pushes you to be teacher-centered though you try not to be, while **tutoring is the opposite. It pushes you to be learner-centered. It makes you exposed to the learner's side more and better understand the meaning of individual needs.** So, I found my balance in tutoring where I learned to look through different lenses and to pay attention to every tutee's need. This added an important skill to the teacher me. **Instead of looking at my class as a whole, now when I go back to teaching, I will definitely try my best to see them as individuals.**

(Layla, Tutoring Internship, Final Paper)

Layla explains that she has learned to put the learner at the center of her tutoring; interestingly, she indicates that she will try to do the same when she returns to her EFL classroom, a statement that perhaps represents the beginning of a shift in her instructional stance from teacher-fronted to what might be described as more intentionally student-oriented instruction. Layla continues by providing an example of what that shift means for her teacher identity, a change that suggests she will ENGINEER PARTICIPATION somewhat differently even when she is back in the classroom with many students:

Excerpt 3

"**Tutoring also taught me to ask questions and resist the urge of the teacher me to give direct suggestions without giving my tutees the chance to think and decide.**"

(Layla, Tutoring Internship, Final Paper)

She has come to understand, and believe, that she can engage students more fully in the learning process by allowing them *to think and decide* for themselves rather than telling them what to do.

As our data suggest, the teaching and learning opportunities the novice teachers have in the first two pillar courses help them make sense of and enact the pedagogical concept of ENGINEERING STUDENT PARTICIPATION. The quality and character of their experiences and the *responsive mediation* provided by the Team-Teach Supervisor and Tutoring Supervisor prepare them to apply this pedagogical concept in their 15-week practicum teaching experience. For this experience, novice teachers are mediated by the Practicum Supervisor and a mentor teacher, and they come to realize that there is still much to learn.

In the following example, Lin is close to completing her practicum teaching in the first-year academic writing class for L2 learners (the same program that provided her tutees in the Tutoring Internship). She has carefully planned a peer review activity for a major writing assignment and reflects on the lesson in her weekly Reflective Teaching Journal. She explains that she had paired students in advance for the peer review based on specific criteria, and reviewed her lesson plan with her mentor teacher, but the specifics of her plan to ENGINEER PARTICIPATION were thwarted because of absences:

Excerpt 4

Recall: The first part of the class is peer review discussion. **We didn't count** [Ed.'s note: count *on*] **any absence**, and this actually happened. **Two students did not show up, and I made their partner together.** After they were paired. **One we-thought-absent student showed up finally, so there ended up three students in one group. And that student did not upload his rough draft on Canvas,** which made their group very hard to do peer review. **So, I pretended to be one of them partner, but I lost to chance to walk around and know other students' difficulties.**

(Lin, Teaching Practicum, Week 9 Journal)

With the help of her mentor teacher, Lin responded in the moment by rearranging the learner groups, decided how to engage the learner who had not submitted an essay draft, and realized that she could not support the other learners because she chose to help the group of three learners. In her reflection, she steps back, reconsiders her instructional decisions, and reasons a set of alternative choices that might have more successfully ENGINEERED PARTICIPATION:

Excerpt 5

RE-IMAGINE: **I would let them to do elevator speech to each other, and they can do peer review at that moment. And I would be free to walk around and hear other groups.**

My concern is maybe there would be not enough time for them to do speech one by one, then how to deal with this situation?

(Lin, Teaching Practicum, Week 9 Journal)

In her reflection, Lin articulates ideas for how to address each of the dilemmas she faced in that moment, and in doing so, stretches herself to reason beyond where she actually is in her L2 teacher development. The key realization she makes in this reimagining is that she recognizes that even if she had implemented these strategies, she still would not have ENGINEERED PARTICIPATION in the way she wanted. Stumped, she reaches out to the Practicum Supervisor, who responds by asking questions to confirm what the novice teacher has expressed, and then offers ideas for concrete steps that Lin might adopt in a similar situation in the future. The Practicum Supervisor also helps Lin begin to think about how to ENGINEER PARTICIPATION when students are absent or have not completed their work:

Excerpt 6

If they don't have a paper, they can't do the peer review, right?? So you might put the student who had a completed paper with another group of two, and have them work out doing the peer review together. Because that student had done the work, you want to provide the opportunity for that person to get feedback. **For the other two, you might give them seatwork**—on their own—maybe they have to write an outline for their topic proposal while in class and turn it in at the end of the hour for points. Or maybe they have to write the introduction in class and turn it in. **Something that requires them to do more than sit there and be 'excused' from the work for that day.**

(Supervisor, Teaching Practicum, Week 9 Response)

The Practicum Supervisor's *responsive mediation* is offered at a distance, well after the teaching dilemma occurred, but it acknowledges Lin's cognitive/emotional dissonance and attempts to prepare her for a future moment such as this.

In addition to the Practicum Supervisor, the mentor teacher is an invaluable resource for mediating teacher learning during the practicum. The next excerpt is an example of how dialogic mediation with the mentor teacher shapes the novice L2 teacher's understanding of how to ENGINEER PARTICIPATION. Hannah has the unique opportunity to participate in both sections of the first-year academic writing course for L2 students taught by her mentor teacher. As such, the mentor and novice L2 teacher would often have lunch together between the classes and discuss their teaching. In this next excerpt, Hannah, the novice L2 teacher, recounts a memorable lunch break moment with her mentor:

Excerpt 7

After the first class, Emine and I ate lunch and we debriefed and **she gave me some suggestions for the next class**, things like: **When you hand out a worksheet, make sure everyone has it before you give the directions** (i.e. don't start talking when they're still passing it around); **after watching a video and filling in said worksheet, maybe students would like to compare their answers with the person sitting next to them**, and **then they will feel better about volunteering their ideas for the whole class to hear**—fairly simple, concrete things overall, and things that seem obvious once somebody mentions them.

(Hannah, Teaching Practicum, Week 3 Journal)

Hannah is grateful for the *fairly simple, concrete things* her mentor suggests to effectively ENGINEER PARTICIPATION and decides to implement them in the next class:

Excerpt 8

I tried making those changes in the afternoon class, and it did seem to make a significant difference in terms of how people participated and understood the activity.

(Hannah, Teaching Practicum, Week 3 Journal)

The Practicum Supervisor, who can see that Hannah has begun to understand how and why ENGINEERING PARTICIPATION matters for student learning, notes Hannah's ability to instantiate that understanding in her teaching activity and uses the opportunity to reinforce the pedagogical concept:

Excerpt 9

That's it—to ENGINEER PARTICIPATION we have to give them a sense of where they are going. Then they can make it happen!

(Supervisor, Teaching Practicum, Week 3 Response)

The data in this section offer a window into our novice teachers' internalization of the pedagogical concept, ENGINEERING STUDENT PARTICIPATION. The excerpts suggest that the quality and character of the intentionally designed learning-to-teach activities and *responsive mediation* by the teacher educators and mentor teachers leads to shifts in novice L2 teachers' understanding of and ability to enact the pedagogical concept of

ENGINEERING STUDENT PARTICIPATION in a variety of teaching and learning contexts.

Provide Relevance

The pedagogical concept PROVIDE RELEVANCE reminds our novice teachers that they have to be able to justify their instructional choices, communicating their reasoning for their instructional decisions with their students, and be sure the students understand what they are expected to know and do by the end of the lesson. We include the pedagogical concept PROVIDE RELEVANCE here for quick reference, and it is also available in Appendix 1:

> PROVIDE RELEVANCE
> a. Tell students exactly *why* you are doing what you are doing
> b. Tell students *why* you are asking them to do what they are doing
> c. Tell students what you expect them to know and be able to do by the end of the lesson

The following excerpts illustrate how *responsive mediation* by the Team-Teach Supervisor mediates the novice L2 teacher's understanding of PROVIDE RELEVANCE as she works with the novice teacher on her lesson. As part of the team's lesson, Bao is responsible for teaching their class of first-year L2 writers how to use American Psychological Association (APA) citations in academic writing. She works closely with her team and the Team-Teach Supervisor to determine how to ENGINEER STUDENT PARTICIPATION in learning the proper format of in-text citations:

> **Excerpt 10**
>
> TE: Here's an idea, **what if you put up three examples of the most common kinds of things they will cite, one is a book, one is probably a website, and one is a journal and you said to the class,** "raise your hand if you cite a book" and people who cited a book will raise their hands and you say, "does it match what's up there? And if it doesn't why doesn't it?" **And then they have to edit their citation**…"raise your hand if you cited a scholarly journal does it match what's up there? If it doesn't revise it," **that's a way you can connect what they did with what you are trying to do here.**
> BAO: Yes, **I think it is good,** and **I think it should be quick.**
> TE: Yeah, **I think it can be pretty quick because, for me APA or any type of citation method is something you just look up, you don't memorize that stuff**…
> (Bao, Teaching ESL, Practice Teach)

The Team-Teach Supervisor helps Bao understand how to make APA citations RELEVANT to her learners. She notes that first-year writers are not expected to memorize the APA style manual, but they are expected to use it as a reference; thus, she suggests ways that the learning activity can be ENGINEERED to help learners practice using the style manual as a reference.

Accordingly, Bao makes adjustments to her part of the lesson plan and leads the activity in the academic writing class during the *actual teach*. During the *stimulated recall session*, she experiences a moment of cognitive/emotional dissonance that appears to spark greater understanding for her. Even though, with the help of the Team-Teach Supervisor's feedback, she successfully planned how to better ENGINEER STUDENT PARTICIPATION, she realizes that she forgot to explain another crucial dimension of the lesson segment, that is, the RELEVANCE of the activity to the learners:

Excerpt 11

> BAO: Actually, I don't know how to use, **I don't know how to start, to guide them to review this part, so I think I got over the beginning and over the end, it's my feeling, like it didn't fit.**
>
> TE: One way you could have couched it is to say, "a really important part of an annotated bibliography is to have a correct citation, you already know how to do citations, you've done it before, let's just do a quick review"...**tell them your reasoning for why you are having them do this... and that's making your thinking explicit to them, so they know why they are doing it.**
>
> (Bao, Teaching ESL, Stimulated Recall)

In her final reflection paper, Bao articulates more fully her improved understanding of the importance of making her teacher reasoning explicit and providing RELEVANCE for her students:

Excerpt 12

> Also, **I remembered I asked Dr. Johnson why is that I felt awkward** when I started teaching my part, **she said that is because I did not say anything about why we today went through this part.** After she talked lots of to me, **I learned that every part of the class should be explain to our students or give them a clear guidance: why we are doing this part.** Like, "I know you are quite familiar with this part, I am going to teach citation part because it is also an important part for annotated bibliography if you want to earn A+, we will review and revise it together."
>
> (Bao, Teaching ESL, Final Paper)

Internalizing Pedagogical Concepts   **153**

In the following excerpt, we see the role of providing RELEVANCE in the Tutoring Internship. In this example, Shu learns that providing RELEVANCE also matters in a one-on-one instructional context. Here, Shu expresses her emerging understanding of why providing RELEVANCE is crucial for tutees in her written reflection:

Excerpt 13

In this tutoring session, I realized that when students do not see or do not agree with the value of an assignment, they would easily lose interest in working on the assignment. **However, when they see the value or the purpose of doing that assignment, they would be more willing to make efforts to complete it.**

(Shu, Tutoring Internship, Session 4 Post)

The Tutoring Supervisor responds by paraphrasing the pedagogical concept of RELEVANCE, using Shu's word *purpose* to validate the insight:

Excerpt 14

Shu, this is a really important insight that you share here: **students who do not understand or appreciate the purpose of a task often cannot find the focus or energy to do it well.** Even if they don't like the task very much, or find it really difficult, **they can often work more successfully on it if they understand what the instructor wants the task to accomplish for/with them.**

(Supervisor, Tutoring Internship, Session 4 Response)

Tutoring interns confront the importance of providing RELEVANCE in different ways. Here, Qing achieves a similar understanding by examining her own activity in the tutoring sessions and the activity of her tutees, a process supported by the *responsive mediation* that she receives from the Tutoring Supervisor. In her final reflection paper for the Tutoring Internship, Qing remembers being struck by the realization that her tutees did not always understand the RELEVANCE of some of the writing activities they were expected to complete in their first-year academic writing class. In the following excerpt, Qing reflects on one tutee's understanding of the annotated bibliography assignment, which was required as part of a research sequence leading to a final argumentative problem-solution essay:

Excerpt 15

"…it seems that for various reasons, **some students just follow the guideline or just answer the questions but don't know the deep** meaning of that they do. I am a little afraid that without those guidelines in the future, some students still not know how to write each phrase of a paper by themselves." **After posted this reflection, I received the comment from my professor and she gave several possible solutions.** For example, there are other kinds of activities for them to understand the guideline, such as in-class discussions, models that are shared by the instructor, workshop activities such as debates, peer review sessions, logical fallacy competitions, etc...**So I always paid lots of attention to explain why my tutees should do so behind their assignment.**

(Qing, Tutoring Internship, Final Paper)

Qing then recalls the excitement she felt when her tutees finally grasped the RELEVANCE of the annotated bibliography for the essay: finally, the tutees actually used the bibliography entries they had prepared to evaluate and connect sources to topics and to find better evidence for their arguments:

Excerpt 16

...in later sessions, I saw both of my tutees can look up their annotated bibliography when they need relate the sources into their topic and find some supportive evidence for their essay. I wrote this gratifying phenomenon in session 8-11. **When I found they could use their annotated bibliographies, I knew they had started to understand the meaning behind their actions.**

(Qing, Tutoring Internship, Final Paper)

Qing notes that working with her tutees and helping them find RELEVANCE in their assignments reminds her of her own learning experiences. She acknowledges that even though her teachers may have provided the RELEVANCE for activities and assignments, she—like her tutees—did not always use this information to make sense of assignments until after they were complete:

Excerpt 17

As for my own learning experience, although there may be lots of activities in class which teachers designed to help us know WHY behind WHAT in each task, I started to realize its intent mostly by myself later. After I finished the whole process of a final paper, I looked back and understood why I should write ABs, proposal, etc. No matter how hard my teachers explained to me before, I cannot fully understand them until I've done them. **So I believe (or hope...) tutees could understand many "WHY" behind tasks by themselves after they finished them...**

(Qing, Tutoring Internship, Session 7 Post)

As we expect and hope, the novice teachers can 'transport' their understandings, in this case of the pedagogical concept of providing RELEVANCE, from one context to another. Qing, in this instance, demonstrates how her weekly Teaching Practicum seminar class informs how she now reasons her instructional choices in her teaching activity. In the next excerpt, we see Qing having been tasked with creating a grammar quiz for her practicum class learners. To make one section of the quiz, she uses an online corpus tool to find sentences for her learners to analyze. However, she is concerned that perhaps the sentences she has selected from the corpus have no RELEVANCE to her learners:

Excerpt 18

When I was working on the first version, **I searched the example sentences from the Corpus of Contemporary American English. However, I found the sentences are so far from my students' daily life.**

(Qing, Teaching Practicum, Week 8 Journal)

After much searching, she remembers a resource she learned about in the Teaching Practicum class and creates another version of the grammar quiz:

Excerpt 19

When I was doing my second version of the quiz, I thought of in APLNG 500 class, we had talked about the Penn State News what we receive in the mailbox every day. **So I read the news and found lots of sentences in news which have the grammar points students just learned and the sentences are also close to their daily life. After all, IECP students need to be familiar with the university, and it is not bad to see some school news on their quiz.** My mentor thought the second version is good and **students did that quiz on Thursday.**

(Qing, Teaching Practicum, Week 8 Journal)

While making the quiz, Qing sees a potential dual purpose for the grammar quiz. She can use the sentences both to test her learners' understanding of the grammar points they have covered and to raise their awareness of interesting and authentic content that may provide RELEVANCE to *their daily life*. Her decision to choose RELEVANT content for the quiz is validated when her mentor teacher approves and uses the revised grammar quiz.

For our novice teachers, the pedagogical concept of providing RELEVANCE reminds them that when their learners understand the reasons, the 'why' behind instructional choices, they are more likely to participate in the learning activities. Choosing to explicitly state the RELEVANCE for their learners means choosing to reason their teaching, think deeply about their instructional choices, and recognize how their choices shape and are shaped by their learners and their contexts.

Create Predictability

Where the pedagogical concept of PROVIDE RELEVANCE focuses on the *why*, the closely related pedagogical concept, CREATE PREDICTABILITY, focuses on the *how*.

We include the pedagogical concept CREATE PREDICTABILIY here for quick reference, and it is also available in Appendix 1:

CREATE PREDICTABILITY

a. Explicitly state what students are expected to say and do
b. Explicitly and overtly link activities through language: provide connections/transitions
c. If working in pairs or small groups, provide students opportunities to 'practice' before they 'perform' or 'present'

A familiar example might be how to follow group work with a reporting task: when leading pair and small group activities, the teacher can CREATE PREDICTABILITY by always allowing learners to prepare and practice their group report in the small group before delivering it to the whole class. Used regularly, this 'rehearsal' segment can make group work feel more comfortable and ultimately make it more productive for shy or hesitant L2 learners.

Our novice teachers encounter the pedagogical concept of CREATE PREDICTABILITY in the first pillar course, Teaching ESL, specifically when preparing the Extended Team-Teach Project. The design of this project includes the requirement that each team deliver a version of its lesson to the other peer teachers in the course. This *practice teach* session provides a critical mediational space for the team of novice teachers to 'try out' their lesson plan. The team receives feedback from the Team-Teach Supervisor and their peer teachers about both the content and the delivery of the lesson plan. Often, it is during this experience that the novice teachers confront the need to think about creating PREDICTABILITY for the first time. Heavily focused on compiling materials and devising activities for a group of learners they barely know, the teams become so immersed in the preparation of the lesson that they tend to forget about the fact that the learners will have no idea what they are expected to say or do during the lesson. Thus, the *practice teach* is a powerful learning exercise. In his final reflection paper for the team teach experience, novice teacher Pavel explicitly invokes the pedagogical concept, noting how the Team-Teach Supervisor's *responsive meditation* on the activity helped him understand the importance of creating PREDICTABILITY:

Excerpt 20

Practice teach was another important step in making our designed lesson much better. **Due to valuable comments that our classmates and instructors gave, we managed to fix the parts that might have caused trouble at our actual teach.** There were two main features I remembered well from the practice teach. **One of them is PREDICTABILITY which meant that I, as a teacher, was supposed to be as explicit as possible while giving instructions to do certain tasks, so that students would know why they were doing the task and what I would expect them to do with it.** Prior to knowing that, I just played the "Zootopia" cartoon review without proper guidelines to students. However, after learning that technique, before showing the video clip I divided students into two groups assigning group A to listen to "descriptive sentences", and group B to "sentences with personal opinion". By doing that, students became clearly informed about what was expected from them.

(Pavel, Teaching ESL, Final Paper)

Here we can see Pavel referring both to the pedagogical concept of providing RELEVANCE, *so that students would know why they are doing the task*, and to the pedagogical concept of creating PREDICTABILITY, *what I would expect them to do*. He seems to understand that the two are closely linked, and he expresses appreciation for the mediation his team received because he can see that without these two pedagogical concepts guiding their choices, the original lesson design *might have caused trouble* when they did the *actual teach*.

PREDICTABILITY is a rather vexed issue in the Tutoring Internship. Like many tutors, Shu is somewhat anxious about the fact that she cannot prepare lesson plans or activities in advance for her tutoring sessions. Instead, she is expected to respond to the tutee in the moment by engaging in dialogue, raising issues and questions about her tutee's writing, and asking and answering questions in dialogue with the tutee. Not surprisingly, this feels dismayingly open-ended and unpredictable both to Shu and to many of the novice teachers when they begin the Tutoring Internship course.

In this excerpt from her final paper, Shu remembers how she felt at the beginning of the Tutoring Internship by naming several emotions and putting into words the tension that she remembers before encountering this new context:

Excerpt 21

When first learning that we don't have to prepare for the tutoring sessions, I was surprised, nervous, yet excited. **I was surprised because I didn't know that teaching can be conducted without preparing beforehand. Even when I tutored in Taiwan, I spent lots of** time preparing for my tutoring sessions. I was nervous because I didn't know how well I can teach without preparation. I was excited because I have the chance to try different 'teaching styles' in tutoring— the teaching style that does not require teachers to be 'well-prepared'.

(Shu, Tutoring Internship, Final Paper)

Shu recounts the shift in perspective that she experienced as the semester progressed, realizing that what constitutes tutoring activity may not be pre-programmed, but it can incorporate familiarity and routine. She describes in some detail how she began to create PREDICTABILITY for her tutees so they could feel prepared to respond to her questions in each tutoring session:

Excerpt 22

One of the challenges that I faced in the first few weeks of tutoring was that I tried hard to resist the impulse to give answers and to remind myself to ask more questions. **Both the tutees and I were very used to 'teacher-lecture-student-listen' mode of interaction in class.** Hence, in the first few tutoring sessions, when I respond to students' questions with questions, they would feel a bit uncomfortable with me not giving the answers. However, as I became more skillful at asking questions, and as my tutees were used to answering questions, I noticed that asking questions was actually very effective in developing tutees' ability to self-editing and fostering them to be a more independent writer. Instead of looking at the miscommunications in the writings as something that I need to 'fix', questions help me look at those as chances to understand what my tutees were trying to convey and why they decided to express themselves this way.

(Shu, Tutoring Internship, Final Paper)

Eventually, the PREDICTABILITY Shu creates for the tutoring sessions leads to more independence on the part of one tutee, something that surprises Shu and even makes her uneasy as she struggles with the way this new development positions her:

Excerpt 23

In this tutoring session, Anika and I worked on revising the first draft of her topic proposal. **As we go over her writing, she would verbalize her thinking process of identifying the parts to be revised and explaining how she will revise it. It was like she's talking to herself and I became more like a listener instead of an** interlocutor. She would ask me how do I think about her revision after she finished revising a paragraph. **At first, I found myself a bit uncomfortable with this change because I felt myself not helping her 'effectively'.**

(Shu, Tutoring Internship, Session 9 Post)

In fact, Shu quickly *adjusted herself* to this change by reframing the tutee's activity as emerging autonomy, an outcome that she can happily align with the stated goals of the tutoring program:

Excerpt 24

However, I adjusted myself by recognizing that what she did was actually demonstrating her developing self-edit ability. This was actually a sign that the 'scaffold' that I used was no longer that much needed. Interacting with Anika actually helped me learn a lot about the change of the role of a tutor (or a teacher) when students became more independent and developed automaticity in learning.

(Shu, Tutoring Internship, Session 9 Post)

Shu has modeled for her tutee how to *verbalize her thinking processes*. She has done this by creating PREDICTABILITY for each tutoring session in the way she asks questions and engages her tutee in dialogic mediation. Over time, her tutee learns to think independently, to ask her own guiding questions, and to use Shu as a sounding board. Importantly, Shu notes that these tutoring experiences, particularly learning how to help learners develop into autonomous learners of academic writing, will be crucial when she takes up her role as a teacher upon returning to the classroom.

We see a similar shift in teacher learning with another tutor, Chul, who has an 'ah ha' moment in which he comes to understand the power of asking guiding questions rather than telling his tutee what to do. As he recounts the incident, we see Chul's understanding of the pedagogical concept BE DIRECT, NOT DIRECTIVE come into focus:

Excerpt 25

I should say this week's session was the most productive of all time. Jaareh brought his second draft of compare and contrast essay. It was almost the same as his first draft. Some of the noticeable features of his writing were very outstanding again this time. His ideas are always clear and well-written (in good level of English). **However, there are no clear distinctions among paragraphs, so it feels like he is talking about the same points over and over again. He doesn't**

usually give examples for his main points, so it sounds very subjective. These features eventually lead to a weak thesis statement. What I usually did was to tell him these things. This time, I changed my mind and asked him to give me an outline of his entire essay.

It took him a while and he told me himself that every idea in his essay sounds the same. I was happy that he actually diagnosed his own problem (I really do not use this word) by himself.

(Chul, Tutoring Internship, Session 4 Post, with Jaareh)

By changing his teacher stance, shifting from seeing himself as the giver of information to using dialogic mediation with his tutee, Chul changes the way he creates PREDICTABILITY in subsequent tutoring sessions:

Excerpt 26

Again, as usual, I asked him to clarify and elaborate on those. He confidently explained and clarified them with relevant examples. Speaking of examples, **I suddenly realized how much progress he has made throughout this semester.** Providing examples **was one of our goals at the very beginning of our tutoring, but seeing him giving instances of his topic and main points now just gave me goosebumps. I was even more thrilled when he thanked me** and told me that he appreciated having me as his tutor. I'm not sure how much of help I gave him skill wise, but **I am proud of myself for getting that kind of comments from him.** I really enjoyed working with Jaareh and am so happy that he is going to pass with the grade he had expected.

(Chul, Tutoring Internship, Session 10 post, with Jaareh)

Chul recognizes that he has increased the PREDICTABLITY by adjusting the way he leads the tutoring sessions and notes that his tutee is participating differently in them. He excitedly reflects on his tutee's development as an independent thinker and writer, a realization that gives Chul *goosebumps* as he thinks about how much his tutee appreciates his mediation.

We share one more example of how the pedagogical concept of creating PREDICTABILTY not only supports student learning but also mediates novice teachers as they learn how to help their learners become more autonomous and self-directed. For the first half of the semester, Layla has been leading the tutoring sessions with her tutee, Munwah, initiating discussion with him through *responsive mediation* and drawing concept maps each week to help him visualize the content and organization of his papers. In what follows, we see evidence that Layla's choice to create PREDICTABILITY in each tutoring session has had a significant impact on how her tutee approaches the activity of writing. Specifically, we see the outcome in Week 8 of an activity that started in Week 1 or 2. Layla enthusiastically recognizes the success of her instructional choice:

Excerpt 27

I want to start this reflection by saying that it was an **amazing** session. Though the whole session was about working on the problem Munwah wants to write about, for me it was an **inspiring** session because I got to see two **amazing** things: **Munwah thinking critically and independently, and Munwah using a technique - that I always use with him- simultaneously without me initiating the act to do it.** So, this reflection might be shorter than the others but its **impact** on me is indeed **stronger**.

(Layla, Tutoring Internship, Session 8 Post)

In previous sessions, Layla has guided her tutee's participation, taking the lead on what to discuss and suggesting the use of a concept map to guide the discussions. This time, however, the tutee excitedly initiates the session as he enters the room by sharing *what concerned him about the problem he wants to write about*:

Excerpt 28

It was a funny moment when Munwah started talking to me about what concerned him about the problem he wants to write about directly after saying hi before even he took off his jacket and sitting down... We talked about it and analyzed it from different perspectives using the sources he found till we fixed it.

(Layla, Tutoring Internship, Session 8 Post)

The tasks Layla usually directs, thinking critically and independently and even drawing a concept map to illustrate the connections among his ideas, are taken up by her tutee:

Excerpt 29

While we were talking **excitingly, surprisingly Munwah stood up and said I think we need a paper. He brought a paper and started drawing a concept map. In all the previous sessions, I was the one who brought out the paper to map our ideas. So, it was an astonishing for me to see him doing this. I am happy because he found it useful and it actually helped us a lot in breaking**

> down his topic. After the session finished, I wished that I have recorded it but anyhow it still feels great.
>
> (Layla, Tutoring Internship, Session 8 Post)

Layla has clearly helped this tutee engage successfully with the ZPD activity of developing essay topics through her use of PREDICTABLE tutoring choices. His ability to be prepared for the session, to initiate dialogue about his topic, and to use a concept map for organizing his ideas for the essay show true development on the part of the tutee and the power of creating PREDICTABILITY for encouraging student learning.

The pedagogical concepts of creating RELEVANCE and providing PREDICTABILITY are infused throughout the program and the pillar courses. Thus, we are not surprised to find extrapolated and extended versions of them in the reflective writings produced the final semester during the Practicum Teaching course, as the novice teachers 'write through' their relationships with these familiar, and accessible, but still emerging, conceptual tools. Hannah, reflecting on the new instructional context of her practicum class, muses on both creating PREDICTABLITY and creating RELEVANCE in her third weekly teaching journal:

Excerpt 30

> Another takeaway was to **give directions one step at a time when there is a sequence of steps to do something. That way, students don't get left behind or overwhelmed wondering what to do first**...Going along with the idea about **presenting context though**, I think I can still introduce the activity in a general way ("Now we're going to do an activity to make our thesis statements stronger,") **so they know where we're headed before I get to "Step one: Move your chairs."**
>
> (Hannah, Teaching Practicum, Week 3 Journal)

Excerpt 31

> SOME TAKEAWAYS: **The point of a lesson plan isn't just to have a list of activities on a sheet.** Even though **everything is connected inside my head** (because I planned the lesson and see how it fits together and how it fits with everything else we're doing this semester,) **the students can't see all that.** So in both introducing and wrapping up an activity, **I need to give it context, explain the purpose for doing it and how it relates to other pieces of the lesson, the homework assignments, etc.**
>
> (Hannah, Teaching Practicum, Week 3 Journal)

Hannah's reflections demonstrate a clear understanding of the pedagogical concepts and an ability to put them into her own words. In this way, she is using the pedagogical concepts, in tandem with the reflective teaching journals, as psychological tools to help her understand and reason her own teaching activity.

Hannah and Layla's reflections illustrate how novice teachers come to understand the value in creating PREDICTABILITY for student learning. For Hannah, it means helping her students understand new content by making explicit connections to previously learned material and to the remainder of the lesson. For Layla, it means recognizing the learning activities she creates really do shape learning, and that becomes particularly clear when her tutee takes up the mediational tools she designs to assist his learning and makes them his own.

Activity Building

The pedagogical concepts of providing RELEVANCE and creating PREDICTABILITY help novice teachers intentionally design instructional activities that invite student participation and create conditions for productive student learning. In this section, we share another important pedagogical concept that mediates novice teacher reasoning, this time at the level of lesson plan design: ACTIVITY BUILDING. We include the pedagogical concept ACTIVITY BUILDING here for quick reference, and it is also available in Appendix 1:

> ACTIVITY BUILDING
> a. Design activities in such a way that they build on one another
> b. Sequence activities so that they lead to a final outcome or 'product' that is a demonstration of what students have learned and are now able to do

As novice teachers come to internalize this pedagogical concept, it becomes a psychological tool for learning how to sequence activities so that they build on one another and lead to the desired outcome: learners who are able to demonstrate that they have learned or can do what is expected of them.

To illustrate this pedagogical concept, consider the Extended Team-Teach Project. An intentional design feature of the project is that the team is required to teach content that is already part of the course syllabus; for example, it is something that the first-year academic writing teacher would normally include in the syllabus for L2 writers. For most teams, this means they need to learn the content first, and then figure out how to teach it. The pedagogical concept ACTIVITY BUILDING becomes an essential psychological tool in this process as the teams attempt to construct their initial lesson plan. As an example of how our novice teachers learn about and begin to engage in ACTIVITY BUILDING, let us trace the *planning journey* of a team of three teachers, Aisha, Leo, and Ana, as they prepare an introductory lesson on applying the scientific method to a new discipline. The lesson was developed for a content-based Applied Science English course in the university's Intensive English Language Program (non-matriculated L2 English learners). The L2 learners in the course were already generally familiar with the scientific method and knew how to develop a research hypothesis. The team was tasked with linking these concepts to the academic discipline of psychology.

Aisha describes in her reflection how the team struggled to come up with appropriate content for their lesson. She recalls an ACTIVITY BUILDING exercise in the Teaching ESL course where MA TESL students are given a textbook unit and asked to adapt it to the needs and goals of different groups of learners in different instructional contexts (i.e., TOEFL prep, tourist English, EFL, etc.). Remembering how, in that activity, she and her classmates physically cut the textbook unit apart, and then rearranged, supplemented, eliminated, and added activities in order to meet the needs and goals of their target learners, reminds Aisha of the importance of relating activities to learner needs and goals. Remembering that experience of ACTIVITY BUILDING based on learner needs and course goals enables Aisha to recognize that while at one point she assumed teaching that without a textbook, where activities are already created for teachers, would offer *more freedom and ease*, her team had to consider a host of critical questions as they attempted to BUILD ACTIVITIES for their introductory lesson.

Excerpt 32

We were having a very difficult time trying to figure out what to teach. I guess it helps to know we were starting a new unit, but it was just so broad - psychology- **how do we start? How much should we give? How can we transition from the previous unit? What basics/foundations should we further integrate and how? All these questions were floating in our minds**, and the fact that we did not have a textbook we could follow made it far more difficult for us. It is funny, because **I always assumed that no textbooks means more freedom and ease**, but **after having our lesson** [from Teaching ESL] **on curriculum and course development, it made me realize that textbooks are just means of guidance, not something that should have complete control on one's teaching and the way they frame the class.**

(Aisha, Teaching ESL, Final Paper)

Remembering how the team struggled to find a focus for their lesson, Leo recalls how they sought to BUILD their ACTIVITIES *in a seamless organic way*. Based on a lecture he had attended, the team decided to use a video that illustrated a psychological experiment on facial recognition and memory constraints as an ORIENTING activity for their lesson.

Excerpt 33

The challenge then was not only thinking about what to do next, but how to connect the following activity to the previous one in a seamless, organic way. It was fortuitous that I had recently attended a CLS [Center for Language Sciences] talk about language chunking and memory constraints in which the presenter showed that same video to illustrate a point he had made. **It was a great way to expand on the topic of face recognition, showing students how overestimated it is, and we all agreed that it would work well in the lesson.**

(Leo, Teaching ESL, Final Paper)

The third team member, Ana, describes how she spent hours reading about *psychology in science* and uncovered *really interesting experiments*, an effort which helped the team link the content of the video to the syllabus goals of the unit (i.e., the scientific method in different academic disciplines):

Excerpt 34

I spent many hours reading about psychology in science and found really interesting experiments. We were trying to come up with something fun, meaningful and professional at the same time. **Afterwards, when we found the video on face recognition and were able to find a link to the content and the goals, the process went smoothly.**

(Ana, Teaching ESL, Final Paper)

In words that resonate with Aisha's, described earlier, we hear how Ana and her teammates reasoned through their instructional choices by asking critical questions that helped them select (RELEVANCE) and sequence (ACTIVITY BUILDING) their activities as they planned this lesson:

Excerpt 35

The three of us contributed with our knowledge and experiences and while planning, we would ask ourselves questions such as: **Is this meaningful? Why are we doing this? Why are we showing this** video? What is the goal? What are we trying to teach? Are we linking activities coherently? Is this relevant? Is the text too difficult? What about the vocabulary? Is it up to their level? Does this lesson match the course's and unit's goals? Is the content appropriate? What would be the students' reactions and expected performance?

(Ana, Teaching ESL, Final Reflection Paper)

Even in the Tutoring Internship, where lesson plans and classroom management do not play a crucial role in the instructional session, we can see Layla trying to create PREDICTABILITY with her tutees by starting each dialogic session with a series of questions. She uses this activity to motivate them to interrogate their writing and follows up on that discussion by co-constructing a concept map with each tutee to visually represent the tutee's ideas. In the sequence below, we can observe Layla in the process of learning about ACTIVITY BUILDING through her series of posts and watch how she makes sense of it for each tutee in a slightly different way. First, working with Whan, Layla starts the session by placing a piece of paper in front of the tutee:

Excerpt 36

I put a piece of paper between us and I asked her to tell me what were the ideas she wanted to include in her essay. After we wrote a list, I drew a concept map for her categorizing her ideas into three main themes. I did this because I thought by showing her her ideas in a map, the idea of organizing would be clearer for her. Working on the concept map made it easier for me to explain to Whan how her ideas were scattered throughout the essay.

(Layla, Tutoring Internship, Session 2 Post, with Whan)

Layla reflects on her choice to highlight the themes that emerged in their co-constructed text by articulating her reasoning: she explains that she did this to help her tutee be prepared to write her paper:

Excerpt 37

We discussed how could she use the same content she wrote but in a different way. So, **I suggested that she could choose three colors for the three themes and highlight every sentence with the appropriate color.** After that, she can put her sentences that belong to the same theme together. By this way, she will not throw away her work but instead she will form the final draft from what she has already.

(Layla, Tutoring Internship, Session 2 Post, with Whan)

However, several weeks later, working with the same tutee, Layla is frustrated because even though she has been carefully mediating each session with this tutee, she worries that Whan neither takes ownership of her writing nor displays investment in her own learning:

Excerpt 38

As I mentioned before in another reflection that I noticed that **Whan forgets what we discuss and talk about in our sessions. I feel like it is a routine for us to repeat points we discuss twice and sometimes more. I try to use expressions such as "as I told you before - I remember we talked about that last time" but I don't think she figured it out.** I am **confused** because I don't know how I can be direct and **not to embarrass her** in the same time to make her aware of this problem. **What is easy about teaching in a class that you can address an issue you face with a student by talking to the whole class. However, when it comes to tutoring, it is totally different.** It is only you and your tutee and anything happens may get personal.

(Layla, Tutoring Internship, Session 8 Post, with Whan)

The Tutoring Supervisor responds by complimenting Layla's *noticing* and acknowledging her ability to articulate the dilemma so clearly. Then the Supervisor offers another ACTIVITY to BUILD into their sessions as a sort of *wrap up* task that, she suggests, may help to shift the sense of who is responsible for Whan's learning from Layla to the tutee:

Excerpt 39

Layla, **it's great** that you have been able to identify and work with this tutee's 'weakness' of not remembering previous discussions. **I wonder if this would work: ask her to make notes in front of you, while she is still at the tutoring session, of the various topics you discussed in each session. She can write them in her L1–the notes are purely to help her pay attention to important things that come** up in tutoring and 015 [Ed's note: the first-year academic writing class]. It would take away 2-3 minutes of time from your sessions, but she might get used to the idea—she could make the notes on her phone, so it would be simple—and then you could regularly ask her to review the notes for 1 minute before beginning the next session. **A good academic study skill**!

(Supervisor, Tutoring Internship, Session 8 Response)

The Tutoring Supervisor provides a concrete learning ACTIVITY to sequence into Layla's tutoring sessions with this particular tutee. She also offers several suggestions for how Layla might ENGINEER the tutee's PARTICIPATION during the new activity. Layla demonstrates her willingness to develop control of this pedagogical concept by BUILDING this final ACTIVITY into the very next session with Whan:

> **Excerpt 40**
>
> By the end of the session, **I summarized everything we did as Deryn suggested** to help her remember and take notes of what we have discussed in this session. **I hope this technique works with her.**
> (Layla, Tutoring Internship, Session 9 Post, with Whan)

The Teaching Practicum offers a very different teaching/learning context than the Tutoring Internship because the novice teacher works on a regular basis with a classroom full of learners. This context provides an opportunity for novice teachers to further develop their understanding and mastery of ACTIVITY BUILDING. Throughout the practicum experience, the Practicum Supervisor and mentor teachers provide responsive mediation to the novice teachers as they plan and lead lessons with sequenced ACTIVITIES that BUILD on one another In this example, we learn from Qing's reflective writing about how she is learning to BUILD a sequence of ACTIVITIES for a practicum class she plans to teach relatively late in the semester. In her post-class reflection, she explains that she decided to give a *grammar lecture* at the beginning of the class and follow that with a game, but she acknowledges that she was concerned, even before class began, that she might lose her learners' interest during the grammar lecture:

> **Excerpt 41**
>
> In the past several classes, I didn't talk about grammar for such a long time. **This time, I had a grammar lecture for 20 minutes and a game for it about 15 minutes. So it is no wonder that this was the first time that I saw some students dozed and nodded constantly. I considered it before the class, so I tried my best to keep interactions with students when I was teaching.**
> (Qing, Teaching Practicum, Week 10 Journal)

As she predicted, her learners do lose interest in the grammar lecture even though she attempts to engage them at different points. Her learners become more responsive when she moves to the game, and Qing considers options to the choice she did make in how to SEQUENCE the two ACTIVITIES:

> **Excerpt 42**
>
> **If I had last Tuesday's class again, I would like to adjust the order of the activities.** I felt hard to grasp their attention again after

their individual work especially in the last few minutes of the class. **In order to make sure everybody heard what I said, in the future, I may finish the part that needs their attention at first, and then, let them do their individual work.**

(Qing, Teaching Practicum, Week 10 Journal)

Fortunately, she actually does have a chance to (re-)enact her understanding of the pedagogical concept of ACTIVITY BUILDING as she plans for the next class. This time, her mentor teacher provides *responsive mediation* that reinforces what Qing learned from her previous class, namely that understanding and predicting how learners might respond should be considered when determining how to sequence the ACTIVITIES in a lesson plan:

Excerpt 42

Moreover, when I prepared to go over their quiz on Thursday, I had thought to move it to the proceeding part of the class. However, my mentor suggested me to put it as the last part because students may feel upset and distracted when they saw their grades. From that, I realized knowing some psychology is also helpful for the class design. I would think of it when I plan for the following classes and make each activity in a good order.

(Qing, Teaching Practicum, Week 11 Journal)

The Practicum Supervisor agrees with Qing's mentor teacher about the sequence of the quiz review within the broader design of the lesson. She also compliments Qing for keeping her focus on the learners' experience:

Excerpt 43

Yes—a good idea to review quizzes at the end of class so you can then address individual questions. Your questions, your ideas for how to make revisions to your plan are very thoughtful and focused on creating the best learning space for your students.

(Supervisor, Teaching Practicum, Week 11 Response)

For our novice teachers, the pedagogical concept of ACTIVITY BUILDING becomes, ultimately, a psychological tool that shapes the choices they make for sequencing activities in their lessons. We close this chapter by looking at the Teaching Philosophy written by Qing, which she prepared as an assignment in the Teaching Practicum. In this document, Qing resorts to a creative and striking analogy to explain how she now understands the pedagogical concept of ACTIVITY BUILDING for her own teaching:

Excerpt 44

In order to reach the final course goals, I decide how to scaffold my students learning by building a concrete structure or foundation with them. Then, I add ample projects which are aligned with the course goals into the structure. I use bonfire as a metaphor to illustrate my beliefs. **Every time I design a lesson, I think of "the bonfire" as my goal and plan my lesson from the macro perspective first. Then, I consider each piece of firewood needed for the fire and focus on the micro perspective.** In order to get the whole picture, I must know every students' language proficiency at the very beginning and teach them in accordance with their aptitude and strengths.

(Qing, Teaching Practicum, Teaching Philosophy)

Qing's description of a bonfire is a powerful visual representation of how the pedagogical concept of ACTIVITY BUILDING informs her instructional choices and how she can help her learners accomplish their learning goals.

Conclusion

The data in this chapter provide evidence for our claim that novice teachers can be seen to gain fluency and versatility in reasoning their pedagogical choices. The data also support and illustrate our belief that praxis-oriented pedagogy drives change in L2 teacher reasoning and teaching activity over time in observable and significant ways. More specifically, the novice L2 teachers learn to ENGINEER STUDENT PARTICIPATION by intentionally designing learning activities that encourage learner engagement with one another and which engage learners in the activities themselves. The novice L2 teachers learn to explicitly provide their learners with the RELEVANCE of the instructional choices that lie behind the lesson plan, so that learners understand why each segment of the lesson, each activity or task, matters for their learning. The novice L2 teachers learn to create PREDICTABILITY in their classrooms so their learners can feel comfortable with familiar routines and ways of engaging in the lesson activities so they can focus on learning new content. Finally, the novice L2 teachers learn the importance of ACTIVITY BUILDING and sequencing of learning tasks in ways that support learning. Whether we are teacher educators with decades of experience or novice L2 teachers just stepping into the classroom, we want our classrooms to be spaces in which learners actively engage in language learning. The pedagogical concepts of ENGINEERING STUDENT PARTICIPATION, providing RELEVANCE, creating PREDICTABILITY, and ACTIVITY BUILDING become valuable psychological tools that help novice L2 teachers as they begin their teaching journeys.

PART IV
OUTCOMES, IMPACT, OPPORTUNITIES

9
RECONCEPTUALIZATION IN NOVICE L2 TEACHER REASONING

Introduction

Novice teachers have different reactions to our praxis-oriented pedagogy, and throughout our program they experience and reflect on different personal, professional, and pedagogical issues. Of course, this is consistent with the principles of Vygotskian Sociocultural Theory (VSCT) because novice teachers have histories, and their histories are shaped by differing episodes of *perezhivanie*: how they understand their lived experiences and how their lived experiences refract the way they experience the new *social situation of development* created through our pillar courses. Recognizing these varied histories is crucial to understanding how they experience our praxis-oriented pedagogy.

In Part IV of this book we examine, in much broader strokes, the outcomes and takeaways of our praxis-oriented pedagogy. In Chapter 9, we offer data from our novice teachers' written reflections and instructional practices that reveal an intentional and significant reorientation in how they conceptualize themselves as language teachers and how they conceptualize language teaching itself. This outcome is reflected in the various ways in which our novice teachers have come to conceptualize teaching as reasoned, deliberate, and student-oriented, and recognize the pedagogical value of and can enact a *teaching as dialogic mediation instructional stance*.

In Chapter 10, we explore the impact of our praxis-oriented pedagogy through interviews with seven post-MA TESL graduates who participated in the original research project but are now teaching, studying, or working in different instructional contexts around the world. We asked these practicing L2 teachers to reflect on the significant concepts, experiences, and/or realizations that have traveled with them from our praxis-oriented pedagogy into

DOI: 10.4324/9781003268987-13

their early professional years and how these concepts have become important facets of their own pedagogy.

Chapter 11 concludes by providing readers with additional information about the way our praxis-oriented pedagogy offers other forms of mediational spaces and input to our novice teachers. It is provided in the hope that readers who want to explore applying some of the ideas laid out in this book will have a deeper understanding of the many kinds of opportunities that can be used for responsive, contingent, and socioculturally focused mediation of novice teacher reasoning.

Reconceptualization in L2 Novice Teacher Reasoning

Since the goal of praxis-oriented pedagogy is to understand language teaching as a reasoned and agentive activity, in this chapter, we focus on the most notable and most significant outcome of our praxis-oriented pedagogy: a major reorientation in the conceptions that novice teachers hold of language teaching. To effect this reorientation, we work to help our novice teachers develop the ability to articulate, create, and enact engaging and interactive language learning environments for the learners they teach. This shift can be characterized as an intentional moving away from a traditional teacher-centered transmission view of teaching to a reasoned, deliberate, student-oriented *teaching as dialogic mediation instructional stance*. The shift involves the building of novice teacher agency, strengthening the novice teachers' knowledge of, and ability to manipulate, a repertoire of linguistic, cultural, pedagogical, and interactional resources that enable them to support productive learning. Unsurprisingly, this process is not smooth, straightforward, or effortless. As we have shown in previous chapters, it often involves intense emotional turmoil, deeply personal critical reflection, and engagement in consistent and constant *responsive mediation* with teacher educators and mentor teachers. The process of reorienting novice teachers' conceptions of language teaching runs through all three pillar courses: this typically begins during the highly controlled and mediated Extended Team-Teaching Project in the Teaching ESL course, continues to be confronted through direct tutoring experiences and engagement in *responsive mediation* throughout the Tutoring Internship, and is materialized and, to varying levels of self-regulation, internalized through intense engagement in and reflection on the daily activities of teaching during the Teaching Practicum. But this description perhaps implies a smooth and linear developmental path for all novice teachers, which is not the case. Some issues and challenges remain constant, appearing and reappearing throughout the three pillar courses. Some reappear at the start of the second or third pillar course, especially as novice teachers are given more autonomy over the decisions they make about teaching and their attempts to enact it in ways that have been modeled for them and which they come to see as an ideal they wish to emulate.

In this chapter, we offer evidence of how engagement in praxis-oriented pedagogy fosters changes in how our novice teachers conceptualize themselves as teachers, as demonstrated in the ways they attempt to carry out teaching/tutoring, shifts in the developmental trajectory of their reasoning, and the emerging of new ways in which they create engaging learning environments for their learners. To illustrate these changes and to support our claims that praxis-oriented pedagogy is a crucial factor behind them, we include excerpts from the digitally recorded *actual teach* and final reflection papers from Teaching ESL, reflective posts from the Tutoring Internship, and digitally recorded lessons and reflective teaching journals from the Teaching Practicum. We also highlight relevant instances of engagement in *responsive mediation* with teacher educators and mentor teachers.

English for No Specific Purpose

The majority of our novice L2 teachers have a long history of English as a Foreign Language (EFL) study, and therefore typically conceptualize language teaching as simply teaching *the language*, i.e., grammar, vocabulary, pronunciation, etc. In the context of our MA TESL program, as a new *social situation of development*, the English language is the means through which *content*, such as academic writing, or instructional language, is taught and learned. One novice teacher with several years of experience teaching EFL described how he once conceptualized his own practice of teaching English as being for *no-specific purposes* but credits the Extended Team-Teaching Project with challenging him to recognize his own long-held conceptions about teaching as being just about *teaching the language*. In his final reflection paper, Leo wrote:

> **Excerpt 1**
>
> Overall, my biggest challenge was to see past my experience of **teaching English for "no-specific purposes." The idea of teaching English through content or content through English is still a novelty for me.** I struggled a little to understand exactly what I was teaching and how that related to my role as a language teacher. I must have asked **"But what exactly are we teaching?" countless times during our first planning meeting. Sometimes it is easier for me to see learning in ways that are easier to quantitatively assess based on grammar or functions, that is, students have learned/ I have taught structure/function X, Y and Z.**
>
> (Leo, Teaching ESL, Final Paper)

Later in the same reflection paper, Leo is able to articulate an alternative way of thinking about language teaching, one that is sensitive to the *ecology of the classroom*, *the sociocultural context*, and *well-reasoned teaching*.

Excerpt 2

This experience has shown me that there are alternative ways of approaching the teaching of languages, which are as effective as the one I have grown accustomed to. **Teaching should not be a one-size-fits-all kind of activity in which the teacher has everything figured out before even knowing the ecology of the classroom; in other words, it should observe who the learners are, the sociocultural context in which they are inserted, as well as their expectations regarding the course and personal goals. Well-reasoned teaching should factor in all these variables,** resulting in a curriculum design with views to ensure that learners succeed in attaining their objectives, and that the process is an agreeable and insightful one.

(Leo, Teaching ESL, Final Paper)

These two data excerpts in no way suggest that Leo can enact a *teaching as dialogic mediation instructional stance*, or has mastered REASONING TEACHING, but they do suggest that the Extended Team-Teaching Project challenged him to confront how he had previously conceptualized language teaching. In addition, he has developed an awareness that there are alternatives available to him and he is able to articulate a range of *variables* to consider in order to offer *well-reasoned teaching*. Conscious awareness is a crucial first step in VSCT concept development, and such awareness was clearly prompted by the intentional design of and how this teacher experienced the Extended Team-Teaching Project.

Shifting Away from a Teacher-fronted Instructional Stance

As they move through the pillar courses, the novice teachers come to realize why, and how, they can become more versatile, expert teachers by shifting their conception of teaching away from the traditional, teacher-fronted instructional stance they brought with them to the program. This is not surprising given the praxis-oriented pedagogy offered by all three teacher educators and the intentional design features embedded in the pillar courses. They read about *reasoning teaching* (Johnson, 1999) and *teaching as dialogic mediation* (Johnson, 2009), and this instructional stance is defined and modeled for them throughout each of the pillar courses. In the Teaching ESL course, as they plan and *practice teach* their Extended Team-Teaching Project lesson, there is an expectation that it will be intentionally designed to orient toward learners' understandings, in other words, how learners learn content through greater engagement and participation. For example, Ai recalls, perhaps for the first time, beginning to *think as a student when teaching* she writes:

Excerpt 3

Now I've been thinking through all the processes we had been in during the group teaching project, **the most valuable experience I've gained is "to think as a student when teaching". When designing the lesson plan, we kept asking ourselves: "if I were a student and the teacher just asked me to do that, what would I think?"** At the first place, to think as a student in fact freaked me out a bit because the students from ESL 015 [1st year academic writing for L2 learners] (both sections) are actually intelligent, fluent in English, and with quite strong personality. **I thought I was not qualified to be their teacher. Now I find myself really "self-centered" at that time. The point of teaching is not just about performing as the "leader" of students but also pushing the students by challenging them, or by making them challenge the authority (maybe the textbooks, the teachers, the material they've been provided with), the habitual thinking and themselves.**

(Ai, Teaching ESL, Final Paper)

Notably, Ai recognizes the cognitive/emotional dissonance she experienced when she faced learners who were very different from the learners she taught in her home country, leading her to question her own qualifications as a language teacher. On the other hand, she rejects the notion of *teacher as performer* and instead embraces the idea that she can challenge learners to challenge themselves and the authorities that surround them. A major challenge for novice teachers is to reconceptualize language teaching in terms of how learners experience their teaching. In line with Daniels (2014) embrace of Vygotsky and dialogic pedagogy, "the teacher is constantly the learner who is trying to understand the consequences of the teaching they practice" (p. 26).

Since REASONING TEACHING is a central principle in praxis-oriented pedagogy, and it is initially introduced in the Teaching ESL course, it is often mentioned in the final reflection papers. Sometimes it is mentioned by the teachers as they begin to first verbalize and then internalize REASONING TEACHING as an alternative way of conceptualizing language teaching, as is evident in Lin's final reflection paper:

Excerpt 4

To be a qualified teacher, I have to explain the reason why I choose this class material and why I design this activity. Before our practice teaching, what concerned me most was how to teach, how to deliver. After our teach practicing, what plays the main role during my teaching is to think from both teacher's perspective and students' need.

(Lin, Teaching ESL, Final Paper)

Others recognize the value of opportunities to engage in REASONING TEACHING. For Zeina, the *stimulated recall session* became a space where the Team-Teach Supervisor *listened to their reasoning* a valued quality of praxis-oriented pedagogy, rather than simply observing and offering evaluative commentary.

Excerpt 5

Additionally, listening to our teacher's comments meant a lot. We watched the video together and **she listened to our reasoning as teachers. She didn't only observe and comment because she knows that is not enough as she taught us. That is one of the most important things I learned from her,** along with many other amazing concepts.

(Zeina, Teaching ESL, Final Paper)

Explicit Mediation

However, often the pedagogical concept REASONING TEACHING is explicitly highlighted by the teacher educators to reinforce how and why it is important to enact a *teaching as dialogic mediation instructional stance*. In the following excerpt from a *stimulated recall session*, Aisha realizes that she forgot to mention a key feature of the lesson (the use of distractors in psychological studies on attention). Ana is able to articulate a rationale for not mentioning distractors in the video that the learners watch. Instead, Aisha offers a rationale for allowing the learners to figure out what a distractor is, as this will have a direct effect on the hypotheses they are attempting to craft. Initially, the Team-Teach Supervisor mediation is offered as 'teacherly talk' (voicing what a teacher could say) as an alternative form of the point that Aisha was trying to make. However, the Team-Teach Supervisor allows Ana to articulate an alternative rationale for why Aisha's *I missed that thing* might actually be a productive instructional strategy (to match their hypotheses). In response, the Team-Teach Supervisor names what Ana is doing—offering a pedagogical rationale—and reemphasizes it as a core feature of REASONING TEACHING.

Excerpt 6

AISHA: Yeah. **I didn't say that. I missed that thing.**
TE: Yeah. That would've been- So you just did this. You had, you know the distractor that wasn't there. You ask them to look for this. **"Now we're gonna look at the video in which we're gonna see how good our attention is"** or something like that.
ANA: Yeah. But I think maybe **if we said, "You're just giving that", right? Like because that would've maybe changed their**

hypotheses. All right? Because we have- **if we wanna them to try and realize (.) ok there's like a distraction**. So, there's gonna be a distraction involved on their mind.

TE: Right, **so what you've just articulated is your pedagogical rationale for why you did what you did,** which is excellent. You can do that! ((laughter)). No, seriously! There're lots of right things that could be done **and as long as you have a strong, pedagogical reason for why you're doing it in a particular way, that is right way to do it.** And that's why when you're trying to decide whether I should do it this way or that way- Ok, what am I trying to accomplish here? And what I suggested was making it explicit, but **you have a better pedagogical reason for what you want them to do (.) that is the right course of action. And the full notion of reasoning teaching that's all I'm trying to get you to do. It's to say ok I know I can do the same behavior five different times, but I might have very different reasons for why I do it.**
(Extended Team-Teaching Project, Teaching ESL, Stimulated Recall)

Dialogic Mediation

Some of our novice teachers, especially those with some prior teaching experience, do attempt to take up a more *teaching as dialogic mediational stance* in the very first pillar course, Teaching ESL. We can see this emerge particularly when, as in the following episode, two team members work together to TEACH OFF STUDENTS contributions and/or questions. During their *actual teach* lesson on the use of hedging and boosting in academic writing, Natalie assists Qing as the latter attempts to respond to a learner's (S1) query about the semantic difference between 'clear' and 'rather clear.' Instead of answering the learner's question directly, Natalie offers Qing a model sentence with the word 'clear' and allows Qing to articulate how she might interpret the meaning of this sentence. Their exchange continues as they engage in dialogue in front of the learners, using each other as resources to make explicit how a writer might interpret the difference between 'clear' and 'rather clear.' Thus, they collectively offer no 'right or wrong' answer in their exchanges; instead, their dialogic interaction makes their reasoning visible, and opens up a space that allows the learner to speculate, and later confirm, that the semantic meaning of 'rather' actually decreases the possibility of something happening.

Excerpt 7

QING: "Strong possibility", "good possibility", "slight possibility" and "little possibility". So here are the answers ((pointing to the slide)). And you may have your own opinions, but I think, most people may agree with this-

> S1: I, I need a, **what is the difference between "clear" and "rather clear", can you give me an example?**
> NATALIE: Ok, uhm.
> S1: Maybe it's just an odd question-
> NATALIE: No, it's not an odd question. (.) **"Clear" and "rather clear". So if I were to say 'it is clear that it is going to rain today'. What do you think I mean? ((directed at Qing))**
> QING: **I'm thinking 100% that it will rain today. If "It's rather clear that is going to rain today", there is also some possibility that it will not rain.** It is very clear, but some people may think it will not rain.
> NATALIE: Yeah, **it's like saying it's mostly true, like it's pretty true,** it's just a li:ttle bit of a (qualifier).
> QING: Yes, it's similar to, 'it's true that blah, blah, blah'. Or 'it's pretty true blah, blah, blah'-
> S1: **so what is (.) if if I add "rather" here, so it means that I decrease the possibility of () frequency?**
> QING: **Yes, it can weaken your statement.**
> S1: If, so if I add "rather" before the possible, so, "it's possible that", and "it's rather possible that". **"It's rather possible that" will be less possible** ((laughter)).
> (Extended Team-Teaching Project, Teaching ESL, Actual Teach)

Other teams are able to garner increased student participation and engagement by asking open-ended questions, which encourage learners to explain or expand upon their ideas, during large group discussions. As they lead a preparatory activity for the Problem-Solution Essay assignment, two team members (Layla & Zeina) work together to support two learners (S1 & S3) as they attempt to articulate both the effectiveness and shortcomings of potential solutions to the 'problem' they have been assigned: mass shootings. They accomplish this by initially asking open-ended questions (*What do you think?* and *Why*) and then by pushing learners to offer more reasoned explanations and to consider the potential shortcomings of each solution *you have to consider every point* and *what is the shortcoming?*. Their dialogic, open-ended stance throughout the *actual teach* creates a safe space for learners to reason through their ideas as they engage in exchanges with each other.

Excerpt 8

> LAYLA: **Do you think it's really the most effective? the least (.) shortcoming do you think? Or is it doable?** (2.0) You can decide. You can say no. Yes, it's your opinion. What do you think?
> ZEINA: So if you- if you're saying one, why? why?
> S1: One as the possibility of not only solving this issue, but the overarching issue of mass shooting as a whole. Two (.) prevents um prev- I know. I wanna find the best one out ().

S3: But this like () we're like early working on is this like like a- like a () team.

ZEINA: One?

S3: Yeah, like the one. It's not like a specific point like kind of law should be. It's like killing is bad, something like that.

S1: **Wait. we're providing essentially guidance. One. Mental health patients should not get it [a gun]. Second. There should be safety measures** such as if you do buy a gun, there should be certain place, where you can () store your gun. Such as not in reach of kids. Others. Colleges should be separated from guns as a whole. **Third. You should not buy ammunitions from internet** such as the bump stock or um even not buying ammunitions.

ZEINA: So. So for our class today I think yeah she she's kind of right because it's kind of a little bit broad like if you're one, two, go to the shortcomings. You have to consider every point.

S1: There's only one shortcoming. [It is the marked one.

S3: Because you can't stop in the middle of a solution or the like the list of- you pretty much have to saying the summary not like just a specific solution.

S1: So. Ok. [().

LAYLA: **What is the shortcoming?**] What is the shortcoming for solution one?

S1: Um **political** ().

LAYLA: Ok. **Politically**. It's not really- we don't really have control over this. Right? What about solution two? What's it drawback?

S3: **Because we're like- espec- especially on top, we (have) social study because better government, it's not allotting like, money to (search for) background checks.** So why do people with like, mental disability () like local gun store because they don't have to like give specific background of their instead of governmental. They say oh it's like a privacy issue and they just go to local store and they just buy the gun with like, id card like just avoiding just like, some (.) thing like um they searched on internet. And it seems they just have to sign the document like the responsibility thing. And they just give them their id and they just buy the gun. And I think it's a big problem.

(Extended Team-Teaching Project, Teaching ESL, Actual Teach)

In this final example, a different team, also working with the Problem-Solution Essay assignment, wrap up their *actual teach* lesson by highlighting the approach of *working backwards from solutions to the problem*. In Excerpt 9, Ethan asks learners if they see value in the *working backwards* approach they have just experienced, acknowledges learners' contributions, and uses INSTRUCTIONAL

PARAPHRASING to link learners' ideas to the focus of the current lesson as well as to the final writing assignment for the course.

Excerpt 9

ETHAN: **So, for today's experience, what do you think are some benefits of beginning with the solution or working backwards through a problem? What were some benefits of this process?**

S1: **Well, one of the benefits is you really, like, you don't miss anything, I guess you could say.** Like, you don't miss a step, I guess.

ETHAN: Okay,

S1: **like the solution, I guess.**

ETHAN: Okay. **How?**

S1: Well, if you think about it, like the earlier example, the guy gave us the tools.

If you read it in one forward fashion, you probably would miss the second "the". **But if you read it backwards, it would, you would notice the two "the"s.**

ETHAN: **Okay, so did you guys feel that working backwards and associating the problem made you realize certain things along the way that you wouldn't ordinarily find?** Do you find that to be true in this?

S2: **I think it makes a problem more specific.** So, if you generally look at this solution, you only focus on the homeless people. Perhaps () you'll get more specific problems and stuff.

ETHAN: Okay.

S2: **And also, like, I feel I would tend to simplify a complicated question.** Like, they're all pretty complicated or hard to solve. And it's easy for us just feel like, Oh, we have a solution. And the solution can help solve the problem. But it's not the case for most of the time, we think from the solution, we'll find out that this specific solution might be pretty partial, and only one side of the problem and you kind of see another side, maybe?

ETHAN: **Okay, perfect, perfect. So, this relates to the final assignment perfectly.** So, the topics you guys end up deciding on will all be complex to a certain degree. If it's too simple, it probably won't pass the process of a topic proposal on stuff? So, I want you to choose relatively complex problems, relatively broad. These are all pretty good examples, um, and then when you're writing your paper, you really want to think about what are the complex different solutions that might solve this problem.

(Extended Team-Teaching Project, Teaching ESL, Actual Teach)

Responsive Mediation in Tutoring

The Tutoring Internship continues to push teachers to reconceptualize their notions about language teaching. In this course, changes in understanding are contextualized in a setting that requires direct contact with learners in a formal, if minimalist, instructional setting, and the teaching experiences are less directly mediated by the teacher educator. While we cannot expect that our novice teachers have completely let go of the lingering concept that teaching means being expected to know the 'right' answer to every question, they are perhaps more able—because of their experience in the first pillar course, with its Extended Team Teaching Project and exposure to several pedagogical concepts—to recognize the importance of collaborative dialogue and *responsive mediation*, especially when the context is stripped down to a one-on-one encounter, as it is in a tutoring session. Thus, tutors are pushed, both through specific mediation and through the very parameters of the setting that they are working in, to see the importance of learning to listen, question, probe, and build a trusting relationship with their learners, all the while co-constructing and maintaining mutual understandings between themselves, their tutee, and the text. It is during the tutoring sessions that novice teachers begin to understand first-hand the central importance of being agents in the reasoning and enactment of their teaching. Fen wrote, when reflecting on the semester's experience:

> **Excerpt 10**
>
> **I would feel anxious in my first several sessions with them because I was not sure about the "right" answers. But later I realized that it was not appropriate for me to give answers. What I should do was to use guidance to push them to think, and this task was not that hard for me.** ... After that time, **I began to ask more questions about their thoughts and reflections on her writing process and encouraged them to speak more in our tutoring meetings.** In this way I could know their expectations, their desires and how I could help them to achieve their goals. **During this process I also gained more confidence, because I realized I did not need to give them the "right" answers towards every question.**
>
> (Fen, Tutoring Internship, Final Paper)

This shift in how tutors conceptualize tutoring is continuously, though indirectly, mediated by the Tutoring Supervisor, who does not observe the tutoring sessions in person but engages in *responsive mediation* using two channels of communication: written responses to the tutors' regular reflective posts (which must be written and submitted within 48 hours of the tutoring session) and formal instruction and discussion in the weekly Tutoring Internship class meetings. Aligned with praxis-oriented pedagogy, the written mediation, which appears within 24 hours of a post being submitted, is responsive to each tutor's immediate experience with a particular tutee. In the following excerpt, from the second week of tutoring, we see that the Tutoring Supervisor's response to Aisha's reflective post serves an explicit reminder of information that had already been discussed in the weekly seminar class, and as an encouragement to draw upon, but not be limited to, previous experience. The Supervisor reiterates how the context of the Tutoring Internship differs somewhat from that of the undergraduate Writing Center, where Aisha previously worked as a tutor for several semesters. A major goal of the Tutoring Internship is for the novice tutors to experience a mediational space for both writing-focused dialogue, in which tutor and tutee examine texts, think about writing, and talk about textual specifics and instructional practice, in which tutors select and adapt teaching strategies and engage in regular reflection on their choices. In this context, tutors develop instructional relationships with their tutees over the 12 weeks of interaction which are, in some ways, echoes of the instructional relationships they themselves have with the Internship Supervisor. Indeed, the Internship class requires the tutors in turn to create mediational spaces for their tutees that enable the work of *reasoned teaching* to be productive and purposeful:

Excerpt 11

> It sounds like you will have some good challenges with this tutee: she seems confident and already very proficient. But of course as a tutoring internship **the purpose of working with actual students is also to give YOU the experience of learning how to make good choices. I'm glad that you agree it is NOT your job to 'write it for her'—I think this will be something you can work on for the whole semester: holding back and not taking charge of the session. You do not, in fact, "know how your tutees think" because you don't know them yet.** This is not drop-in tutoring, where you might meet a novice writer once and you want to give him/her the best possible feedback. This is a long-term tutoring relationship and **it's crucial for you to BRING your knowledge and your enthusiasm and also to LISTEN and ASK about your tutee's knowledge and enthusiasm! So I'm glad you reverted to questions!** She has lots to say, if she is really so proficient, and you will learn even more about novice writers if you use follow-up questions and let HER choose what to talk about sometimes. **I truly appreciate your enthusiastic and eager attitude. Your tutees will get a lot from**

you. But remember that we also want you to get a lot from them—what you learn from your tutees will stay with you for your whole career!

(Supervisor, Tutoring Internship, Session 2 Response)

Strategic Use of Questions

An important instructional practice that helps novice teachers take on a *teaching as dialogic mediation instructional stance* during tutoring sessions is learning how to use questions strategically. This topic is introduced during one of the early class meetings and is repeatedly reinforced by the Tutoring Supervisor's *responsive mediation*, but for some teachers the subtlety of what distinguishes a strategic and effective question from a 'vague' one is an ongoing challenge. By comparing two posts written by the same tutor working with the same tutee, from sessions that occur several weeks apart, we can see how Chen's understanding of, and use of, questions to engage her tutee change from early in the semester (Session 2) to late in the semester (Session 13):

Excerpt 12

I asked my tutee how many points he wanted to say and what were they. He said at "the first point is freedom is important and the second is I have different ideas from dictionary definition". **Then I asked him cut off every unrelated and unimportant sentence. Next, I polished his language such as using conjunctions to connect sentences, summarizing his meaning with less words etc.**

(Chen, Tutoring Internship, Session 2 Post)

In this early tutoring session, Chen is relatively directive in her approach and seems to adopt the goal of making the tutee's text *better* by asking a question with a simple numerical answer and then following it up with directives. Indeed, she even takes over the authorial voice to *polish* the tutee's language. Some weeks later, in Session 13, she demonstrates a more nuanced and responsive use of questions in her work with the same tutee:

Excerpt 13

First, I asked my tutee to introduce his assignment (a kind of retelling). He made a very detailed introduction, but it was less logical, I think. So, **I asked him "how did you organize it"**. He seemed a little confused and gave an answer which is very similar to the previous one. **I think my instruction is not clear enough. So, I change a way to ask: "what is the main point of your assignment? Tell is just like the retelling we made before. For example, I can see you** briefly introduce the topic and argue for one solution." Then he knew what I mean. He made a very clear and concise summary about his assignment and meanwhile, I know he read the requirements for this assignment very carefully.

(Chen, Tutoring Internship, Session 13 Post)

Another tutor, Yan, writing at the end of the semester, recognizes that to ask effective questions means recognizing both the reader's and writer's perspectives. As she notes in her final paper, this recognition fostered her own development in *asking questions more effectively*:

Excerpt 14

Asking effective questions is a strategy which is not so easy to get. After all the tutoring sessions, I could see I got some improvement on it but it's still not enough. **It requires tutors to think both from a writer's perspective and from a reader's perspective. Why didn't the writer think about what the reader would like to know? ... I can feel that the questions I asked were becoming more and more effective through the semester. At the very beginning, I could only ask "why do you think so", or "what else".** At the last several sessions, I could lead them to think backward to get what they really want to write when they didn't have ideas.... [A]s the most important part, **asking questions more effectively is what I hope to continue developing.** Sometimes tutees still didn't go towards where I wanted them to go, which requires me to think more from tutees' perspectives.

(Yan, Tutoring Internship, Final Paper)

Instructional Choices

As tutors recount their experiences with their tutees, they begin to articulate their reasoning about particular instructional choices and why those choices support tutees as they talk about and think through their writing. In this exchange, Ana describes how she asked her tutee to talk through a class activity done in preparation for the upcoming compare and contrast essay by recounting similarities and differences between two assigned readings. As the tutee does this, he names the very *connectors* that are *important for comparing and contrasting*:

Excerpt 15

Afterwards, we passed on to his new assignment: compare and contrast essay. He showed me an activity they did in class in which they were given two articles telling the same story differently and then asked to complete a similarities and differences chart. He said that when he was given the similarities and differences sheet **he thought it was going to be really difficult but when he started reading the articles, the charts made sense.** I asked him to tell me a bit about the two articles and to choose two similarities and two differences to share with me. During his explanation he even used connectors such as while, on the one hand, on the other hand. I drew his attention to them and we talked about their importance for comparing and contrasting.

(Ana, Tutoring Internship Session 2 Post)

In her response, the Tutoring Supervisor both expresses support for the tutor's choices in the session and labels the specific actions the tutor took (listen, respond, showed interest, and reinforced student understanding), a response that helps the tutor conceptualize these simple but effective strategies as central to the dialogic, student-oriented, responsive, and interactional nature of the tutoring sessions:

Excerpt 16

Ana, in this session **you listened to the student carefully, tried to respond helpfully and productively to his concerns, took a personal interest in his connection to the material used in the lesson, and successfully (I think & hope!) helped him to see that through asking, reflecting, participating and trying hard, he will continue to grow as an academic thinker and writer.** He does sound like a hardworking and serious student!

(Supervisor, Tutoring Internship, Session 2 Response)

As tutors progress through the Tutoring Internship, they often recognize changes in their interactional and interpersonal relationship with their tutees. As we hear from Qing, often this repositioning entails a shift from being perceived as *finishing their drafts* to *just talking about our thinking and confusions*. The Tutoring Supervisor names this repositioning as functioning as a *sounding board* and *advisor* in the interaction, and that her tutees have learned from her the *power of talking through ideas*:

Excerpt 17

One thing I am appreciated is that both two of my tutees don't regard me as a person to finish their drafts, **most of the time we just talked about our thinking and confusions.**

(Qing, Tutoring Internship, Session 10 Post)

> Qing, **I completely agree that it's great to hear that your tutee see you as a 'sounding board' and advisor rather than just as someone to 'finish' their work for them!** That shows that they have learned (from you) the power of talking through ideas, using discussion as a kind of brainstorming (in the early stage) and revision (in the later stages) for writing.
>
> (Supervisor, Tutoring Internship, Session 10 Response)

Additionally, working as a writing tutor, by its very nature, places tutors in a somewhat tenuous position in that they are not the ESL writing instructor, who ultimately has the final say on the content and quality of these tutees' written work. Instead, the focus of the tutoring work is to ensure that the tutee fully understands the ESL instructor's expectations and is cognizant of the parameters of the particular writing assignment. Qing realizes that discrepancies between her tutoring advice and the instructor's expectations can sometimes occur, but by deferring to the ESL instructor, she is reminded of an important fact about writing instruction: that writers are getting feedback and suggestions from multiple sources:

> **Excerpt 18**
>
> Furthermore, sometimes during the tutoring, **I realized that the contents I talked about have overlaps with what her teacher said in her class, and our requirements can be different.** For example, I said introduction part can be 10% of the whole essay, in which means around 150-200 words here. But Yao said her teacher asked them to write 200-300 words for the introduction. When such things happened, **I always respected her teacher's and explained to Yao why we have different requirements.** I think her teacher's requirement will more focus on the targeted assignment, in which will be more appropriate to Yao's assignment and **I am also still a novice tutor who need listen to more others suggestions. This reminds me that [my tutee is] receiving more than one teaching input on each of her assignment, and I should try to be correspondence with what she received in class and also keep my own ideas in the meanwhile.**
>
> (Qing, Tutoring Internship Session 10 Post)

Reinforced by the Tutoring Supervisor's response, Qing has created an intentional goal for herself in her tutoring sessions, namely, recognizing and managing varied interpretations and expectations, while she remains mindful of aligning her tutoring advice with the ESL instructor's expectations:

Excerpt 19

And of course this is exactly what we WANT them to learn from the tutoring sessions. It can be a bit challenging to fit in all the varieties of interpretations: yes you can include your own opinion; no you must write only about expert opinions; yes you need to have three solutions; no you can choose two or three or four solutions, etc And **I think you have managed to negotiate pretty well in that maze of differences!** In the end, it is the classroom instructor who has the final authority, so all questions can end up there if necessary. It's also good to hear that you used your experience with another tutee to shape your activity with this tutee.

(Supervisor, Tutoring Internship, Session 10 Response)

At the conclusion of the Tutoring Internship, tutors not only have become comfortable with a more dialogic, student-oriented instructional stance, they also have come to appreciate the importance of building rapport with their learners as people and not only as writers: through theoretical discussion and concrete material activity, they recognize the personal and pedagogical value of conceptualizing the activity of tutoring/teaching as responsive engagement. This shift, from conceptualizing tutoring/teaching as being in a position where one is expected to provide right answers, to understanding that tutoring/teaching is in fact the creation of a mediational space for writers to talk about, and think through, the activity of writing is abundantly evident in Aisha's final reflection paper:

Excerpt 20

I became more understanding than I already am, and **I found myself finding the importance and value of talking to a tutee as a person; knowing where they came from, what type of environment they grew up in, and their views on writing and so much more.** It is interesting because Dr. Verity has mentioned this various time, reflecting how important it is. **Let them talk. Give them the avenues to talk.** That is the job of the tutor, and while it may be very frustrating doing this, we should never give up because truly it can reveal you to a different side of your tutee that may help you understand them and know the teaching method and learning style that suits them the best. **Tutoring is more than just the act of tutoring – it is expanding your bandwidth on the different ways of tutoring that can only be acquired by having experience tutoring all kinds of different people from all over the world who have different needs and who struggle with different things.**

(Aisha, Tutoring Internship, Final Paper)

Learning to Think Like a Teacher

Novice teachers' reconceptualization of language teaching is often solidified during the Teaching Practicum. Over a 15-week period, they are confronted with daily opportunities to plan and enact lessons with real learners, learners they come to see as unique individuals with specific instructional needs. Yet, at the start of the Teaching Practicum, they often experience the lingering effect of their long 'apprenticeship of observation' (Lortie, 1975) and find themselves struggling with how to position themselves as teachers, reverting back to a more comfortable teacher-fronted instructional stance. Fen spent time imagining her new teaching context and envisioned creating a *community of learners* but her ideal of a student-centered classroom faded away as she found herself enacting what she had experienced as a language learner. Fen writes:

> **Excerpt 21**
>
> However, in the first week of my practicum teaching, **I realized that the real teaching context is much more complex than the imagined community of learners I had envisioned. I thought I was prepared with my many strengths and my creativity, but the truth was that I could barely find my position and authority in the classroom. And when I first had a change to lead an activity, I made it more like a lecture which involved a mass majority of teacher talking time.**
>
> (Fen, Teaching Practicum, Final Paper)

The role of the mentor teacher throughout the Teaching Practicum is critical in enabling novice teachers to shift their conception of language teaching to be more reasoned, deliberate, dialogic, and student-oriented. As such, the relationship between the mentor and the novice teacher is at the heart of the learning process, a relationship that involves trust and develops gradually over time through standing weekly planning meetings, impromptu and sometimes planned preparation and debriefing meetings before and after each class, ongoing email communication, and of course, phone calls and texts. Mentor teachers are typically experienced teachers who model a *teaching as dialogic mediation instructional stance* and are skilled at making their reasoning accessible to novice teachers, but they also play a key role in supporting, both emotionally and professionally, their developing confidence as they reflect on and critically analyze their emerging conception of language teaching. Fen describes her mentor teacher as enabling her to transform her professional identity through his mentoring style. She writes:

> **Excerpt 22**
>
> **As for transformation of my professional identity, the pedagogical and emotional support from my mentor teacher played a**

crucial role. During the whole teaching experience with Adam, **my legitimacy, agency and voice as a teacher are demonstrated by my teaching practice thanks to his supportive, sensible and considerate mentoring style.**

(Fen, Teaching Practicum, Final Paper)

She recognizes that the mentor teacher's guiding questions and both the modeling and *remodeling* of her activity designs encouraged her to think through her instructional choices, orient to how the learners might experience her instructional activities, and articulate what she expected the learners to learn as a result. As is clear below, Fen is becoming future-oriented, recognizing that what she is experiencing is preparing her to make appropriate instructional choices in whatever instructional context she finds herself in the future.

Excerpt 23

Every time I had ideas about an activity, he facilitated my thinking about teaching with guiding questions such as "What would be the focus of her activity? What do you want the students to do in each step, and what do he expect them to learn from it?" And in these discussions of activity design, he often used his experience to model the class with me and drove me to think about every detail of activity design. In this way, I did not only learn to prepare one specific lesson, **but I had perceptions of how different choices of activity details could work differently in various contexts.** After the classes that I participated, **he often did a remodeling with me to guide me reflect on my practice and provided me with suggestions on future teaching, which enhanced my ability to reflect on and analyze critically about my teaching.**

(Fen, Teaching Practicum, Final Paper)

The Practicum Supervisor is the other linchpin in mediating and reinforcing novice teachers' reconceptualization of language teaching. This is accomplished through engagement in *responsive mediation* via weekly reflective teaching journals, practicum meetings, and post-observation discussion of multiple novice teacher-led lessons. Novice teachers need to be worked gradually into their roles as teachers, often feeling anxious about being an outsider when they first enter their practicum placement:

Excerpt 24

I also found myself challenged by the questions raised by my mentor teacher during the class, and I felt that I was not confident in providing examples for students' assignments. **I did not feel like a teacher or**

> even a teaching assistant, in my teaching journal I called myself an "outsider student" during that period.
>
> (Fen, Teaching Practicum, Final Paper)

Our novice teachers are still MA TESL students themselves enrolled in graduate classes at the same time they complete their practicum, yet in the Teaching Practicum classroom, they are teachers. This creates a very real tension for them as they sense their shifting identity yet lack clarity as to who they are. It is particularly important at the beginning of the semester for the mentor teacher and Practicum Supervisor to provide *responsive mediation* emotionally and cognitively for novice teachers because they are more likely to feel discouraged by many aspects of their teaching as they struggle with who they are as teachers. When Fen expresses disappointment at being unable to garner learner participation during an initial lesson, the Practicum Supervisor encourages her to use the cognitive/emotional dissonance she experienced as a space for learning about her teaching. In this case, her emotional response might be an indication that something about the activity design, choice of materials, and even her instructional language might need to be reconsidered:

> **Excerpt 25**
>
> At that time my emotions were kind of complicated. **I felt regretful that I did not guide them better, I felt disappointed about myself, and I felt really sorry that I did not help Adam more when he was not in good condition.** Then I left my seat and sat in the chair in the front of the classroom behind the desk, and I encouraged the first two groups to share their ideas. **I remembered they still have more to share. They reported their ideas well and I kind of felt better.**
>
> (Fen, Teaching Practicum, Journal 5)

> I can understand your disappointment with their participation, and this is also an indicator that **the activity may need a redesign so that all students can complete it successfully. So allow that moment of cognitive emotional dissonance to be your teacher, your guide, and think about how you might revise the activity and your materials choice for another time.**
>
> (Supervisor, Teaching Practicum, Journal 5 Response)

By taking a *teaching as dialogic mediation instructional stance* in her response, the Practicum Supervisor opens the door for the novice teacher to see her moment of struggle as an invitation to reimagine her teaching rather than something she had not done well.

Ultimately, by the time they reach the end of the Teaching Practicum, our novice teachers have established their own voice, they have learned to *think like a teacher* and recognize the value of *constantly revaluating and reevaluating* their own teaching and student learning. Hannah recalls her initial identity struggle in the practicum classroom but has come to realize that she does, in fact, belong in the classroom and belong as a teacher capable of making appropriate instructional choices for her students and recognizing the socially situated nature of learning to teach:

Excerpt 26

Overall, the value of this semester has been in **learning to think like a teacher—that is to say, constantly evaluating and reevaluating my own work and how my students are responding to it.** From the first day, not knowing where to sit, to this last week, giving feedback on final paper presentations, **I have grown in my sense of belonging in the classroom, thanks to the support and constructive critique of observers, as well as my own deciphering of how to more effectively think about writing and communicate my understanding to novice writers.** Looking ahead, I hope to continue this process, **learning from my students, other experienced teachers, and making use of reflection to stimulate ongoing development.**

(Hannah, Teaching Practicum, Final Paper)

In response to Hannah's realization of her own ability to support her students' learning about how to write, the Practicum Supervisor reiterates that facilitating student learning *is at the heart of teaching* and by orienting to the learners, she will continue to *think differently about your teaching*:

Excerpt 27

This is an important realization and one that is at the heart of teaching—**how to facilitate student learning. You are starting to think beyond teaching content to teaching students particular content. When you put the students first, you will think differently about your teaching.**

(Supervisor, Teaching Practicum, Final Paper Response)

In the following exchange with the Practicum Supervisor, Fen comes to the same realization, that facilitating learning is *at the heart of teaching*. She looks back at her prior *lecture-based* teaching style and is now able recognize her *transformation* to a teacher who *endeavors to facilitate students' learning....* Emphatically acknowledging what the Practicum Supervisor describes as *transferrable*

194 Outcomes, Impact, Opportunities

pedagogical knowledge, she praises the qualities of this teacher and encourages her to bring these qualities and her reorientation to language teaching into her future teaching contexts:

> **Excerpt 28**
>
> When I reviewed the lessons that I did in my previous classes, I noticed that my teaching was lecture-based and there was a large portion of teacher talking time. I thought that was my teaching style before although I never appreciated that style, **but now I have become a teacher who endeavors to facilitate students' learning by helping them seek for answers with their own approaches or perspectives. I feel very satisfied with this transformation, and thank the Teaching Practicum class for making it happen!**
>
> (Fen, Teaching Practicum, Final Reflection)
>
> Yes!! **And you have 'transferrable' pedagogical knowledge now, and you may just have to add the content knowledge depending on what you have to teach in the future.** ... You are thoughtful, insightful, and always introspective—and together, those qualities have led to your incredible growth and development. **I know you will continue to push yourself as you move into your career and that you will touch the lives of your students in meaningful ways!**
>
> (Supervisor, Teaching Practicum, Final Paper Response)

Learning to teach is a process filled with emotions, and this novice teacher's positive response to the *transformation* she has experienced through the *responsive mediation* of her mentor teacher and Practicum Supervisor can lead to changes in how novice teachers conceptualize what it means to teach.

Instructional Stance

During the Teaching Practicum, the third pillar course and typically the culminating experience of the MA TESL program, our novice teachers typically demonstrate how adept they have become at enacting a *teaching as dialogic mediation instructional stance*. In the following two excerpts, Gan is teaching the rhetorical devices Ethos, Pathos, Logos in the first-year academic writing class. He has asked his learners to listen to and analyze a speech by President Obama. In Excerpt 29, Gan TEACHES OFF HIS STUDENTS as he uses INSTRUCTIONAL PARAPHRASING to confirm their responses as well as encourage them to dig deeper for examples of these rhetorical devices. He accomplishes this by CREATING PREDICTABILITY, explicitly offering a model for how to find examples of these rhetorical devices. Both learners, S1 and S2, take up his model and provide very specific explanations of how the example they found represents Pathos. We see Gan modeling the academic labels he has just taught the class to encourage them to use these terms in their responses:

Excerpt 29

GAN: O:h yup, "can be canceled", cool, **so that can be an Ethos, yeah.**
S1: **And in the very same paragraph, he uses (renowned) names** like (David Cameron), Obama, and adds (mentions) to the students (is) associated with those big names, **which adds to the credibility of what he's talking about.**
GAN: **Yeah, that's also Ethos because Obama is a powerful person and he kind of agree with the solution so that can be an Ethos here, right, so, cool.** So, we have abundant evidence for Ethos, so can you find some other evidence for Pathos? (2.0) I think it's, **it's a little bit hard to find evidence for Pathos, right, so did you find some?**
S2: **Yeah, on the first page, the fifth paragraph, the last sentence, ((S2 reads line))** (8.0)
GAN: **Yes, trying to put that problem on the audience, so audience should think of this problem, right, so it is not that far, it is close to your life, right?**
S1: **Yeah, I think () Pathos on the second page, second to last paragraph**, he talks about () so like, stuff like that really appeals to the emotion of the audience because everyone shares a level of emotion with children and where they go, and when you associate, when you talk about offenders (2.0) the emotions of the audience, **I think that's a very good example of Pathos.**
GAN: **Yeah, exactly, that can be a Pathos here, because there are many evidence the presenter can find, right,** but why the presenter choose the children as an example, because he can appeal to many person's emotion here, right, because there are many adults in the audience here, so you can see that it can appeal to the emotions, right, uh, another thought?

(Gan, Teaching Practicum, Digital-Recording #3, 4/3/2018 – Week 12)

Later in the same lesson, Gan expands upon this activity (identifying rhetorical devices) by assisting S2, who is attempting to recognize an instance of Logos in the text of a TED Talk. At first, S2 doesn't see any examples of Logos, and Gan accepts his response. Rather than pushing S2 for a better response, Gan opens up the question to ask if anyone else sees an example of Logos, which gives S2 a chance to offer a concrete example. This enables S1 to make sense of the concept of Logos, and he then is able to find another example of Logos in the text. Gan's instructional decision to allow S1 to listen to and learn through the contributions of classmates is another example of TEACHING OFF, NOT AT, HIS STUDENTS:

Excerpt 30

> GAN: Yeah, he uses graphic aids to show the ideas, right, that can be Ethos, okay, so let's move on to talking about what is the Logos evidence in this TED Talk? (.) **Can I have some other volunteers to talk about this? (3.0) (), can you give us some evidence from this TED Talk? The Logos one?**
> S1: **I don't really see the logos.**
> GAN: **You didn't find Logos, right? So does anyone find Logos here?**
> S2: **Um they introduce the idea that () is that the author or the presenter give any statements or definition of terms.**
> GAN: **It can be both, right? So, yup, that can be Logos here**, so did you find some other evidence? **Uh, (S1), did you find some evidence for logos?**
> S1: Uh (3.0) **Every statistic used.**
> GAN: **Yeah, statistics can be Logos here, right?** But it also can be Ethos, like some other folks have talk about, right? So, like, when I talk with (), there are some overlapping here between Logos and Ethos because both of them have the statistics...
>
> (Gan, Teaching Practicum, Digital-Recording #3, 4/3/2018 - Week 12)

Of course, not all novice teachers are equally able to display a dialogic instructional stance at all stages of the Teaching Practicum. Especially in the early weeks of this pillar course, many still need explicit mediation, as we see in Excerpt 31. In this episode, the *responsive mediation* offered in-the-moment by the mentor teacher guides Qiao's instructional language, enabling her to formulate questions that will facilitate greater learner participation in the large group discussion:

Excerpt 31

> QIAO: **Okay, anyone from article two read the problem summary for us?**
> TIMOTHY: **Oh, no, they don't have to read it, they can just talk about it (.) (2.0) ((Timothy walks to front of room, saying a few words in private to Qiao and scrolling down on the document on the screen))**
> QIAO: **Yeah, so you know what is the solution here, so how do you come up with the problem?** (.) (2.0)

S1: Come up with the solution or the problem?
QIAO: Problem (.) (1.0) So you know like what's the topic and you can think about what's the causes, right? **You know the solution but how can you combine the solution with the problem ()?** (18.0)
TIMOTHY: **Could you repeat the question?**
QIAO: So, um, if you know what is the solution, so, um, how can you think about how you can () into a problem, **so what's the steps for you to imagine what's the problem (.) yeah (.) so, any ideas?**
S1: **I think basically you have to think about what the solution is trying to solve, so basically ()**
QIAO: T1: **Yeah, (so what elements about the solution you tried to solve)?**

        (Qiao, Teaching Practicum, Digital-Recording #1, Week 7)

Later in the semester, however, during the final weeks of the Teaching Practicum, Qiao is about to lead the class in a debate, the goal of which is to help learners understand why they have to provide support for the solutions they propose in their Problem-Solution Essay. Having them participate in a debate is an interactive, engaging way for them to form and present arguments. Unlike in the previous excerpt from earlier in the semester, Qiao is now able, after a few restarts, to formulate questions that help to ORIENT the learners to the lesson. As the discussion continues, she becomes more comfortable asking questions that facilitate learning, demonstrating that she is now much more able to TEACH OFF HER STUDENTS, something she was unable to do earlier in the Teaching Practicum:

Excerpt 32

QIAO: So before we start, I have a question for you, what is a debate? What is debate, do you think what is? (2.0) Can anyone have a definition about debate, (think about what does it mean)? (16.0) **What is debate?**
S1: **It's like formal argument**
QIAO: **Formal argument?**
S1: **Each side kind of opposes their own viewpoint on each other ()**
QIAO: **That's true, anyone else?** (5.0)
S2: **It's arguing () make the person () different viewpoints and let him (come to the same side as yours)**
QIAO: So debate in, so debate in dictionary definition will be two, "the discussion between two opposition", and one, one the other definition will be, "() by words or argument", so the key word for debate will be "argument" or "discussion" ((S enters the room and

T1 shows her where to sit))...**so do you know why should we debate? Can you think about any benefits of debating?** (.)

S3: **Understanding the opposing people's viewpoints, because normally, uh, normally when you take a stance and argue something you don't fully understand why the other person is also arguing their points, so understand and, like, start a conversation**

QIAO: **Yeah, understanding what your opponents are saying and you need to walk a mile into someone's shoes**

S3: Yeah

QIAO: **So, do you think it also can translate into real life skills, how to get along with people?** (.) anything (that you use) () the debate (that is the benefit of debating)?

S4: **We learn how to convince people**

QIAO: **How to convince people, yeah** (.)

S5: **And how not to offend people**

QIAO: **How not to offend people? Okay, can you explain that a little more?**

S5: Uh, when you're debating, **you have to be careful with your own words, take the other person's () backgrounds into account, not using offending words**

QIAO: **Hm-hm, that's a really good point, thank you.**

(Qiao, Teaching Practicum, Digital-Recording #3, Week 12)

Because the majority of our Teaching Practicum teachers are placed in the first-year academic writing course for L2 learners, which has as its final writing assignment the Problem-Solution Essay, conducting an oral debate in class is a common instructional choice. In the following excerpt, Ping has just completed leading such a debate and is now asking the class to reflect on what they learned through the process of preparing for and participating in the debate. As Ping listens to their ideas, she uses INSTRUCTIONAL PARAPHRASING to confirm their contributions and then connects what they say they have learned directly to the purpose of the Problem-Solution Essay:

Excerpt 33

PING: ...so, um, **we need to move on to the reflection part**, so I will choose one group, maybe group six (.)

S1: so, uh, **basically we learned () skills, and how we should be having () skills, and how we should be supporting our viewpoint by evidence,** you know, () prove that your point is right, and also like if you point out any mistakes ((cell phone ringer sounds, obscuring voice)) and have any disagreements, you can always point it out and make a feasible statement to show how you're right and the other person is not, even though that

PING: Okay, **so you mean supporting enough evidence is very important in a debate.**
S1: **Yeah, and valid evidence**
PING: Okay, so, **how can you relate this debate to the problem-solution essay?**
S2: So, like, **in the argument section, you know like how we're going to compare our solutions and also compare feasibility, you can use evidence (or like) how these solutions have been implemented (), and has it really impacted in a positive way, and if it has, you can compare and make a conclusion on which one's better** () (2.0)
PING: **So you mean () to [compare]?**
S2: [Yeah, to compare] with them the examples, yeah.
PING: **Very good**, examples, so how about group three, where is group three?
(Ping, Teaching Practicum, Digital-Recording #3, Week 13)

Each novice teacher has a slightly different journey through the three pillar courses and through the MA TESL program. Each person will experience, and demonstrate, changes in their conceptualization of teaching in different ways and at different times in their trajectory. The data presented in this chapter provide strong illustrative evidence for our claim that transformation is happening at every stage, and can be observed, documented, and reflected upon because of the mediational spaces that we create for it to occur. Over time and through active engagement, novice teachers can understand, enact, and adapt their abilities to TEACH OFF NOT AT their students.

Conclusion

As we have noted throughout, the mediational spaces that we construct for our novice teachers are infused with the notion of praxis-oriented pedagogy and our novice teachers experience what that means, directly, through the three pillar courses. In this chapter, we offer evidence, captured through our novice teachers' voices and our engagement in responsive mediation, that characterizes their shifting conceptions of language teaching as they move through the three pillar courses. We hear them shifting toward conceptualizing teaching as reasoned, deliberate, and student-oriented, and that they understand the pedagogical value of and can enact a *teaching as dialogic mediation instructional stance*. This final excerpt best encapsulates the dramatic reorientation of Leo's conceptions of language teaching that now inhabit his stated teaching philosophy:

Excerpt 34

I do not see language as a mere system of rules and constraints that learners have to memorize and by which they are to abide. Rather, **I view** language as social practice; as a means to enable individuals to 'get things done' and gain membership into the communities to which they aspire to belong. Thus, before I teach students, I find it imperative to find out what their needs, learning styles, and purposes are so I can best align my practice with the specific demands of the classroom. **This whole understanding of the situatedness of the classroom is best summarized in the words a great teacher educator once told me and that became one of my secular mantras: Tell me what you need English for and I'll tell you the kind of English you need.**

(Leo, Teaching Practicum, Teaching Philosophy)

References

Daniels, H. (2014). Vygotsky and dialogic pedagogy. *Cultural-Historical Psychology*, *10*(3), 19–29.

Johnson, K. E. (1999). *Understanding language teaching: Reasoning in action*. Boston, MA: Heinle & Heinle.

Johnson, K. E. (2009). *Second language teacher education: A sociocultural perspective*. New York: Routledge.

Lortie, D. (1975). *Schoolteacher: A sociological study*. Chicago, IL: University of Chicago.

10
POST-GRADUATION TRAJECTORIES

Our novice teachers in the world

Introduction

As teacher educators and graduate faculty members, we often wonder what becomes of our teachers once they leave the MA TESL program. Do the academic and pedagogical concepts we ask them to engage with remain present in their reasoning and teaching activities? Do the changes we have observed—how they conceptualize themselves as language teachers and the activity of language teaching—carry over into new, and presumably, very different instructional contexts? And if so, in what ways have these reconceptualizations become facets of their professional identity and daily pedagogy? In this chapter, we take up these questions by engaging in dialogue with seven of the original teachers who participated in our research project, 2–3 years after graduating from our program. All seven who were contacted agreed to be interviewed. A relatively small group, they are quite diverse, both male (3) and female (4), from different languages, nationalities, and ethnic backgrounds (Argentina, Brazil, China, Saudi Arabia, USA).

Furthermore, we intentionally designed the interviews to be both dialogic and targeted. Specifically, this means that we did not just ask questions, but engaged with their responses; also, we directed their attention to several specific experiences and writings from the pillar courses they took in our program. To accomplish this, we read and re-read the final Extend Team-Teaching papers, the final Tutoring Internship papers, and the final Practicum paper with an analytic eye for evidence of what Veresov (2017) calls "dramatic moments," that is, turning points that seemed to have developmental significance. The excerpts we chose from their writings seemed to indicate that they were experiencing some sort of cognitive engagement: an 'ah-ha' moment of insight, a moment of

DOI: 10.4324/9781003268987-14

cognitive-emotional dissonance, or a sustained process of 'working over' a new concept, a new realization, or a critical incident that perhaps pushed them to rethink or reimagine their identity or their activity. The dialogic and intentional design of the interviews align with Vygotskian Sociocultural Theory (VSCT) and praxis-oriented pedagogy in that we were not simply interested in gaining access to their perceptions of the program, but also hoped to make the interview an engaging and meaningful dialogic experience that could continue to have developmental value for their reasoning and teaching activities.

Prior to the actual interviews (which were conducted via video chat), each teacher received several (four or five) excerpts selected from their reflective writings. They were invited to reflect on how, looking back, they perceive these moments of development now and what, if anything, noted in that excerpt might have had a lasting impact on their professional development and identity. Some of the teachers chose to provide written comments for each excerpt, but all seven teachers engaged in dialogue with the interviewer (an advanced PhD student versed in VSCT and L2 Teacher Education) for approximately one hour. They were also asked to reflect on any significant concepts, moments, or incidents that were particularly meaningful for them throughout the program. Finally, they were asked to describe their current teaching context and their future plans. Each teacher also received a link to the recorded interview which was automatically transcribed.

To give readers a sense of the nature of the selected excerpts, we have included three examples below, each written by a different teacher for a different pillar course. Excerpt 1, from the final paper written for Teaching ESL, was selected because it focuses on Yan's concerns over the unpredictable nature of teaching and her uneasiness about handling unexpected student responses (TEACH OFF YOUR STUDENTS). She indicates her discomfort with the phrases *I'm not sure* and multiple uses of *what if* and clearly anticipates her struggle to respond appropriately if *unexpected things happen*. We were curious to know what she thinks now about the unpredictable nature of teaching after several years in the language classroom:

Excerpt 1

I expected the class could go smoothly according to our lesson plan and I knew it's very likely that there would be some **unexpected things happen.** However, when the unexpected things happened, **I'm not sure whether I could handle them well.** When we were making the lesson plan, I was more focused on the students' reaction to our activities. I was considering whether they would like the activities or not, what if they didn't like it and were unwilling to cooperate, **what if they didn't know what they're supposed to do**, etc.

(Yan, Teaching ESL, Final Paper)

Excerpt 2, from the final reflective paper for the Tutoring Internship, was selected because Leo clearly recognized the reasoning behind the design of the Tutoring Internship and conceptualized both teaching and tutoring as *socially situated* and *responsive to students' needs*. In addition, he explicitly cites the phrase TEACH OFF YOUR STUDENTS, NOT AT THEM, as a pedagogical concept that informed his thinking and teaching. We were interested in his understanding of this pedagogical concept today and if and how it continues to shape his reasoning and teaching activity:

Excerpt 2

Despite my discontentment with the apparent lack of structure of my future sessions, **I understood the reasoning behind it.** If there is one lesson I have derived from my experience in this MA TESL program so far is that **teaching (or tutoring, for that matter) does not happen in a void. It is socially situated and should be responsive to my students' (tutees') needs.** Professor Karen Johnson's words became imprinted on my brain, **"Teach off your students!"** That was my mantra throughout the semester and I strived to comply with it as much as I could.

(Leo, Tutoring Internship, Final Paper)

Excerpt 3, written for the Teaching Practicum class, was selected because it indicates that engagement in reflection not only enabled Ana to *develop self-awareness* but also *unpack* her experiences, *verbalize* her thinking, and recognize *the why* behind her instructional decisions. We wondered if Ana continues to engage in critical reflection and were interested to hear how she reasons about her teaching choices today:

Excerpt 3

My **teaching journal reflections** were also **instrumental in developing self-awareness**. I had never had the opportunity to engage in this kind of reflection. At the beginning it felt strange and I was not quite sure of what to write but later in the semester, I found myself looking forward to writing them after every class. These journals, the interactions with my classmates and the opportunities you opened up for me to deploy my teaching knowledge, **helped me unpack my experience as a teacher and verbalize my thinking and the why behind each decision I make in my classes.**

(Ana, Teaching Practicum, Final Paper)

As articulated in Part I, praxis-oriented pedagogy attempts to transform novice teachers' conceptual understanding of teaching by allowing them to confront, engage with, and experience new concepts and new ways of understanding and enacting the complex activity of language teaching. In our interviews, we were interested to see how the pedagogical concepts (new concepts) and the VSCT orientation of our praxis-oriented pedagogy (new ways of thinking and enacting) have been taken up and carried over into our former graduate students' current conceptualization of language teaching and, especially, into their current instructional context. To accomplish this, we used the discourse-analytic techniques of grounded content analysis (Bogdan & Biklen, 2007), which allowed us to inductively create themes that were directly drawn from close, repeated readings of the data (three final reflection papers, oral and written video chat interviews). In essence, the themes give us insight into the dynamics behind these teachers' current conceptualization of language teaching through the meanings they ascribe to their past, present, and future teaching experiences.

The two predominant themes that emerged, not surprisingly, reflect the central tenets of praxis-oriented pedagogy: *reasoning teaching* and *teaching as dialogic mediation*. The first theme highlights characterizations of the various ways in which these teachers continue to reason about why they do what they do, how they came to these realizations, and how their reasoning continues to shape their current instructional choices. The second theme reflects the unique ways in which these teachers have taken up the pedagogical concepts that permeate our three pillar courses and reinforces their commitment to a *teaching as dialogic mediation instructional stance*. Two other themes that emerged in the interviews include *developing a professional teaching identity* and *teaching in a new instructional context*. These themes capture how these teachers conceptualize their own developmental trajectory as professional language teachers and the many challenges they face in the instructional setting in which they are currently teaching.

Overall, these four themes highlight how these teachers experienced our praxis-oriented pedagogy and how those experiences shaped, and continue to shape, the ways in which they conceptualize language teaching, how they position themselves as language teachers, and the kind of teachers they have become. These themes also inform us, as teacher educators, to better understand our teachers' professional development experiences and highlight how pedagogical concepts from our praxis-oriented pedagogy have shaped their teacher personas and pedagogies as they navigate new language teaching contexts.

Reasoning Teaching

Throughout this book, we have argued that a VSCT-informed praxis-oriented pedagogy positions reasoning, rather than techniques, methods, or skills as central to the development of language teacher expertise, building off

Johnson's (1999) original definition: "reasoning teaching reflects the complex ways in which teachers conceptualize, construct explanations for, and respond to the social interactions and shared meanings that exist within and among teachers, students, parents, and administrators both inside and outside the classroom" (p. 1). By fostering reasoning teaching through our praxis-oriented pedagogy, we expect our teachers will take up an expert stance as reasoning teachers and make theoretically and pedagogically sound instructional choices as they address the institutional affordances and constraints inherent in the instructional contexts in which they teach.

How Teaching Should Be Done

As Johnson's quote suggests, courses, such as our three pillar courses, informed by praxis-oriented pedagogy are intentionally designed to focus on the *how* of teaching rather than the *what*. In the following excerpt, Ethan's caricature of traditional teacher-fronted delivery of content knowledge stands in stark contrast to his main takeaway from the program: his conceptualization of *how teaching should be done*. Now teaching North American undergraduate students as a teaching assistant in his doctoral program, he remains committed to the *academic perspective they* [the program] *represent* (i.e., praxis-oriented pedagogy) and a belief that success in teaching requires a tremendous amount of teacher preparation and attention to teaching and student engagement:

> **Excerpt 4**
>
> I can say that when it comes to thinking about how I teach, or teaching in general, **how teaching should be done,** I often think about Sharon, Deryn and Karen, and also **the academic perspective they represent.** Because when you get outside of Applied Linguistics, or Education departments, very few other departments focus on **how teachers teach their classes or care about it,** ... there's very little thought about how teaching should be done, it's really just you have the content or content knowledge, and then deliver it to them or put it whether it's an PowerPoint or a lecture or reporting, you can just give it to them, and then the good students will take it. So I've learned that that's not really how it works…but based on their teaching, that's really kind of how I feel that a lot of the success of a teaching classroom has to do with how you prepare the class, how you prepare yourself, how you prepare the materials, how you respond to their questions. And that's, yeah, all those things.
>
> (Ethan, Post-Graduation Interview)

Thinking Seriously about Teaching

In this excerpt, Aisha describes a persistent effect of our praxis-oriented pedagogy on her teaching. After reading an excerpt from her final reflection paper in which she recalls how a comment from a teammate, which channeled the Team-Teach Supervisor, pushed her to provide a rationale for her instruction choice: *I'm Karen, how does this connect to what you are teaching, why are you showing them the video, what is the point? How is it connected to the orientation?* Aisha now describes *a little voice in my head* that continues to help her think *seriously* and *deeply* about her teaching. She also notes that over time, this way of thinking *seriously* about teaching *naturally comes to me that way*:

> **Excerpt 5**
>
> This was iconic! **A little voice in my head** actually asked, do experienced educators, like Dr. Karen Johnson, actually **think about the content they incorporate that deeply? I answered that question finally during my first year of teaching...You should think about these things seriously...** Whenever if you are gathering materials, what whenever you, gathering up and preparing a lesson plan, **you should think seriously about that.** You know, and **over time, obviously, I've learned you do have to, to a certain degree** doesn't have to be this literal, but yeah, **it naturally comes to me that way.**
>
> (Aisha, Post-Graduation Interview)

Why Am I Doing What I Am Doing

Reasoning teaching asks teachers to be conscious of their instructional choices and to have a reasonable rationale for making such choices based on the particulars of the instructional setting. Leo credits engagement in *introspective reflection* on his teaching throughout the program with enabling him to conceptualize language teaching as more *localized*, more responsive to *students' needs and goals*, and more contingent upon the instructional *setting*:

> **Excerpt 6**
>
> **Observing teachers do stuff and then reflecting upon them and trying to find the rationale behind them. And then looking at ourselves, and, you know, like analyzing what we did, which was like so humbling. And sort of like, Okay, so what were you thinking, what are you doing that, you know, this sort of like introspective reflection,** ... you know, start like realizing why you do certain stuff or realizing that you haven't been doing what you think you're doing. That was the case though. Like I remember watching myself and doing stuff. I was like, why did I do that? That was not

my plan, like why am I repeating myself so much? Why, you know? But, yeah, I think my takeaway from the whole experience is that **teaching should be a lot more localized in the sense of like, to students are to be taken into consideration, their goals are to be taken into consideration, the setting is to be taken into consideration.**

(Leo, Post-Graduation Interview)

Purposeful Lessons

The concept of *reasoning teaching* requires teachers to evaluate their instructional choices as being purposeful (goal-directed), substantive (content-rich), meaningful (matters for your goals and the students' goals), and engaging (involves all students all the time). Thus, when teachers engage in reasoning teaching, they can better justify their instructional choices and articulate their thinking. Yan continues to contemplate making teaching purposeful, not just when she is planning, but also knowing *where they* [L2 learners] *are after today's lesson*, so she can ensure that her *next lesson is purposeful* as well:

Excerpt 7

Sometimes, yeah, sometimes it made me a little stressful because I just presume that **I have to make every activity purposeful in my lesson.** I shouldn't waste time or I shouldn't. Like, say some nonsense in my lessons to my students. **I think the purposeful thing, kind of pushing me to really pay attention to my lesson plan.** Yeah. And and it also make me do reflection, every lesson after each lesson, **because if I want to make my next lesson, purposeful, I have to know where they are after today's lesson.**

(Yan, Post-Graduation Interview)

Dialogue and Reflection

Throughout the MA TESL program, engagement in written reflection creates multiple and sustained mediational spaces where teachers externalize their thinking, write about what they are experiencing, describe how they are feeling, explore new ideas and ways of teaching, seek answers to questions, and confront common classroom dilemmas. We consider this kind of written reflection to be dialogic in that we typically respond to them, usually also in writing, in a short time frame, so that continuing exchanges are possible. During the Tutoring Internship and the Teaching Practicum, particularly, the Supervisors are not always in the room, so to speak, but their mediation is offered 'at a distance' through immediate and individualized responses to the tutoring posts and the reflective journals. Our goal, in line with praxis-oriented pedagogy, is to direct our written responses toward the novice teachers' ZPD activity. In the following excerpt, Ana discusses how she came to the MA TESL program from an instructional context where reflection on teaching was neither supported nor valued. Here she describes the various ways in which engaging in written reflection offered her a *new way of interacting with my thoughts* and *a layer of understanding that I had not had before*:

Excerpt 8

> Reflecting in writing was new for me. Before starting my MA, I worked in a context that did not necessarily allow this practice. My reflections were more in the form of conversations with colleagues, family members or friends. However, the fact that in this instance **I had to write provided a new way of interacting with my thoughts and my emotions. Sitting and writing about my week helped me: 1. organize my thoughts, 2. think about where my emotions were coming from, 3. question my own beliefs and ideas about teaching, 4. go back to past teaching experiences and see them through a different light, I added a lens of empathy and a layer of understanding that I had not had before.**
>
> (Ana, Post-Graduation Interview, Written)

Developing a Teaching as Dialogic Mediation Instructional Stance

A *teaching as dialogic mediation instructional stance* highlights the importance of the teacher's mediating role in supporting learners' conceptual and language development. In our program, we provide novice teachers with accessible, meaningful pedagogical concepts that allow them to understand, and engage in, *responsive mediation* with their learners from their earliest days in the program.

In our post-graduation interviews, we found that the teachers we interviewed continue to reference the pedagogical concepts they encountered throughout the pillar courses, using them as lenses for understanding and *reasoning teaching* activity. Some teachers made explicit reference to specific pedagogical concepts, for example, *to not teach at your students but teach off your students. It's really impressive for me, because I always think about what she said to us*, whereas others made more indirect references; *By asking, yeah, by asking these questions, I can kind of want to give them the idea of the purpose of their writing*. The post-graduation interviews suggest that these pedagogical concepts continue to support teachers attempts to create spaces for learners to make their thinking explicit, to foster productive instructional dialogues, and to promote conceptual thinking by linking academic knowledge (subject matter content) to practical everyday activity (meaningful language use). The data excerpts presented in this section illustrate how they understand these pedagogical concepts now, and how they continue to shape the ways in which they engage with their students and lesson materials.

Teach off Your Students, Not at Them

The pedagogical concept TEACH OFF YOUR STUDENTS, NOT AT THEM was regularly mentioned during the post-graduation interviews. Despite its simple play on prepositions, as a pedagogical concept it has powerful consequences for how teachers orient to their students and how students' histories and current understandings are both valued and made part of any instructional conversation. For Yan, TEACHING OFF her students has become both an overarching instructional stance and a psychological tool that informs how she thinks about her teaching every day:

> **Excerpt 9**
>
> And I remember, she taught she told us that like, **to not teach at your students but teach off your students.** It's really impressive for me, because **I always think about what she said to us.** Yeah, it normally works when I before I met our new group of students, but for the students I'm teaching, they are different every day. So after today's lesson, they are kind of a different person for me because they learn something new today. So for tomorrow, **I have to think about, okay, teach off the students again.** So what they got what they gained yesterday, makes them different for tomorrow, **now what should I do with them?**
>
> (Yan, Post-Graduation Interview)

Asking Questions

In adopting a *teaching dialogic mediation instructional* stance, teachers create spaces for learners to make their thinking explicit, thereby opening it up to social influence. Asking questions is an essential tool for teachers to determine and engage with their learners' level of understanding (i.e., intersubjectivity); the strategic use of questions allows the teacher to engage learners with the subject matter content in ways that promote deeper understandings and conceptual thinking. In essence, the strategic use of questions forces teachers to TEACH OFF their students. For Bei, *forcing* himself not to give learners the answers right away, but to create a space for learners to think, to react, and to explore arose from his learning to wield questions strategically. Now, he continues to recognize the value of asking questions as a means of gaining access to learners' insights and ideas:

Excerpt 10

But I think every time when I am teaching students, **I always use the skill of the artist to ask questions.** Yes, I think this is the thing that is very important for being a teacher, **a qualified teacher.** And I just tried on my best to tell myself, **to force myself to hold before I like to give the answers directly to the students like after five seconds, I like to give them more time to think to react to see if they have the potential to explore....Because most of the time my students could come up with very insightful, very interesting ideas and responses. If I do not give them those chances, they will never do this... So asking question, I guess, is a very important thing.** And the experience I got from this two years program changed my old way of teaching in schools.

(Bei, Post-Graduation Interview)

Other teachers described ways in which strategically asking questions can enable them to make the content they are teaching more transparent and accessible for learners. In this excerpt, Yan describes how she used questions to enable her students to understand both the purpose and structure of a written review:

Excerpt 11

So firstly, when I was teaching them how to write a review, **I use a lot of like effective questions.** For example, what do you expect? When you are reading a restaurant review, what do you expect? In the first paragraph? What do you want to read? Read in the first paragraph? Or what do you want to read in the last paragraph? Or like, well, after reading this review, what information do you want to get like this? **By asking, yeah, by asking these questions, I can kind of want to give them the idea of the purpose of their writing. So sometimes they don't know how to write what is review. But by answering this question, they kind of know, like, this is a review.**

(Yan, Post-Graduation Interview)

Teaching as Connecting

The pedagogical concept TEACHING AS CONNECTING was often mentioned in the post-graduation interviews. Teachers stressed the importance of establishing an instructional relationship with learners, which means not only building rapport with and among learners, but also making meaningful connections between the content being taught and learners' lives. For Ana, TEACHING AS CONNECTING is an *emotional activity* and at the same time involves making a *human connection* with learners:

Excerpt 12

Like my biggest takeaways? Yeah, um, that **teaching is a crazy emotional activity**. That it's incredibly important that there's *human connection*. For me, it's vital. It's vital. Like you can give me all these amazing articles to read on. **But if, I think that if I don't connect with my students, I have the feeling that I don't know certain things, the techniques, the things like, yeah, I can read them, I can put them in practice.** But that **connection that in that you feel with your, with your professor, or your supervisor, or a mentor, or teacher, whoever is in charge of your learning process**, I think that it's very, very important.

(Ana, Post-Graduation Interview)

Engineering Participation

Several teachers recalled the importance of not assuming that learners know how to participate in classroom activities and thus spoke of continuing to make a concerted effort to ENGINEER PARTICIPATION as a means of achieving their instructional goals. Yan explains that even when planning a lesson, she considers how to best ENGINEER PARTICIPATION in order to support learners when they are confronted with challenging content:

Excerpt 13

So when **I was making the lesson plan, I was thinking**, if I should ask them to answer all six questions, like, every, every one of them, also the six questions, or should I divide them into two groups? And each group work with three? Three questions. Yeah. **So, like, when I was thinking about why I, I was doing that. So, I think the lecture was quite hard for them so maybe working with all those six questions was, well, what was a little bit too challenging for them.** So, I think at last, I chose to divide them into two groups. And each group had three questions.

(Yan, Post-Graduation Interview)

Developing a Professional Teacher Identity

Most of the teachers we interviewed describe their experiences in the program as enabling them to develop a resilient and confident professional teacher identity. However, not surprisingly, their developmental trajectory differed based on their prior and current learning and teaching experiences; their histories vary, as do the experiences they had in the program and their current teaching contexts. Ana entered the program with many years of English as a Foreign

Language (EFL) teaching experience; thus, she recalls having to *unpack* what she already knew, realizing that before joining our program, she had never had the opportunity to *articulate it*:

Excerpt 14

Because what happened to me is that, at the beginning was like, well, **it's obvious why, like, for me in my head, but then when I got to write it, I said, well, whoa, wait, I actually cannot articulate these, why am I having such a hard time? So it helped me unpack.** But I had the feeling that during my whole program, I was doing the opposite. I've already had that. I knew what I had to do and, and, and why I had to do it. But I never have the chance to articulate it.

(Ana, Post-Graduation Interview)

Our teachers often recalled that confidence in themselves and a growing confidence in a more dialogic approach to language teaching emerged gradually throughout the three pillar courses. The Tutoring Internship stood out for several interviewees as the key experience in enabling them to think differently about how they could interact with learners. Given the unpredictable and spontaneous nature of tutoring interactions, it seems that this course in particular enabled them to become competent at using questions strategically and engaging in *responsive mediation*. Leo, with considerable years of EFL teaching experience, credits the Tutoring Internship as a *watershed moment* that not only reinforced his confidence in his ability to tutor novice writers but to do so dialogically. He recalled initially feeling *insecure* and *nervous* about the prospect of tutoring, but through the experience of working with his tutees he realized he could focus on more *global aspects of language* and *take a more holistic approach*. He also noted that the fact that this *transformative* experience preceded the Teaching Practicum was key to giving him the confidence to think about language and classroom language instruction more holistically:

Excerpt 15

INTERVIEWER: And it's [tutoring] a different kind of instruction, right? Because you had all these years of teaching experience, but then you're thrust into the situation. Exactly. You're gonna do something with this person for 30 minutes or an hour or whatever, whatever. Without planning it. Right, exactly. Right.

LEO: And in even though I've been, as you know, I was no spring chicken, you know, when it came to teaching, but **that was something that I was a novice again**, I was like, doing this for the first time. So **I was a little, like insecure and, and nervous about**

it. It took me a minute, you know, to get my footing. But once I did, that was **very transformative, like a watershed moment**. You know, I started saying, **Man, I'm good at this**, you know? ... Because that's another thing, to think about a more **global aspects of the language, as well as local like to make sure to blend both of them rather than just checking for grammar or whatever**...I started **taking a more holistic approach**, you know, so who's your audience? Right. Thinking about tone, or do you think that this is clear enough? ... That [tutoring] **was a very important experience especially because it preceded the practicum, ...so that was the moment I realized, I can do this, and I'm going to be able to do**, okay, so that was **for me, that was really important**.

(Leo, Post-Graduation Interview)

Others described feeling confident but noted that they continue to experience the normal anxiety of teaching new content or working with students at a higher level of English language proficiency. Many seemed open to learning along with their learners and yet confident they had much to offer. Bei, who is originally from China but is now a resident of the US, stayed in the area to teach English at a university-level intensive English language program and continues to believe there is always more to learn, describing himself as a teacher as *a half empty cup* and *always welcoming more* yet realizing that despite his non-native English status, by *teaching something, you know, very interesting* he had much to offer his learners, and this helped him regained his confidence as a teacher:

Excerpt 16

INTERVIEWER: And now that you've been teaching for a few years after that, would you consider yourself a confident teacher?

BEI: **Not a 100% as I believe that it should always be, you know, a half empty cup.** So you always welcome more, you know, nutrients or juices or wines to get in? ... Yeah, so, not always, **I actually still feeling out a little bit nervous when teaching some courses.** Like, you know, that two semesters ago, I was teaching that science course. Because the students were all the highest level here, almost, **most of them could speak very fluent when using English very perfectly.** But luckily, **I was teaching them something very interesting, a little bit different way from their core courses, like literature, writing, readings,** something like that, of course, I was teaching them sciences. **So, I regained my confidence in my abilities as a teacher.**

(Bei, Post-Graduation Interview)

Aisha, despite her lack of teaching experience, felt her *willingness to understand the students* allowed her supervisor at work to have confidence in her abilities to adapt as a language teacher in a new and unfamiliar teaching environment:

> **Excerpt 17**
>
> **I was still kind of nervous about teaching**, right? Because again, I was still very young and inexperienced. And even my boss told me even though you're very inexperienced, in a way, to a degree inexperienced. **She felt like she saw something in me,** which was I guess, **this kind of willingness to understand the students and come to a degree to adapt**, right?
>
> (Aisha, Post-Graduation Interview)

When asked about the most important lessons, concepts, or takeaways from the program, Aisha expressed appreciation for the fact that the program practiced what it preaches and that she could observe her educators engaging in praxis in the pillar courses, which ultimately convinced her of the value of the instructional stance of the program:

> **Excerpt 18**
>
> …. it was more of like, a package and everything kind of like, are **interconnected**. But I think I really appreciated, some people say, **you should preach what you should do what you preach or something.** Yeah. **I saw that, in our program. Whenever they said about student centered, whenever they talked about reflection, whenever they did that, I can see that being done. And that was, that is what convinced me.** And that's what I really appreciated about our program the most.
>
> (Aisha, Post-Graduation Interview)

New Instructional Contexts: Cultures, Constraints, and Challenges

Teaching in a new instructional context places extra demands upon teachers, even experienced ones; for a new teacher, who is perhaps facing their first full-time instructional position while adapting to a new set of expectations and perhaps unwritten rules, the demands are greater. Like all teachers who enter, or re-enter, the professional world with a new credential, our graduates need to calibrate their responses to these demands.

Some of the teachers we interviewed noted that they continue to wrestle with issues that they confronted throughout their graduate program, as they adapt and respond to their new teaching contexts. Others described institutional constraints, such as mandated curricula or high-stakes exams, which curtail their ability to maintain a *teaching as dialogic mediation instructional stance*. Perhaps the most frustrating constraint many of them face is what they perceive as a lack of student interest or engagement which makes it difficult for them to construct productive instructional dialogues.

Lack of Student Participation

Many of the teachers we interviewed expressed frustration with the lack of student participation in their instructional activities and discussions. For those now teaching in instructional contexts where active student participation is not the norm, their ability to engage in *student centered teaching* can feel thwarted by this kind of social convention. Aisha, for example, notes that she does not *get that participation that I'm looking for* from her current students and comments on her frustration with what she calls *dead silence* in the room:

Excerpt 19

But **I still don't get that participation that I'm looking for. And I still don't get that. That involvement that I'm looking for,** I would ask the students a very simple question. for example, I remember I asked them, we were having a discussion about something about woman, what do women struggle with, you know, now in our modern day, and they're all women, they all should know, have an answer, and I kid you not. It was like dead silence. dead silence. And **I remember feeling so, I'm very patient but in that moment, I felt very upset, and very frustrated.** Because, how **I mentioned about student centered teaching, that became so me, this is me, this is my style.**

(Aisha, Post-Graduation Interview)

At times, it seemed that the structured nature of the required curriculum was also a deterrent to garnering student participation. Having little freedom to adapt the curriculum, Aisha experienced outright revolt from learners when they were asked to write *five sentences* with *five vocabulary words*. Her frustration was not so much with the learners, but with her inability to *see* their learning/growth:

Excerpt 20

I don't really have the freedom to kind of change the curriculum, and they already have a lot going on, that if I did add reflections, I feel like they're going to despise me for it. **I remember from one of the courses I had them do like five sentences, including five**

vocab, you know, five. And I remember, they were like, **Can we not do that? I'm just like, I'm doing it for you. So that you're learning?** You know, whenever I saw all of them agree, I mean, okay. **I'm just trying to see how I can see their learning, how their growth**

(Aisha, Post-Graduation Interview)

Teacher Talk

Teaching in quite a different context, Ethan, when prompted by the interviewer to recall his prior concerns about dominating classroom talk as a language teacher, notes that he continues to feel a certain level cognitive-emotional dissonance over the need to *stop me from dominating the whole classroom*. In his new instructional context, where he teaches 'content' courses rather than language courses, he continues to be concerned that he dominates the class. Nevertheless, he is able to articulate strategies for circumventing this problem, such as *working through the materials* and *planning so that this doesn't become an issue* and he credits the MA TESL program with making him aware of this, that he *doesn't want to talk so much*, but with increased *awareness* he *continues to work on it*:

Excerpt 21

INTERVIEWER: And so it's what does this look like now? Right, in your current teaching, or your current instructional context? Are you more aware of like the distribution of talk? Or do you still think you, you know, you dominate, so to speak? or What is that like? Now?

ETHAN: It's a good question I've taught some classes that are similar to ESL 015 [1st year academic writing] here, quite similar. And I've also taught very different classes. And some of those classes demand more of a lecture style. In some of those classes I talk a lot. But the interesting thing there's not much difference, because at that time, **I felt that I didn't want to talk so much. And at this time, I also feel like I don't want to talk so much. But in both times, I still talk a lot. And so I'm constantly working on how to design lessons better to, you know, stop me from dominating the whole classroom, basically working through the materials and the plan so that this doesn't become an issue. But it still happens.** …I'll say if anything's changed, **at least my awareness that that's not the best way to go about all lessons or all teaching has at least increased. And so my awareness is there. And I'm still just kind of continually working on it.**

(Ethan, Post-Graduation Interview)

Institutional and Instructional Constraints

One of the most striking features we heard from the post-graduation interviews was how self-aware the program graduates have become, both of themselves as teachers and of their own teaching. This is not altogether surprising given the intensity with which we ask them to engage in critical dialogic reflection on their teaching/tutoring and on their own development as a teacher/tutor throughout the three pillar courses. But moving to a new instructional context, especially where the institutional expectations are different, can mean that this self-awareness confronts severe challenges. Some teachers idealized the experience they had in our MA TESL program, expressing the disappointment of returning to instructional contexts, such as their home countries, and feeling unable to use much of what they knew they had gained from the program. As Yan put it:

Excerpt 22

I think **our program kind of may give us very ideal circumstance of teaching. Like, I think everything was perfect.** When I was there, like the practicum, or the teaching project, **everything was perfect**. And when I went back to China, and started to teach my kids here, **I got, wow, what is that? The classroom was totally out of control.** And, like, I, **I feel a little bit disappointed**. The first because I feel like **80% of what I learned in Penn State was not working now.**

(Yan, Post- Graduation Interview)

Similarly, Fen told us about a job interview she had in China (her home country) where the headmaster who was interviewing her explicitly questioned the value of her American educational experience: *You had a nice degree in the US, that's good. But what you learnt about teaching in the US is not suitable in China, you cannot use that knowledge here.* She expressed confusion and disappointment that the transformation of understanding and expertise that she had experienced in our MA TESL program would be neither valued nor respected in her new context:

Excerpt 23

I was really confused about her words since I did not even tell her anything about what I learnt in graduate study. She continued that: "**Here is China, the context is totally different, but you will have chance to study how to teach when you become a teacher in our group.**" I tried to explain the knowledge and skills about teaching that I learnt, but she did not want to listen and just held her opinion that **to be novice teacher means knowing nothing about teaching.**

(Fen, Post-Graduation Interview, Written)

Other teachers faced challenges, such as teaching learners of age levels different than they had worked with during the MA TESL program or coping with mandated curriculum or high-stakes tests. When asked what she learned overall from the program, Aisha claimed, *I learned a lot about myself*. However, now teaching children, she feels she cannot be herself, that she must *mask* her true personality, since in this context, she has to *be very strict*, and do things like *raise* [my]*voice* and *repeat* [myself], behaviors she feels are not authentic to her teaching self: *I'm not like that. I'm the opposite*:

Excerpt 24

Oh, my God, **I learned a lot about myself.** Sometimes I appreciate these things for happening, because it makes you learn about yourself, sure it's not really on your path. **But it's still so important to know about yourself. I realized teaching kids is not for me, because it made me mask my personality.** And you know, **when you mask your personality, you're draining yourself.** You need to be very strict with kids. You need to have this strictness, and you need to kind of raise your voice a little bit, you need to repeat yourself. **I'm not like that. I'm like the opposite. I'm so chill. I'm so calm.**

(Aisha, Post-Graduation Interview)

Yan noted that despite learning about the value of ENGINEERING PARTICIPATION and making her instruction predictable, she describes her current instructional context as *too predictable*. By this, she means that she is tied to the textbook. Given the value placed on high stakes testing in this new context, she laments the fact that she must *teach based on the tests*. She regrets being unable to make her lesson *fun* but is resigned, given the institutional constraints, to a less responsive approach: *I just follow the textbook* which she feels is *really boring*:

Excerpt 25

Yeah, is too predictable. And, each unit starts with two examples, and then grammar points, and then two more example centers, and then some exercises, and then finished. So each unit goes like this, and students didn't have any fun activity. And I have to based on, **I have to teach based on the tests that because of our, it's like exam plans or something.** So and because there are only three or four pages in each unit. And **I don't have very enough time to make very fun classroom activity** for them every day. So sometimes **I just follow the textbook, the structure, and it's really boring.**

(Yan, Post- Graduation Interview)

Even though he did not return to his home country to teach, Bei remains very aware of the differences between the instructional contexts he was familiar with in China and where he teaches now. He demonstrates a commitment to a *teaching as dialogic mediation instructional stance* that goes beyond his own personal classroom and suggests that it holds potential value for education even in an old-school, old-fashioned context such as China. While he has not yet faced the challenges described by Yan, Fen, and others who did try to maintain their *teaching as dialogic mediation instructional stance* in the Chinese context, he expresses optimism about the possibility of change in general:

Excerpt 26

Because my vision is so different here in America, even back in China, the situation has been changing quickly. Not always stayed the **old ways the old, old school, old fashion.** Back in China, there are a lot of people, new teachers coming back from other countries learning I mean, equip, equipping, being equipped with a lot of new knowledge, skills, techniques, they learn from other countries like America. So all schools have been challenged back in China. That's why we need to change, right?… **And the experience I got from this two years program changed my old way of teaching in schools.**

(Bei, Post-Graduation Interview)

Fen notes that she probably would have left the teaching profession entirely if she had not encountered the new ways of thinking and understanding teaching that the MA TESL program offered her: *I did not have the program from Penn State, I may give up, teaching*:

Excerpt 27

I'm going to say that I think that if I, **if I did not have the program from Penn State, I may give up, teaching.** I think if, if I did not have that experience, **I may feel that or maybe this is the real teaching. Maybe I feel not comfortable doing that was because I was not a suitable, teaching is not suitable for me.** Because I, I see that some teachers with children and they worked there for maybe two or three months, and **they left give up teaching.** I saw many outstanding teachers at Penn State. And they don't work that way. **I think that gave me confidence**…Because just like what I said, so from time to time, I still think of the moments in Penn State, maybe just some, some moments when Sharon and Karen do their teaching in a class, **I realize more and more about why they do that.**

(Fen, Post-Graduation Interview)

Conclusion

As we have said so many times throughout this volume, framing the MA TESL teacher education program around the principles of VSCT means that we are committed to what Vygotsky called a 'genetic' or historical development-over-time perspective on human activity. Tracing the ways that novice teachers learn, grow, change, and transform their understanding, their activity, and their identities while they are with us makes our work meaningful and fulfilling. Hearing from those teachers years later how the lessons they studied with us have taken root in new contexts brings a level of gratification to the work that would otherwise remain invisible.

Human development is open-ended, and we do not have a template or model that we want all our novice teachers to fit. With decades of teaching and teacher educating behind us, we understand that careers and lives often take unexpected turns or thrive in ways that cannot be imagined earlier. Because we focus on helping teachers develop new ways of seeing, understanding, and reasoning, rather than on gaining mastery of specific techniques or skills, we expect that the outcomes and trajectories of each person who passes through our MA TESL program to be different from every other, while at the same time being resonant with the concepts we introduce. These interviews illustrate the immanence of change in every professional endeavor and give credence to the VSCT-informed commitment to supporting growth and change through a principled mix of theoretical and practical engagement.

References

Bogdan, R. C., & Biklen, S. K. (2007). *Qualitative research for education: An introduction to theory and methods* (3rd Ed.). Boston, MA: Allyn and Bacon.

Johnson, K. E. (1999). *Understanding language teaching: Reasoning in action*. Boston, MA: Heinle & Heinle.

Veresov, N. (2017). The concept of perezhivanie in cultural-historical theory: Content and contexts. In M. Fleer, F. González Rey, & N. Veresov (Eds.), *Perezhivanie, emotions and subjectivity. Advancing Vygotsky's legacy* (pp. 47–70). Singapore: Springer.

11
PRAXIS AND PROGRAM DESIGN

Introduction

When we share our ideas and experiences at conferences, the most common questions we get from audience members are the following, as we noted in Chapter 2: *How can I, working alone/without supportive administrators/without interested colleagues/without knowledge of Vygotsky Sociocultural Theory (VSCT), manage to accomplish what you have done? How do I initiate a similar coherence of engagement in my own program? What are some of the design features of your program that can be adapted to my context?* Of course, the answers are not simple, and that is because the underlying question is a complex one: What are the limits of individual effort and where does collaborative, supported effort become necessary? This chapter provides the reader with additional information about the ways in which our MA TESL program sets up, identifies, includes, and makes available forms of mediational spaces and input to the novice teachers enrolled in the program. It is provided in the hope that readers who want to explore applying some of the ideas laid out in this volume will have a deeper understanding of the many kinds of opportunities that can be used for responsive, contingent, and VSCT-focused mediation of novice teachers.

This chapter will not try to cover this topic exhaustively; there are many ways of looking at, and understanding, the efforts of individuals working in less-than-supportive environments. But we will try to discuss some of the features of the program that have been built into it—either through tradition or through conscious application—that seem to us to be available for appropriation and adaptation. Little we do in our teacher education program is done by chance; but like all human activity, our program is shaped by various contextual factors and represents an historical journey of change, stasis, and conscious decision-making.

DOI: 10.4324/9781003268987-15

In this chapter, we discuss professional development opportunities that exist at the program level, the department level, and the university level. It also explains how we strive to support the development of our novice teachers in their completion of the program and institutional requirements that shape the program; describes extra-curricular and off-campus opportunities for volunteer teaching and consulting; and identifies departmental resources and projects that provide professional development in collaborative research and study.

Opportunities for Professional Development

Job Searching

We encourage the novice teachers to use their e-Portfolios when searching for jobs. To this end, we offer a workshop every year that focuses specifically on job searching topics, such as how to prepare an accurate and appropriate professional CV and how to identify and make productive use of various job-hunting resources. Some of our students, after they graduate from the program, plan to teach English overseas, either in their own home country or in another country. On the other hand, many of our international students hope to stay in the United States on an Optional Professional Training (OPT) visa, which allows them to maintain their student visa status while engaging in paid work that is relevant to their degree program. With our help and through their own initiatives, they have landed interesting positions with exchange programs, private schools, research projects, and other language-related opportunities. For some of these MA TESL students, the workshop is the first time that they understand the breadth of opportunities available to them. We encourage them to combine our TESL-oriented workshops with training sessions offered by the campus office that oversees visas and international student paperwork, because we do not view ourselves as experts in visa-related questions.

Extra-curricular Teaching Opportunities

To the extent that our large university is located in a very small town in a relatively rural area, readers of this volume should understand that their teacher education programs may have one enormous advantage over ours: being located in an urban area, or within easy travel distance of several urban areas, or in a place with a widely diverse set of linguistic communities, you do not have to work quite so hard, perhaps, to identify and develop outside opportunities for your novice teachers! So, this section of the chapter is written about our local situation, but we encourage you to seek out similar kinds of opportunities in your local area.

All parts of the MA TESL program come to bear on other parts, though not predictably, and the influences are not always equal or mutual. Because we view our program as a kind of 'functional system' in which every element has the potential to change an outcome or an experience; one characteristic of the work that we do is that it is not limited to the formal classroom. This fact is true and important despite the value and weight we give to formal instruction and formally organized, strategically provided mediation.

One major goal of any educational or training program is the autonomy of the learner. The program, the classroom, the textbook...they all disappear. The learner, if the program has been successful, has internalized a lot of important conceptual and practical information, but, as theory predicts, concrete material activity is crucial for this information to be fully realized and appropriated. To this end, we cultivate local opportunities for our novice teachers where they can work on developing their skills independently, away from our oversight, but still within a communal effort of a program, center, or office.

Community-based Literacy Center

A mainstay of our local community is the community literacy center (CLC), a large volunteer-dependent tutoring center that offers tutoring and small classes to support adult literacy, ESL skills, test-prep such as TOEFL and GED, profession-specific communication skills, and general English language support. Free or extremely low-cost tuition, volunteer teachers and tutors, and a supportive but limited professional tier of administration characterize this center. They have become our eager and welcoming partners over the years, as we encourage our MA TESL students to get involved as volunteer tutors and teachers.

At the CLC, our novice teachers can perform needs analysis, create curricular materials, co-teach, and collaborate in ways that the more formal university program does not necessarily allow, have autonomous standing in their own classrooms, and work on consolidating through material practice the scientific and taxonomic information they are learning in their graduate education. As one novice teacher stated in her e-Portfolio:

Excerpt 1

This course was a wonderful experience for me, who was a novice teacher and just started TESL Program. It inspired me to teach more courses voluntarily.

(Yan, E-portfolio text)

Because of the relationship that has been created between our department, our program, and the CLC, exchanges between our department and the CLC have included the following:

- An MA TESL student doing their required teaching practicum at the CLC
- A doctoral student collecting data for their dissertation on tutor education at the CLC, a project that included training workshops and feedback that improved the overall quality of tutor training there
- Observations by us, carried out informally (not as part of a credit-bearing class), giving us more chances to talk to our novice teachers about teaching as a reasoned activity
- Visits from the CLC administration to our MA TESL graduate classes, to talk about the teaching of reading and writing to adult literacy students, materials preparation, and the cultural context of American adult literacy programs

We actively seek opportunities to engage with the CLC as teacher educators, validating it in the eyes of our MA TESL students, and opening doors to future collaborations. Members of the CLC staff have been invited to MA TESL classes as outside speakers, and the novice teachers themselves are recruited to talk about their own experiences there every year when the call goes out for new volunteers.

Campus-based Family Literacy Tutoring Center

As a large research university in an area that attracts a small but significant number of migrant families, international families and spouses, and other adults and children who need language and cultural support, our university hosts a family literacy center (FLC) on the campus. As a unit of the College of Education, separate from our own department and college, the FLC is another place where our MA TESL novice teachers are warmly welcomed as creative instructional volunteers. Most of the FLC work they do is one-on-one tutoring in English skills. As they do at the CLC, they have the opportunity to diagnose linguistic needs, to respond to expressed and perceived learner needs and preferences, and to create teaching materials. The director of the FLC's tutoring program provides broad oversight, but this opportunity gives the novice teachers a chance to consolidate what they are learning through concrete, material activity.

Local Schools and Church-based Language Programs

Our university is not located near many private schools and academies, which tend to be the kinds of institutions that are legally able to hire international students to work part-time, but there are a few such institutions. Many of our MA TESL students, especially those who speak Chinese, have been hired to tutor at a local school that hosts Chinese high schoolers who live with local host families. There is also a heritage Chinese language school in the community, which occasionally has positions for our novice teachers to do classroom instruction. Another local private school has hired our novice teachers for both part-time and full-time work teaching languages. Of course, all these hires are subject to visa status and relevant regulations. Several houses of worship in the area sponsor tutoring programs, especially ESL for families, and MA TESL students are welcome as volunteer tutors in those programs.

Intensive English Program

An active unit of the department where our MA TESL Program is located is the Intensive English program (IEP), a program that provides pre-matriculated students with language classes, academic skill training, and cultural orientation. The IEP runs a busy tutoring center and regularly engages volunteer tutors; we encourage the MA TESL students to volunteer there, and, occasionally, an MA TESL student is hired on wages to coordinate the IEP tutoring center. Similar to the community-based tutoring opportunities, this program provides structure and independence in a productive balance.

The University Undergraduate Writing Center

While the peer tutors at the main undergraduate writing center are undergraduate students and thus cannot include our graduate students, there have been opportunities for our MA TESL students to give workshops for the peer tutors at their weekly training sessions, attend grammar clinics as 'local experts,' work as an hourly paid assistant to the director of the Writing Center, and carry out informal observations for class projects or out of personal interest. Every university's writing center is unique, but as a place where the focus is on language, on the composition process, on conceptualizing academic writing as a reasoned activity, and on responsive pedagogical interaction, it can be a particularly fruitful place for engagement with novice MA TESL teachers.

The Teacher in Residence Program: A Post-doc for MA Students

For several years, we were able to invite a small number of outstanding graduates of our MA TESL program to stay with us for one year to teach as a full-time lecturer (Teacher in Residence) in the first-year academic writing program for international students (the program described in several other places in this volume, where many MA TESL students do their practicum work and where the Extended Team-Teaching Project is often hosted). While this initiative, for all the positive things it offered to its participants, did not become a permanent fixture in our department, it could be a model for another campus or program or department. At the beginning of the fourth semester of study, MA TESL students were invited to apply to be a Teacher in Residence for the following year. Applications were considered in terms of pedagogical promise, and a strong record of reliability, academic strength, and general collegiality and department citizenship. Successful applicants were hired for one year, a limitation clearly stated in the contract (as well as the application) and assigned to teach in the first-year writing program for L2 writers (the ESL program, as it is called). The pay that the Teachers in Residence received was much the same as that of a fully funded Graduate Teaching Assistant, and they did, as full-time employees, receive benefits such as retirement and health insurance coverage for the year.

The Teachers in Residence were assigned two first-year writing classes per semester, plus tutoring duties and sometimes curriculum development work. For two semesters, these newly credential teachers were invited to become full members of our department and to experience to a limited but legitimate extent what it is like to hold a full-time job teaching English to international students. Both domestic (American) and international students were offered Teacher in Residence status during the years that the program ran.

Conferences: Local, Regional, and International

Graduate students can find conferences expensive and inconvenient, yet such academic events are crucial for networking and for professional development. Many of our MA TESL students not only manage to attend conferences but also present posters, papers, and symposia talks. Working alone, or in collaboration with a doctoral student or faculty member, our MA TESL students often present at conferences ranging from the very local (on campus) to the international (in Europe and Asia). While no MA TESL student is required to attend conferences, we strongly encourage them to find professional meetings that work with their budget and their schedule. The department occasionally manages to provide travel funds for MA TESL students, which of course is a great incentive.

Professional Development on the University Campus

ESL Days

On campus, the ESL program sometimes sponsors an *ESL Day* meeting, best described as a micro-conference for professional development, a two-hour block of time dedicated to a theme or topic relating to the teaching of ESL.

Everyone in the department and on campus with an interest in English language teaching, pedagogy, materials design, and international student support is invited. The number of participants has ranged from 10 to 60. Our novice teachers serve as audience members, presenters, and organizational helpers. Though the events are by design, small in scale, they offer a chance for the novice teachers to engage in discussions, debates, and exchanges of ideas with a wider variety of interlocutors than a single class or lecture can provide.

Themes are chosen through brainstorming, consultation with ESL instructors, questions that come up in MA TESL classes, and conversations that take place with students and colleagues from other units of the university. Sometimes the topic is practical teaching strategies (The Power of Index Cards) and sometimes it is conceptual understanding (Metaphor and Teacher Development). While the format is almost always small-group discussion, there are various kinds of prompts and follow-up activities: Sometimes each group is given a typical 'dilemma' or 'classroom management challenge' and asked to come up with creative solutions. Sometimes participants are asked to create drawings or concept maps. Role-plays and group tasks are common. Every ESL Day stems from two deeply held beliefs: First, talking with other people who care about the same things that you do is a great way to learn, and second, there is always something new to learn, no matter how long (or short) a time you have spent in the field.

Departmental Speakers and Seminars

The department that houses our MA TESL program has a faculty who are all prominent in their various fields of research, and we host many well-known and even iconic representatives of recent scholarship. While we do not specifically require our MA TESL students to attend every guest lecture, we strongly encourage them to attend at least a few such events every semester. We also promote relevant talks on campus sponsored by other departments, by using our departmental mailing list and specific MA TESL announcements. After a lecture, we sometimes hold follow-up sessions with the novice teachers, asking them to reflect upon what they learned, or how they see the research they heard about connecting to what they are learning in their classes.

Several times each semester, the department also hosts a roundtable, a kind of seminar for members of the department, faculty and graduate students, to share works in progress, dissertation research, and other topics. Again, while MA TESL students are not formally required to attend, they are encouraged and invited, and are occasionally invited to join the line-up of speakers.

On top of outside speakers and events, there is a unit of our department that specializes in creating language and cultural bridges among cultures on campus; this unit sponsors several workshops every semester, two conversation groups for undergraduate and graduate-level international students, training sessions, tutoring and consultation, and other events and services that help international and domestic scholars and students communicate and collaborate more successfully. We encourage the novice teachers to attend workshops, volunteer to help if possible, and to participate in ongoing activities such as the conversation groups as bilingual and bicultural informants.

Research and Publishing Opportunities

In general, MA TESL students tend not to be under the same kind of pressure to publish as doctoral students are. However, it can be exciting and motivating for a faculty member or doctoral student to invite an MA TESL student to work on a research project that may end in a publication. Several of our faculty members have hired MA students to join larger projects as research assistants (typically unpaid or paid at an hourly wage), copy editors, and mailing list curators. Whether the work is paid or volunteer, this kind of engagement with the profession "behind the scenes" strengthens an application to further graduate study, consolidates a personal interest or research direction, and spreads the professional development work more broadly to all members of the department. Conference presentations often come out of these experiences, as do impressive letters of recommendation for further graduate study.

Conclusion

The opportunities that we have created or that we have identified for the novice teachers we are educating come from many sources. Not every such opportunity directly reflects our commitment to VSCT principles or to the pedagogical concepts that infuse so much of our work. But we try, consciously, to help the novice teachers engage with and reflect upon such opportunities in ways that are consonant with those principles. The message we share, in workshops, orientation meetings, post-lecture discussions, and classes, is coherent: connect this new idea or new piece of information to what you have already been learning and try to find a place for it in your own future, as you currently visualize it and as you will visualize and materialize it later in your career.

There is no question that it takes effort and the commitment of a certain amount of time to identify, create, and incentivize opportunities for novice teachers that help them engage with the profession. But we have also learned, to our benefit and to the benefit of our novice teachers, these things:

- In any given community, there are people who would appreciate targeted, responsive help with gaining and improving stronger proficiency in spoken and written English
- Scholars and administrators are often eager to meet new members of the academic community who can provide volunteer labor or who will work

for a small wage in return for mentorship and exposure to a new dimension of academia
- Classroom instructors are usually happy and ready to welcome novice teachers into class to observe, to give feedback, to participate as conversation partners or assistants

As one novice teacher wrote in her e-Portfolio about her experience designing a class and then teaching it to adult learners at the Community Literacy Center:

> **Excerpt 2**
>
> This course is a great chance for us to apply our knowledge and teaching experience in another contexts beyond the school. We combined our contents with cultural factors and communicate strategies to help the students behave more confidently in their future studies and research in American academic contexts.
>
> (Ai, e-Portfolio text)

In this chapter, we have described some of the many extra-curricular opportunities that we have either created, or identified, for our novice teachers on campus and in the local community that can contribute in powerful and often unexpected ways to the development of academic and professional knowledge and expertise. These experiences help develop autonomy, self-awareness, and professional engagement.

APPENDIX 1: PEDAGOGICAL CONCEPTS IN L2 TEACHING

Below is a collection of pedagogical concepts that we have extrapolated from our work with Vygotskian Sociocultural Theory (VSCT) L2 novice teacher education. As pedagogical concepts, they are not specific to any particular topic or language skill but are relevant to all L2 instruction and L2 teacher education. We use each of the concepts listed here differently to support the development of novice teacher reasoning, that is, for different purposes and in different ways in our individual courses, but all of them encapsulate fundamental principles of praxis-oriented pedagogy. Taken together, this collection becomes a set of powerful psychological tools that enable novice teachers to instantiate *teaching as dialogic mediation* (Johnson, 2009), or, to phrase its value in the form of a pedagogical concept itself, TEACH OFF YOUR STUDENTS, NOT AT THEM.

ACTIVITY BUILDING

a. Design activities in such a way that they build on one another
b. Sequence activities so that they lead to a final outcome or 'product' that is a demonstration of what learners have learned and are now able to do

BE DIRECT, NOT DIRECTIVE

a. Be explicit about what language point you are focusing on
b. Do not tell the learner what to write or say in place of their own contribution
c. Use targeted mediation to support the learner's use of language

CREATE PREDICTABILITY

a. Explicitly state what learners are expected to say and do
b. Explicitly and overtly link activities through language: provide connections/transitions
c. If working in pairs or small groups, provide students opportunities to 'practice' before they 'perform' or 'present'

EMBODIMENT IN TEACHING

As a performative act, teaching is filled with gestures and positionings that hold meanings for both teachers and learners. Consider the following when you teach:

a. Where do I stand? How do I stand? Where do I look?
b. How do I use gestures and positioning to support student learning?
c. What do I do when learners are working in small groups?

ENGINEER PARTICIPATION

a. Don't assume learners know how to participate
b. Be explicit about HOW you want them to participate
c. Arrange the classroom in ways that invite participation
d. Continue to monitor participation throughout the lesson

INSTRUCTIONAL PARAPHRASING

Whatever learners say, rephrase or paraphrase it out loud so that you:

a. Acknowledge the learner's contribution
b. Make it comprehensible to everyone
c. Provide appropriate language input/model
d. Relate it to what you are teaching (i.e., take learners from where they are to where you want them to be)
e. Establish a pattern that any and all learner contributions are welcome (i.e., lessen face-saving threats)
f. Give yourself an opportunity to 'comprehend' it

ORIENT STUDENTS

a. Situate/connect the concept, skill, or content within the 'bigger picture'
b. Highlight salient and relevant features that learners should pay attention to and state why
c. Help learners relate to it in some concrete or personally meaningful way

PROVIDE RELEVANCE

a. Tell learners exactly *why* you are doing what you are doing
b. Tell learners *why* you are asking them to do what they are doing
c. Tell learners what you expect them to know and be able to do by the end of the lesson

REASONING TEACHING

Justify your instructional choices. Are they *P.S. ME?*

a. P = Purposeful—goal-directed
b. S = Substantive—content-rich
c. M = Meaningful—matters for your goals and your learners and their goals
d. E = Engaging—involves all learners all of the time

TEACHING AS CONNECTING

a. Connect content with learners, learners with content
b. Establish instructional relationship and rapport with and among learners
c. Design activities so learners connect with content/one another in different ways (individually, round-robin, pairs, small groups, whole class)

Note: The pedagogical concepts are listed in alphabetical order, to avoid suggesting that any one of them is more important than any other, or that any particular concept should be taught ahead of any other.

Reference

Johnson, K. E. (2009). *Second language teacher education: A sociocultural perspective*. New York: Routledge.

APPENDIX 2: TEACHER DEMOGRAPHICS

Name	Gender	Home country	L1	Years of teaching experience			Appearances throughout book
				<1 year	1–2 years	3+ years	
Ai	F	China	Mandarin	X			75–76, 82–84, 113–114, 124, 176–177, 229
Aisha	F	Saudi Arabia	English	X			123, 164–165, 178–179, 184, 189, 206, 214–216, 218
Ana	F	Argentina	Spanish			X	122–124, 164–166, 178, 186–187, 203, 208, 210–212
Azadeh	F	Iran	Farsi	X			120–121
Bao	F	China	Mandarin	X			151–152
Bei	M	China/ United States	Mandarin			X	209–210, 213, 219
Chen	F	China	Mandarin	X			72–73, 114–115, 145, 185–186
Chul	M	Korea	Korea		X		80–81, 127–129, 159–160
Emine	F	Turkey	Turkish			X	86, 110–111, 138, 140–141, 150
Ethan	M	United States	English		X		79, 181–182, 205, 216
Fang	F	China	Mandarin	X			107–109
Fen	F	China	Mandarin	X			77, 87, 183, 190–194, 217, 219
Gan	M	China	Mandarin	X			101–106, 194–196

(Continued)

Teacher Demographics

Name	Gender	Home country	L1	Years of teaching experience			Appearances throughout book
				<1 year	1–2 years	3+ years	
Hannah	F	United States	English		X		110–113, 116–117, 137–142, 149–150, 162–163, 193
Lai	F	China	Mandarin		X		78–79
Layla	F	Saudi Arabia	Arabic		X		71–73, 88, 126–127, 147, 160–163, 166–168, 180–181
Leo	M	Brazil	Portuguese			X	123, 164–165, 175–176, 200, 203, 206–207, 212–213
Lin	F	China	Mandarin	X			109, 112, 117, 148–149, 177
Mei	F	China	Mandarin	X			117–118, 124–126, 135–137, 145
Natalie	F	United States	English		X		93–98, 179–180
Pavel	M	Kazakhstan	Russian, Kazakh			X	81–82, 145–146, 156–157
Ping	F	China	Mandarin	X		X	198–199
Qiao	F	China	Mandarin	X			87, 93, 196–198
Qing	F	China	Mandarin		X		71, 93–99, 110, 129–135, 153–155, 168–169, 179–180, 187–188
Shu	F	Taiwan	Taiwanese, Mandarin		X		88, 111–112, 153, 157–159
Yan	F	China	Mandarin	X			86–87, 186, 202, 207, 209, 214, 217–219, 223
Zeina	F	Saudi Arabia	Arabic			X	78, 178, 180–181

INDEX

Note: *Italicised* folios refers figures in the text and CAPITALIZED entries refers to important concept.

academic concepts 18; cohesion in 104; conceptual development of 25–26; scientific and 28n1
ACTIVITY BUILDING 116, 144, 163–170, 230
actual teaching/teach 17, 40–42, 96, 122, 157, 175, 181; in academic writing 179; activity of 21; novice teachers engagement in responsive mediation 113; *perezhivanie* 125; stimulated recall session 122, 152
American Psychological Association (APA) 151–152
asking questions 88, 101–102, 116, 149, 158, 186, 197, 209–210
authorial voice 52–53, 185

Barnes, D. 65–66, 93
BE DIRECT, NOT DIRECTIVE 22–23, 26, 71, 74, 76, 99–106, 159, 230

capstone project 11, 35–36, 60; e-Portfolio 58; MA Workshop Series 55–59; *see also* MA TESL program
challenges 23, 184; in instructional setting 204; novice teachers 38; post-graduation 214–219; in tutoring 158
charts and visuals 85–87

Childs, S. 66
cognition 78, 124, 128, 137, 139; emotions and 13, 63, 119, 120; human 9; of L2 teacher 3; social events and 65; in VSCT 16; Vygotskian sociocultural theory 4–7
collaborative lesson planning 39–40
community literacy center (CLC) 223–224, 229
community of learners 77, 190
conceptual tools 162; MA TESL program 35–36; pedagogical concepts 20, 75, 82
constraints: institutional affordances and 205; institutional and instructional 217–219; of learners 199; memory 165; post-graduation 214–219; Teaching Practicum 42
Cook, L. S. 96
CREATE RELEVANCE 84
CREATE/CREATING PREDICTABILITY 78, 80, 100, 156–163, 166, 170, 194, 231
critical literature review 53, *57*
cultures: cultural bridges among 227; historical practices of 19; human 18; post-graduation 214–219; role in shaping learners and activity of language learning 38

curriculum development 34, 53, 57, 226

Daniels, H. 177
data-driven project 53, *57*
departmental speakers and seminars 227–228
dialectic/dialectical: materialism 10; tension 23–24, 69; unity 9–10, 15–17, 23–24, 26, 46
dialogic instructional relationship 43, 92, 99–106
dialogic mediation 159–160, 179–182; with mentor teacher 149; teaching as 8, 10, 13, 19, 21–22, 41, 92–93, 107–108, 112, 113, 118, 173–174, 176, 178, 185, 190, 192, 194, 199, 204, 208–209, 215, 219, 230
dialogue 56, 86, 92, 179; instructional 91, 92–99; and reflection 207–208; responsive 118; between teacher educators and novice teachers 20; between tutor and tutee 43
dramatic moments 97, 201

e-Portfolio 36, 51, 54–55, 58, *58–59*, 222, 229
EMBODIMENT IN TEACHING 82, 126, 231
emotion 119–142; body language and 110; cognition and 13, 41, 63, 94, 192, 202; in Extended Team-Teaching Project 122–142; practice 121
empty verbalism 9, 70
ENGINEER/ENGINEERING PARTICIPATION 56, 77, 82, 131, 135, 144–150, 152,170, 211,218, 231
English as a Foreign Language (EFL) 33, 147, 164, 175, 211–212
English as a Second Language (ESL) 33, 36; instructional settings 34; students 39–40; tutoring 17
English for Specific Purposes (ESP) 38
ESL Day 226–227
everyday concepts 18, 37
Extended Team-Teaching Project 11, 38–40, 41, 45, 86, 93, 98, 113, 122–142, 146, 174, 176, 226
extra-curricular teaching opportunities 222–223

Feryok, A. 3
final reflective paper 44, 77, 104, 203

focus on learners 112, 133–142
focus on self 133–142
Freeman, D. 65

Golombek, P. R. 24, 120–121

Holzman, L. 17

imitation 27, 70–73, 96, 226
institutional constraints 217–219
instructional choices 23, 47, 110–111, 144, 155–156, 186–189, 191, 193, 198, 204–207
instructional constraints 217–219
INSTRUCTIONAL PARAPHRASING 92–99, 181–182, 198, 231
instructional relationship 42–43, 46, 92, 99–106, 184, 210, 232
Intensive English Communication Program 39
Intensive English program (IEP) 225
intersubjectivity 79, 82, 209

Johnson, K. E. 24, 65–66, 87, 120–121

Kubanyiova, M. 3

language programs: church-based 224–225; English 213
Lantolf, J. 66, 68–69, 71, 79
learning: to create instructional dialogues 92–99; dialectic tension of 23–24; to engage in responsive mediation 107–113; Extended Team-Teaching Project 126; of L2 teacher 17; language 20, 170; practice teach 156; practicum teachers 49; school 4; spaces 46; to think like a teacher 190–194

MA TESL program 4–5, 10–11, 13, 33–50; conceptual tools 35–36; goals and structures 66; MA Checklist 35; MA Paper 33, 51–58, *57*; MA TESL Handbook 35; MA Workshop Series 55–58; material and 35–36; objectives *59*; program goals 35–36; student 24, 164, 192, 222–228; Teaching ESL 37–42; Teaching Practicum 46–50; three pillar courses 36–37; Tutoring Internship 42–46

material and MA TESL program 35–36
materialism *see* dialectical materialism
mediation 40–42; contingent 13; dialogic 179–182; explicit 178–179; formal and intentional 4; modalities 26–27; pedagogical concepts as means of 20–27; spaces 17, 39–40, 69, 199; successful ZPD activity 73–74; teaching as dialogic 8, 10, 19, 176, 208–209; Teaching ESL 40–42; Teaching Practicum 50; Tutoring Internship 45–46; verbal 85–87; ZPD activity 73–74

novice L2 teacher reasoning, reconceptualization in 173–200; dialogic mediation 179–182; explicit mediation 178–179; instructional choices 186–189; instructional stance 194–199; learning to think like a teacher 190–194; responsive mediation in tutoring 183–185; strategic use of questions 185–186; teacher-fronted instructional stance 176–178

obuchenie 24, 82, 92, 118
Optional Professional Training (OPT) 222
oral presentations 88
ORIENTING 41, 66, 71, 84, 116, 165, 231

pedagogical concepts 63–89; academic and 16; charts and visuals 85–87; conceptual development of novice teachers 79–88; creativity and innovation in ZPD activity 82–84; engineering not only thinking but writing 88; history of 64–67; in L2 teaching 230–232; as means of mediation 20–27; mediation ZPD activity 73–74; oral presentations 88; in practical activity of teaching 70–79; and reasoning goals 74–79; supplementing verbal mediation 85–87; theoretical framework of VSCT 67–69; as tokens of shared meanings 79–82; tools for creating, maintaining, and engaging in ZPD activity 67–69; as tools for meaningful imitation 70–73; VSCT-informed 18

pedagogical concepts, internalizing 144–170; ACTIVITY BUILDING 163–170; CREATE PREDICTABILITY 156–163; ENGINEERING STUDENT PARTICIPATION 144–151; PROVIDE RELEVANCE 151–156
pedagogical imperative 15
perezhivanie 86, 120, 173
pillar courses 5, 10–11, 15, 17, 20–21, 24–26, 36–37, 85, 91–93; emotions 122–127; Teaching Practicum 133–142; Tutoring Internship 127–133
placement class, Teaching Practicum 48–50
Poehner, M. E. 68–69, 71, 79
Portfolio Planning tool 58
post-graduation 201–220; challenges 214–219; constraints 214–219; cultures 214–219; new instructional contexts 214–219; professional teacher identity 211–214; reasoning teaching 204–211
practice teach 11, 39, 41–42, 94, 96, 98, 113, 145, 155–157, 176–177
practicum *see* Teaching Practicum
practicum class 46–48, 81, 107, 109, 155, 162, 168
praxis 9, 15, 27, 51, 75
praxis-oriented pedagogy/courses 4–5, 8, 13, 15–28, 120, 144; contingent mediation and 73; means of mediation 20–27; REASONING TEACHING 19–20, 177; responsive mediation 20; teaching as dialogic mediation 19; transformative model 18; VSCT and 17, 204
presentations *see* oral presentations
professional development, opportunities for: campus-based family literacy tutoring center 224; church-based language programs 224–225; community literacy center (CLC) 223–224; departmental speakers and seminars 227–228; ESL Day 226–227; extra-curricular teaching opportunities 222–223; Intensive English program (IEP) 225; international conferences 226; job searching 222; local conferences 226; local schools 224–225; regional conferences 226; research and publishing opportunities

228; Teacher in Residence Program 225–226; on the university campus 226–228; University Undergraduate Writing Center 225
professional teacher identity 211–214
prolepsis 37
PROVIDE RELEVANCE 66, 71–72, 77, 78, 88, 100, 144, 151–156, 232
psychological tools 5, 63, 74, 93, 100, 107, 112, 113, 144, 163–164, 169–170, 209

reasoning goals 74–79
REASONING TEACHING 8, 19–20, 21, 38, 69, 72, 75–78, 84, 177–178, 232; post-graduation 204–211
reflection 153, 163, 217; described 87; and dialogue 207–208; paper 40, 42, 99, 101, 109, 111–112, 124, 136, 175–177; written 11, 208
reflective post 44, 56, 76, 80, 86, 100–104, 120, 127, 130, 175, 183–184
responsive mediation 13, 20, 37, 43, 63, 74, 89, 91–118, 160; BE DIRECT, NOT DIRECTIVE 99–106; Extended Team-Teaching Project 146; instructional paraphrasing 92–99; instructional relationship 99–106; learning to create instructional dialogues 92–99; learning to engage in 107–118; novice teachers learning 120, 168; TEACH OFF YOUR STUDENTS, NOT AT THEM 107–113; Team-Teach Supervisor 146, 151; in tutoring 183–185

SEQUENCE ACTIVITY 88
shared meanings 19, 65, 79–82, 205
social situation of development 4, 8, 173, 175
sociocultural context 3, 175–176
stimulated recall session 40, 42, 152, 178
strategic use of questions 185–186
stress 125, 138, 207, 210
structured mediational spaces 4, 10, 16, 20, 118
student centered teaching 215
student participation 215–216

TEACH OFF YOUR STUDENTS, NOT AT THEM 21–22, 25–27, 66, 68, 77, 107–113, 197, 199, 202, 203, 209, 230
teacher development *see* emotion
Teacher in Residence program 225–226
teacher talk 120, 190, 194, 216
TEACHING AS CONNECTING 23, 26, 66, 78, 80–81, 210–211, 232
teaching as dialogic mediation instructional stance 13, 19, 21, 41, 92, 93, 107–109, 112–113, 118, 173–174, 176, 178, 185, 190, 192, 194, 199, 204, 208–209, 215, 219
Teaching ESL 5, 11, 37–42; course 37–38; Extended Team-teaching Project 38–40; mediation 40–42
TEACHING AS CONNECTING 77, 81–82
TEACHING OFF STUDENTS 108–110
Teaching Practicum 5, 11, 46–50, 133–142; course 46; mediation in 50; placement class 48–50; practicum class 46–48
teaching/learning: dialectic tension of 23–24; journal 47–49, 92, 110, 162–163, 175, 191, 203; the language 175; practical activity of 70–79; well-reasoned 175–176
Team-Teach Supervisor (TE) 39–42, 93–98, 113, 122–126, 145–146, 148, 151–152, 156, 178, 206
the ideal 8, 18, 21, 108
tool-and-result 17, 54
transferrable pedagogical knowledge 193–194
tutoring 42, 44; an ESL student 17; consultation 45; experience 81; intern 71; as real teaching 45; sessions 21, 24, 42–46, 75, 83, 86, 88, 101, 104, 158–161, 185–186, 188–189
Tutoring Internship 5, 11, 42–46, 88, 100–101, 104, 114, 127–133, 147, 157, 166, 168, 174, 184, 187, 189, 207, 212; course 42; instructional work 42–44; mediation in 45–46; novice teachers 24; tutoring as real teaching 45; writing work 44–45

Veresov, N. 201
Verity, D. 66
Visual Depiction 85, *85*
Vygotskian Sociocultural Theory (VSCT) 3–13, 15–17, 34, 96, 119,

173, 202, 230; complexities of 25; dialectic tension 24; dialectical unity of theory-practice 7–9; e-portfolio 54; instruction and cognition 5–8; multi-modality 26–27; praxis-oriented pedagogy 204; principles 67; theoretical framework of 67–69; zone of proximal development (ZPD) 7–9

Vygotsky, L. S. 4, 8, 9, 18–19, 65, 70, 93

well-reasoned teaching 175–176; *see also* teaching/learning

zone of proximal development (ZPD) 7–9, 27, 77; creativity and innovation in 82–84; mediation 73–74; tools for creating, maintaining, and engaging in 67–69

For Product Safety Concerns and Information please contact our EU
representative GPSR@taylorandfrancis.com
Taylor & Francis Verlag GmbH, Kaufingerstraße 24, 80331 München, Germany